A World
in Disarray

ALSO BY RICHARD HAASS

Foreign Policy Begins at Home
War of Necessity, War of Choice
The Opportunity
The Bureaucratic Entrepreneur
The Reluctant Sheriff
Intervention
Conflicts Unending
Beyond the INF Treaty
Congressional Power

EDITED VOLUMES

Honey and Vinegar
Transatlantic Tensions
Economic Sanctions and
American Diplomacy
Superpower Arms Control

A World
in Disarray

AMERICAN FOREIGN POLICY AND

THE CRISIS OF THE OLD ORDER

RICHARD HAASS

PENGUIN PRESS | NEW YORK | 2017

PENGUIN PRESS
An imprint of Penguin Random House LLC
375 Hudson Street
New York, New York 10014
penguin.com

ISBN 9780399562365 (hardcover)
ISBN 9780399562372 (e-book)

Printed in the United States of America
10 9 8 7 6 5 4 3 2 1

Designed by Gretchen Achilles

To my teachers:
Robert Tufts, Tom Frank, Albert Hourani,
Alastair Buchan, and Michael Howard

Contents

PART III

Foreword

A *World in Disarray* concludes with the chapter "A Country in Disarray." The 2016 presidential campaign, which ended after this book was completed, underscored this judgment by highlighting multiple divisions within American society that are both long-standing and deep.

One result of the election is greater uncertainty over the future trajectory of U.S. foreign policy. As the subtitle of this book suggests, support for the old order has crumbled, the result of heightened economic anxiety at home (often associated with globalization, free trade, and immigration) and growing doubts about the costs and benefits associated with what the United States has been doing abroad, including fighting several open-ended wars in the Middle East and supporting allies in Europe and Asia. It is significant that Donald Trump, the winning candidate, called for putting America First.

The rest of the world has taken note. Assumptions about

the willingness of the United States to continue doing what it has been doing in the world are being questioned as never before by friends, foes, and everyone in between.

All this, along with an inbox best described as daunting in the quantity and quality of the challenges filling it, is what awaits the forty-fifth president, who, like his predecessors, will enjoy great latitude in matters of national security. It is of course impossible to know what sort of foreign policy will emerge from the United States and how other countries and entities will react. Still, it is difficult not to take seriously the possibility that one historical era is ending and another beginning.

Introduction

On June 23, 2016, a narrow majority of those British citizens who went to the polls voted in favor of a referendum that called for an end to their country's membership in the European Union. Those voting for "Brexit" may have wanted to voice their frustration with low levels of economic growth, anger over immigration, fears of unemployment, or unhappiness with a portion of their taxes going to an institution based in Brussels that often seemed remote in order to support countries that often seemed to be profligate. Some voters may simply have wanted to register a protest against the politicians ruling the country. But whatever the motives, the results were profound, affecting not just the future of the United Kingdom and Europe but that of the United States and the entire world as well.

If Brexit actually happens, depending on its terms it could lead to the breakup of the United Kingdom and a partial unraveling of the EU. If this was to occur, the historic project of

European integration born in the wake of the Second World War, an accomplishment that has brought unprecedented prosperity and stability to a continent that had all too often known war, would be placed at risk. Also at risk would be the so-called special relationship between the United States and the United Kingdom, often America's closest and most important partner and ally in the world.

But even if Brexit or the worst of it is somehow avoided, that it garnered the support it did in a country such as the United Kingdom tells us that there are fewer givens in the world than many of us—indeed, most of us—assumed. Populism and nationalism are on the rise. What we are witnessing is a widespread rejection of globalization and international involvement and, as a result, a questioning of long-standing postures and policies, from openness to trade and immigrants to a willingness to maintain alliances and overseas commitments. This questioning is by no means limited to Great Britain; there are signs of it throughout Europe, in the United States, and nearly everywhere else.

All this is a far cry from the optimism and confidence that were just as widespread a quarter of a century before. One source of this mood was the fall of the Berlin Wall on November 9, 1989 (11/9 of all days), an event that heralded the peaceful and successful demise of the Cold War, the unprecedented struggle between the United States and the Soviet Union that had defined much of international relations for the four decades following the end of the Second World War.

This was followed less than a year later by a remarkable coming together of the world to turn back Saddam Hussein's effort to conquer Kuwait, something that would have had enormous consequences if it had been allowed to stand. The administration of George Herbert Walker Bush, the forty-first president of the United States, saw what Iraq had done and its likely consequences not just in immediate and local terms but also historically, as the opening event of the post–Cold War era. The president and those around him (including me, then a special assistant to the president and the principal adviser for the Middle East, Persian Gulf, and South Asia on the National Security Council staff) saw developments as constituting a precedent that could well give the new geopolitical era its character. Depending on what was done in response to Saddam's aggression and act of conquest, the post–Cold War world could be one of international order or disorder on a large scale.

It was thus for reasons both local and global, direct and indirect, that the United States did what it did and in the way it did it. Toward that end, the United States worked closely with the other fourteen members of the United Nations Security Council to repudiate Iraq's aggression and to establish and subsequently enforce a sanctions regime designed to ensure that Iraq would not benefit from its conquest and would pay an enormous price for it. A large coalition of dozens of countries contributing in different ways was built to make sure Iraqi aggression did not threaten Saudi Arabia and, when diplomacy backed by sanctions failed to dislodge Iraq from Kuwait, to force Iraq out of that country and to restore Kuwait's independence and government.[1]

The policy succeeded for the most part, and both Bush and his national security adviser, Brent Scowcroft, spoke of their hope that the collective effort to reverse Iraqi aggression and restore Kuwaiti sovereignty would set a precedent for what would follow. This was something the president highlighted in his September 1990 address to a joint session of Congress:

> The crisis in the Persian Gulf, as grave as it is, also offers a rare opportunity to move toward an historic period of cooperation. Out of these troubled times . . . a new world order can emerge: a new era—freer from the threat of terror, stronger in the pursuit of justice, and more secure in the quest for peace. An era in which the nations of the world, East and West, North and South, can prosper and live in harmony. A hundred generations have searched for this elusive path to peace, while a thousand wars raged across the span of human endeavor. Today that new world is struggling to be born, a world quite different from the one we've known. A world where the rule of law supplants the rule of the jungle. A world in which nations recognize the shared responsibility for freedom and justice. A world where the strong respect the rights of the weak. This is the vision that I shared with Soviet president

Mikhail Gorbachev in Helsinki. He and other leaders from Europe, the Gulf, and around the world understand that how we manage this crisis today could shape the future for generations to come.[2]

Now, some twenty-five years later, it is clear that no benign new world order materialized. What exists in many parts of the world as well as in various venues of international relations resembles more a new world *disorder*. If there were a publicly traded stock called "World Order Incorporated," it would not have crashed, but it would have suffered a correction, losing at least 10 percent of its value. The world might even be entering bear market territory, something normally associated with a fall of 20 percent. What is worse, no rally is in sight; to the contrary, the trend is one of declining order.

This is not to deny the existence of important examples of stability and progress in the world, including an absence of great-power conflict, a degree of international cooperation managing some of the challenges associated with globalization, and considerable coordination among governments and institutions in regard to many aspects of international economic policy. There is as well the fact that more people than ever are leading longer and healthier lives, that hundreds of millions of men, women, and children have been lifted out of extreme poverty, and that more people enjoy what can be termed a middle-class life than at any other time in history. Indeed, there is a body of writing that argues just this: we are better off than the apostles of doom and gloom would have you believe. Or to paraphrase that old saw about Wagner's music being better than it sounds, the world is better than it looks.[3]

As attractive as this optimistic worldview might be, it doesn't hold up. To the contrary, it is difficult to argue that what took place with the end of the Cold War and the defeat of Iraq constituted a historic turning point for the better. Saddam Hussein's thwarted attempt to use military force to accomplish his foreign policy goals turned out to be anything but an exception. With the advantage of a quarter century of hindsight, his illegitimate challenge to the status quo looks more like a harbinger of what was to come than the arrival of a new and more stable world. Indeed, it would be naïve and even dangerous to ignore worrisome developments and trends in the world, including increased rivalry among several of this era's major powers, the growing gap between global challenges and responses, the reality of and the potential for conflict in several regions, and political dysfunction and changes going on within many countries, including the United States, that are likely to make it more difficult to design and implement a foreign policy that can help the world contend with all the threats to order.

As for the title of this book, I want to say before going any further that the word "disarray" was chosen advisedly. I scoured the dictionary and thesaurus alike and could not find another word or term that better captured what exists. I say this to highlight that "anarchy" and "chaos" were rejected. Neither applies to the world, although, as will be discussed, what is taking place in the Middle East is too close for comfort. All that said, to speak of there being a new world order is to indulge in fantasy. "Disarray" captures both where we are and where we are heading in the world better than any other word.

The questions that flow from this assessment are many and important. Why and how did this happen? How did the world get from that moment of optimism to where it is today? Was this journey inevitable or might things have turned out differently? And where are we precisely? What about today's world should be thought of as simply the latest chapter in the long march of history and what constitutes something fundamentally different? To be sure, many things look bad, but how bad in fact are they? Might they get worse? And of course there is the question of what, if anything, can and should be done about them.

The purpose of A World in Disarray is to address these and related questions. The book, as often seems to be the case in my experience, was not planned. It began with a phone call in 2014 from Richard Dearlove, the former head of MI6 (the UK external intelligence service, akin to the CIA) and then the master of Pembroke College at the University of Cambridge. He explained to me that the university had a lecture series and asked whether I might be interested in being the "scholar-practitioner" during the coming academic year.

Any resistance on my part evaporated once I learned the title: the Humanitas Visiting Professor of Statecraft and Diplomacy. It was too good a name and opportunity to pass up.

I prepared and delivered three lectures in April 2015; each went on for about an hour and was followed by some thirty minutes of questions and answers. I also participated in a symposium in which three academics and numerous others were given the opportunity to criticize what I had to say, after which I was given the opportunity to criticize the criticisms. As is often the case, the discipline of writing and speaking helped me to develop ideas I had been working with and on for some time. The feedback of others was icing on the cake—or what I hope is cake.

This book is substantially different from those lectures. In part this reflects the different formats: what works as a talk tends not to work if simply transcribed on paper. But the difference between what I had to say in Cambridge and what I am putting forth in these pages also reflects the evolution in my own thinking. There was more to the subject—much more, actually—than I initially realized.

The lectures and subsequent writing did not take place in a vacuum, much less against a backdrop of relative peace and prosperity. To the contrary, 2015 and the first half of 2016 were a time of considerable turbulence and difficulty in the world. The post–World War I order was unraveling in much of the Middle East. Iran's nuclear ambitions and the growing reach of the Islamic State had put much of the region on edge. Syria, Iraq, Yemen, and Libya all shared many of the characteristics of failing or failed states. Syria in particular emerged as an example of what could go wrong: hundreds of thousands of Syrians had lost their lives and more than half the population had become internally displaced or refugees, in the process threatening to overwhelm not just Syria's neighbors but Europe as well. In part as a result, the number of refugees and internally displaced persons in the world swelled to more than sixty million. Russia had seized Crimea for itself and was actively destabilizing eastern Ukraine; it also demonstrated for the first time in decades a willingness and an ability to act boldly in the Middle East. Greece and its various creditors were having difficulty arriving at a formula by which new loans could be extended; the risk was a crisis that would begin but not necessarily be contained within Greece and the Eurozone. The prospect of Brexit raised existential questions for the future of both the United Kingdom and Europe. Seventy years after the end of the war in the Pacific, China was expanding its claims in the South China Sea amid growing nationalism and tensions in a region characterized by numerous territorial disputes and much historical bitterness. Internally, Chinese authorities, fearing the political fallout of a slowing economy, were cracking down politically and intervening in currency and stock markets alike.

Slower economic growth was by no means limited to China; to the contrary, it had become a worldwide reality, both a cause and a result of lower energy and commodity prices. Central bankers could only do so much in the absence of sound fiscal policy and serious structural reform. Many of the most important countries in Latin America, including Argentina, Mexico, and in particular Brazil, were mired in domestic political problems that were undermining confidence in their respective governments and, as a result, their economic performance. Three African countries were contending with an outbreak of the Ebola virus; countries everywhere were bracing for homegrown signs of the disease. Months later yet another disease—the Zika virus—broke onto the world scene. Climate change was outpacing global efforts to contend with it despite the efforts of Pope Francis and others to galvanize more of an international response. It was far from certain that the December 2015 climate conference in Paris, widely described as a success, would lead to significant changes for the better in either the behavior of individual countries or the scale of the problem. Cyberspace was a new frontier of growing capabilities and threats but few rules, with North Korea's hacking of Sony in apparent retaliation for a film that depicted the assassination of its young leader but one example. More traditional terrorism was becoming commonplace not just in the Middle East but far beyond, including Paris, Nice, Brussels, and San Bernardino, California.

Making matters worse were developments at the national level. An increasing number of governments were having difficulty dealing with the domestic political consequences of slowing economic growth, reduced levels of employment (or higher levels of unemployment), widespread concerns over how retirement and health care were to be funded, and increased inequality. Adding to the difficulty in some instances were dysfunctional politics (related to parties, persons, or both) that made it more difficult than ever to foster compromise around needed policies. Populism and extremism gained ground in mature democracies and authoritarianism in other countries. The result was the opposite of a virtuous cycle: challenges stemming from globalization contributed to many of these domestic developments, while these same developments made it more difficult for governments to deal effectively with global challenges.

All this is what is visible. But below the surface are structural changes that are also certain to have significant effects. States, long the dominant building blocks of international relations, are losing some—and in select cases much—of their sway to other entities. Power is more distributed in more hands than at any time in history. The same holds for technology. Decision making has come to be more decentralized. Globalization, with its vast, fast flows of just about anything and everything real and imaginable across borders, is a reality that governments often cannot monitor, much less manage. The gap between the challenges generated by globalization and the ability of a world to cope with them appears to be widening in a number of critical domains. For its part, the United States remains the most powerful entity in the world, but its share of global power is shrinking, as is its ability to translate the considerable power it does have into influence, trends that reflect internal political, social, demographic, cultural, and economic developments within the United States as well as shifts in the outside world. The result is a world in which centrifugal forces are gaining the upper hand.

I am not alone in such thinking. It is instructive that the most senior American military officer, the chairman of the Joint Chiefs of Staff, started off his foreword to the country's new military strategy as follows: "Today's global security environment is the most unpredictable I have seen in 40 years of service. . . . [G]lobal disorder has significantly increased while some of our comparative military advantage has begun to erode."[4] Half a year later, in early 2016, the U.S. director of national intelligence stated, "Emerging trends suggest that geopolitical competition among the major powers is increasing in ways that challenge international norms and institutions."[5] Just days earlier, Henry Kissinger had opined that "the momentum of global upheaval has outstripped the capacities of statesmanship."[6] Such pessimism grew exponentially in the aftermath of the British vote to leave the EU. One British columnist put it this way: "Make no mistake about it. Britain's vote to leave the EU is the most damaging blow ever inflicted on the liberal democratic international order created under U.S. auspices after 1945. Pandora's box is well and truly open."[7]

Those looking for a partisan agenda in these pages will come away disappointed. I take issue with many of the policies of recent Democratic and Republican presidents alike.

Quite simply, my motivation for writing this book grows out of a judgment that the twenty-first century will prove extremely difficult to manage, representing as it does a departure from the almost four centuries of history—what is normally thought of as the modern era—that came before it. I am deeply concerned about the potential consequences. Mark Twain said that history may not repeat itself but it rhymes. On occasion this is true. But my larger point is that the future is less likely to rhyme with the past (much less suggest harmony) than it is to strike a note that is qualitatively different and more often than not discordant.

This book is divided into three parts. The first traces the history of international relations from the rise of the modern state system in the mid-seventeenth century through the two world wars of the twentieth century and on to the end of the Cold War. The premise is that there was considerable continuity in how the world worked during that stretch (think of it as World Order 1.0) even though the history itself varied dramatically, both for good and very much for ill.

The second part looks back at the last quarter century. The argument here is that the past twenty-five years since the end of the Cold War constitute a break with the past and that something very different is afoot in the world. The analysis extends to the principal regions of the globe as well as to the world as a whole. It attempts to depict not just where we are— the state of the world—but also how we got there and what it portends.

The third and final section of the book is more prescriptive. It makes the case that it is important to do everything possible to constrain great-power competition so it does not come to resemble history's norm. At the same time, the world needs an updated operating system—call it World Order 2.0—that takes into account new forces, challenges, and actors. U.S. foreign policy, along with the foreign policies of many others, will need to adjust. One critical element of this adjustment will be adopting a new approach to sovereignty, one that embraces the obligations of governments as well as their rights. Another component will require implementing a new approach to multilateralism, one more flexible in terms of structure and more open as regards participation than the relatively permanent and state-dominated arrangements we have grown used to. Yet a third new element of foreign policy will require accepting a more conditional approach to relationships with other countries, one less fixed than is normally the case. A fourth and final aspect of what the United States needs to do to succeed in the world is to define national security in broader terms than is traditional, taking into account to a much greater degree (and doing something about) what are normally thought of as domestic challenges and problems. I realize that such thinking represents a challenge to a good deal of what passes for current orthodoxy, but these are no ordinary times. It will not be business as usual in a world in disarray; as a result, it cannot be foreign policy as usual.

PART I

1. From War Through World War

It is tempting to begin this book with answers to the questions of what is wrong with the world, why, and what to do about it, if for no other reason than there is no shortage of material to consider. But it is better, and in fact necessary, to take a step back, first, to understand how we arrived where we are and, second, to discern what about this world is genuinely new and different.

The best place to begin is with the concept of world order. For many reasons, the concept, from its modern inception nearly four centuries ago to the present, is central to this book. "Order" is one of those terms that is used a great deal, but like a lot of popular terms, it is used differently by different people and can obscure as much as illuminate. It is best used and understood in a neutral, descriptive way, as a reflection of the nature of international relations at any moment. It is a measure of the world's condition. It includes and reflects arrangements that promote peace and prosperity and freedom as well as developments that do not. In short, "order" is not the same as "orderly"; to the contrary, the term "order" implicitly also reflects the degree of disorder that inevitably exists. One can have world orders that are anything but stable or desirable.

The term is experiencing something of a revival. *World Order* is, among other things, the title of a recent book by Henry Kissinger.[1] Kissinger, the preeminent foreign policy practitioner of the second half of the twentieth century, is also one of the most influential writers not just on this subject but on many aspects of diplomatic history and international relations. And for these and related reasons I will come back to him more than once in the course of this book. I want to begin, though, with another academic, an Australian, Hedley Bull.

I came to know Hedley when I was a graduate student at Oxford in the mid-1970s. We became friends, and his thinking and writing came to have a major influence on me. Bull wrote in 1977 what I find to be the most important contemporary book in the field of international relations, *The Anarchical Society*. Its subtitle, appropriately enough, is *A Study of Order in World Politics*.[2]

Bull writes about international *systems* and international *society*. It is a distinction with a difference. An international system is simply what exists at the international level absent any policy decisions, in that countries and other entities along with various forces interact with and affect one another. There is little or nothing in the way of choice or regulation or principles or rules. An international society, by contrast, is something both different from and very much more than a system. What distinguishes a system from a society is that the latter reflects a degree of buy-in on the part of participants, including an acceptance on their part of limits on either what is sought or discouraged, how it is to be sought or discouraged, or both. It is rules-based. These rules (or limits) are accepted by the members of the society for the simple reason that they determine it is their best (or least bad) course of action given the choices that are realistically available. Such rules as there are can be enshrined in formal legal agreements or honored tacitly and informally.

In the international sphere, the notion of "society" as described by Bull has specific meaning. First, the principal "citizens" of this society are states, a word used interchangeably here and elsewhere in these and other pages with both "nation-states" and "countries." Second, a founding principle of this society is that states and the governments and leaders who oversee them are essentially free to act as they wish within their own borders. How those individuals come to occupy positions of authority, be it by birth, revolution, elections, or some other way, matters not. Third, the members of this international society respect and accept not just this freedom of action on the part of others (in exchange for others in turn accepting that they can act as they wish within their own borders) but also the existence of other members of this society. States therefore seek to avoid war among themselves. It is not far off to describe this approach to international relations as being something of a "live and let live" cross-border understanding.

But history is always more than just the narrative of consensus; it is also at least as much a narrative of disagreement and friction. The mix of success and failure, of order and disorder, is central to the work of Bull. As suggested by the title of his book, history at any moment or in any era is the result of the interaction between forces of society and anarchy, of order and disorder. It is the balance between the two, between society and anarchy, that determines the dominant character of any era.

This is a useful framing concept for approaching and understanding the world. At any moment, it provides a snapshot of where things are. And if enough snapshots are saved and strung together from days or months or years before, it provides a moving picture of trends.

Before going any further, it is essential to make clear just what is required for there to be order. Here I want to return to Henry Kissinger and to an early book of his, *A World Restored*.[3] The book was published some sixty years ago and based upon Kissinger's doctoral dissertation, something that should probably give every graduate student more than a little pause. Replete with vivid character portraits, it is a wonderfully written book, one that darts back and forth between specific history and larger lessons. Kissinger writes about the building of a new international order, about a world that was in large part resurrected in the aftermath of revolution and the Napoleonic Wars in the late eighteenth and early nineteenth centuries. It is the history of an international, that is, European order that was recognized at the Congress of Vienna—a gathering in 1814 and 1815 where, among others, the foreign ministers of Great Britain, France, Prussia, Russia, and Austria met to shape Europe's future—and that survived for much of the nineteenth century.

The Congress of Vienna is noteworthy as an early example of an effort to promote peace and stability. The final product included any number of territorial arrangements, land swaps, recognitions of rightful rulers, and more. It is also noteworthy for what it did not do. While it did help bolster Europe's peace for several decades, it ultimately came undone amid the emergence of revolutionary movements in or near several of the participants, a changing balance of power that reflected both Prussia's (and later Germany's) rise and the fading and ultimate disappearance of multiple empires. This is worth highlighting as it is a reminder of how orders can come to an end and in so doing become disorders.

It is useful to deconstruct the concept of order, to break it down into its most essential elements. One critical element of order is the concept of "legitimacy," defined by Kissinger to mean "international agreement about the nature of workable arrangements and about the permissible aims and methods of foreign policy."[4] Used in this fashion, legitimacy is a big idea, as it not just defines the rules of international relations—what is to be sought and how, as well as how these rules are to be set and modified—but also reflects the extent of their acceptance by actors with real power.

But just as essential to this notion of order, just as essential as this concept of legitimacy, was something much less intellectual. Here again I quote: "No order is safe without physical safeguards against aggression."[5] Thus Kissinger, writing sixty years ago about a very different world, made clear that order depended both on there being rules and arrangements to govern international relations and on a balance of power.

Bull and Kissinger have a good deal in common. Both were mostly concerned with order between states, especially the major powers of a particular era. Order reflects the degree to which those with substantial power accept existing arrangements or rules for conducting international relations, as well as the diplomatic mechanisms for setting and modifying those rules. It also reflects the ability of those same powers to meet the challenges of others who do not share their perspective. Disorder, as explained by both Bull and Kissinger, reflects the ability of those who are dissatisfied with existing arrangements to change them, including through the use of violence. This emphasis is hardly surprising. After all, great-power rivalry, great-power competition, and great-power conflict constitute much of what we think of as history. This was certainly the case for the twentieth century, which was defined by two world wars and a third that mercifully remained largely cold.

Order can be understood in this way, reflecting efforts by

FROM WAR THROUGH WORLD WAR | 23

states to discourage the use of military force to achieve foreign policy aims. Tied to this view is that order is a respect for sovereignty, defined as allowing fellow states (and the governments and leaders in charge of them) to do much as they please within their borders. This approximates what is best understood as the classical view of order. The premise of this approach is that the principal objective of the foreign policy of any government ought to be influencing the foreign policy of other governments rather than the nature of the society over which they preside. As will be discussed later, this definition of order is not universally shared; to the contrary, it is too much for those who do not accept existing borders and not enough for those who worry most about what takes place within borders wherever they may be drawn.

The classical notion of order described above is normally attributed to the Treaty of Westphalia, the pact signed in 1648 that ended the Thirty Years War, a part-religious, part-political struggle within and across borders that raged across much of Europe for three decades. The treaty was something of a breakthrough, in that disorder and conflict born of frequent interference inside the borders of one's neighbors had been the norm. The Westphalian order is based on a balance of power involving independent states that do not interfere in one another's "internal business."

The historian Peter Wilson, who wrote one of the finest books on the Thirty Years War, put it this way: "Westphalia's significance lies not in the number of conflicts it tried to resolve, but in the methods and ideals it applied . . . sovereign states interacting (formally) as equals within a common secularized legal framework regardless of size, power or internal configuration."[6]

All this constituted a significant change in how the world operated. Secular sovereign states had become preeminent; empires founded on religious identity no longer dominated. Size or power didn't necessarily matter the most, as states (all being sovereign entities) had equal rights in principle if not in practice. This approach to order may seem terribly narrow through the lens of the second decade of the twenty-first century, and in many ways it is. But in its time, in its day, in the first half of the seventeenth century, this was an enormous breakthrough. Until then, there was little order in the world other than that imposed by the strongest entity. War was a frequent occurrence between and among this or that principality or state or empire. The idea of trying to bring about a world in which there was not, to use modern parlance, nonstop intervention in the internal affairs of others was a major advance. And it helped set the stage for a considerable period of relative stability in Europe.

As noted, the Congress of Vienna in the second decade of the nineteenth century was convened to come up with a post-Napoleonic diplomatic settlement.[7] The leaders of the day were so traumatized by what had just taken place that they operationalized the concepts of the Westphalian model, resulting in the Concert of Europe. The concert, as the word suggests, was an orchestration of how international relations in Europe would be conducted given the mind-set of those involved at the time, about how they would accept current borders and for the most part leave one another alone within their territories.[8] It encompassed frequent high-level diplomatic consultation among representatives of the major powers. In the words of one historian, the concert "had a deeply conservative sense of mission. Based on respect for kings and hierarchy, it prioritized order over equality, stability over justice."[9] It was hardly the only time in history when a great shock—in this case, revolution in France and the fear it might spread—changed collective behavior. And that is what happened. And for all the problems of the nineteenth century, it compares well in many ways with the century that followed.

Indeed, it was not until the late nineteenth and early twentieth centuries that we witnessed wholesale breakdown of the Concert of Europe, and with it the Westphalian order. (The midcentury Crimean War between Russia and both Great Britain and France was a struggle more about who was to control territory of the fading Ottoman Empire than about anything fundamental.) What occurred were two dramatic developments. First, there arose new nation-states (most prominently Prussia, the forerunner of Germany) unwilling to accept the territorial and political status quo that had developed. They rejected the legitimacy of existing international arrangements. And they were strong enough to act. The balance of power no longer precluded action or deterred them from acting. This last point suggests the second development that so shaped the history of this period. Many of the entities that had dominated the world for centuries were failing and in some cases literally falling apart. This was true of Austria-Hungary, Russia (soon to be ravaged by revolution), and the Ottoman Empire. The United States was only decades out of its civil war and was focused on continental expansion and industrialization. Europe seemed a long way off. All these changes gathered momentum in the second half of the nineteenth century and reached their climax when in the early part of the twentieth century the world experienced the grim effects of a wholesale breakdown of order.

Some of this history can be explained by the limits of the ability of orders to endure in the absence of great diplomatic dexterity. The Congress of Vienna, which led to the post-Napoleonic settlement and subsequently to the Concert of Europe, succeeded in no small part because it involved individuals of rare diplomatic skill. For this reason Castlereagh, Metternich, and Talleyrand, respectively the ministers of Great Britain, Austria, and France, remain significant historical figures.

An optimist would take a moment here to point out the power of human agency, the quality of diplomats, to affect the course of events. This was and remains true. One reason why the Concert of Europe got off the ground and lasted for as long as it did was the ability of some of the people involved in its creation. One factor, though, increasing the odds that a

world order will survive is that it *not* require talented states-
men, the supply of which is likely to be insufficient. One has
to assume that as often as not individuals of mediocre or poor
skills will enter into positions of responsibility. When it comes
to order, something robust and resilient is preferable to dependence on diplomatic dexterity. Indeed, one explanation
for why order broke down in the early twentieth century is
that Prussia, forged by the extraordinarily talented Otto von
Bismarck, came to be led by individuals who inherited a powerful state but not the wisdom for managing its relations with
its neighbors.[10]

The bottom line is that diplomats can and do matter, but
if countries become fundamentally stronger and are willing
to use that power, and if other countries become qualitatively
weaker and/or are less willing to use the power they have,
diplomats will be limited in their impact. Technological innovations and uneven rates of absorbing them matter, as do
demographics, leadership, culture, policies, and fortune. The
result of these and other factors was a first half of the twentieth century that was unprecedented in its disorder, and a
second half characterized by considerable order, however different in its origins and however unexpected.

The unprecedented disorder is that of the twentieth century's two world wars, which were phenomenally expensive
by any and every measure. But the two situations were fundamentally different and offer very different lessons for subsequent generations, including our own. Order broke down in

what became the First World War less by design than by hap-
penstance. There is something of a cottage industry of books
on the origins of the war, some placing the lion's share of
the blame on Imperial Germany, others on military mobiliza-
tions that took on a life of their own, still others on additional
factors.[11] But common to most of the books is a recognition
that the war did not have to happen, even if they are unable
to agree on just why it did. To be sure, there was a failure of
deterrence and of diplomacy, and a lack of communications
mechanisms, but what makes the history so frustrating even
one hundred years later was the carelessness of it all. Even
with the benefit of considerable hindsight it is difficult to understand just why the war came about and why it was fought.
But it also holds some important lessons for us today.

One is that orders are not automatic or self-sustaining
even when they are patently in the interests of all who benefit
from them. History is filled with examples of individuals and
countries acting against their own self-interest. World War I
was obviously not in anyone's interest, but it happened all the
same. Every protagonist lost far more than it gained. What it
shows is the limits to the balance of power, that even though
there was a rough balance in place (as the war demonstrated
on a scale matched only by its costs), military balance alone
was not enough to keep the peace.

Another lesson is the limits of economic interdependence.
Trade was extensive and growing. Indeed, a whole school of
thought grew up at the time that argued that war would never

happen on a large scale in Europe because it made no economic sense. No one would start a war, it was maintained, simply because too many people and firms were realizing too much profit in the current trading and investment arrangements. Too many countries were benefiting as a result. But war nevertheless broke out.[12]

What this teaches is that neither a balance of power nor economic interdependence is a guarantee against conflict and disorder. To this I would add one other point relating to World War I, which has to do with both the fact that war occurred and the way it was fought. History also revealed the limited effect of the body of thought that had grown up over the centuries, essentially known as the laws or rules of war, about the moral or legal basis for both going to war and conducting one.

Policymakers of the time largely ignored this body of thought despite its deep roots in Christian theology. The existing guidelines stated that for a war to be just, it needed to meet several criteria: it must be fought for a worthy cause, have a high chance of success, be sponsored by a legitimate authority, be undertaken only as a last resort, use no more force than was necessary and proportionate, and be fought in a manner that respected the welfare and rights of noncombatants.[13] World War I failed to meet any of these standards. Also largely ignored was the legal tradition that emphasized the illegitimacy of war except in cases of self-defense. Narrow political agendas reflecting nationalist sentiments and based on faulty military projections prevailed. What is obvious is that there was and is a fundamental difference between order as a concept and order as a reality. What international society there was turned out to be both narrow and shallow, lacking a mechanism for seeing that desired norms were honored and enforced.

The Second World War could not have been more different in its origins. Not surprisingly, the lessons to be learned are very different from those to be drawn from the run-up to World War I. Germany and Japan embraced goals in the 1930s that could not be accommodated within the existing international order. Both had become hostage to political systems at home that eliminated checks and balances on those wielding political power. Both invested heavily in the means to wage war. Both did their part to upset the balance of power that had developed. The result was that whereas World War I was largely an accidental and avoidable war, World War II was anything but.

Of course, there were other explanations for the war. This is nothing new. All wars are "fought" at least three times. First, there is the debate about whether to go to war and, in retrospect, its causes. Second, there is the war itself, what takes place on battlefields. And third, there is the debate about the lessons of the war and, quite often, the wisdom of what was done in its aftermath.

This was the case with World War II. Already noted is the

majority perspective, which holds that Germany and Japan were largely responsible for overturning an order they had come to view as illegitimate. But there are other perspectives. John Maynard Keynes, the great economist who was part of the British delegation to the Paris Peace Conference that formally ended World War I, famously wrote a few years later about the impact of the Treaty of Versailles and the failure to integrate Germany into global arrangements.[14] For him and others who shared his thinking, the seeds of the Second World War were sown in the punitive peace that followed the First. Even if too much can be made of this argument, it is true that nationalism in Germany fed off the resentments that grew up around Germany's being forced to pay severe reparations, forfeit territory, and accept stringent ceilings on what it could do in the military sphere.

There is also the argument that European and American actions (or lack of them) were responsible for World War II. Here one could point to the element of fecklessness, for want of a better word, represented by the unrealistic hopes placed in the League of Nations, something made worse by the breakdown in relations between the White House and the Senate and the subsequent unwillingness of the United States to join and support the new body. American retreat into isolationism and then hopes for an order based upon concepts of legitimacy that were aspirational rather than shared played their part as well. What comes to mind is the Kellogg-Briand

Pact, the international pact signed by governments in 1928 that committed them to avoiding war as a means of settling disputes.[15] And obviously the arrangements of the day were not buttressed by a balance of power. To the contrary, there was inadequate arming on the side of the Western democracies coupled with the unsuccessful diplomacy of appeasement. The great European democracies were depleted; they never really recovered from World War I. For its part, the United States (which had paid a far smaller price in the war) was weakened and distracted by the Great Depression. And as was the case with the previous world war, trade and mutually beneficial economic ties were not enough to discourage governments from eschewing aggression that could threaten those ties.

And the result for the second time in the span of a generation was war—the second great war of the twentieth century, one of breathtaking expanse and expense in every way: militarily, economically, in human terms. But unlike the First World War, it ended in a much more definitive way.

There was a clarity about the end of World War II. Of course there was the unconditional defeat of both Germany and Japan, but even more interesting was the fundamental difference in how they were treated afterward by the victors. If the First World War was followed by a punitive peace, the Second was followed by a transformational one. Both Germany and Japan were integrated fully into Western institutions, but more fundamentally, both were remade. The two defeated imperial powers were occupied—by the United States, the Soviet Union, Great Britain, and France in the case of Germany; by the United States in the case of Japan. The occupying powers reformed the countries in their image, which translated into democracy for all of Japan and in Germany as well but for the part (which became East Germany) controlled by the USSR. Nearly three-quarters of a century later, Germany and Japan stand out as among the few successful examples of what today would be called regime change followed by nation or state building.

It would be reassuring to be able to make the case that this approach to the vanquished resulted from a considered assessment of what had failed after the First World War, when Germany in particular was the subject of harsh treatment. The humiliation and economic difficulties contributed to bringing about an environment of radical populism and nationalism that created a political opening for Adolf Hitler and his supporters. And to be fair, there was some of this thinking, to avoid what might be termed national recidivism on the part of either country that had demonstrated authoritarian tendencies at home and bellicose ones abroad. Germany and Japan, it was thought, needed to become fully functioning democratic societies with meaningful political checks and balances to make sure authoritarianism did not return. And only if that was done—only if there came about a democratic internal order—could external stability be ensured. The re-

sult was something of a departure from the Westphalian notion of order, because rather than merely making sure that
neither defeated country would be allowed to possess the
military means to harm others, what was agreed to was an
approach to order that recognized that what goes on within a
country's borders matters not just to its own citizens but to
others. And what the victorious Allies thought they needed
to do to ensure that there would not be a World War III, as
World War II had followed World War I, was to remake their
former adversaries, Germany and Japan.

But one should not make too much of this. Unlike many
contemporary calls for spreading democracy, what was done
in Germany and Japan after their defeat was born more of
realism than idealism. Indeed, the principal reason why both
Germany and Japan were treated differently after the Second
World War was the perceived exigencies of the emerging era,
the Cold War. The United States and what became known as
the West needed a strong, non-Communist Germany and
Japan to anchor their efforts to resist the spread and reach of
Soviet power and influence in Europe and Asia.

Whatever the balance of motives, the experiment worked,
possibly because both societies were characterized by a respect
for authority, an educated citizenry, a clear divide between the
political and the religious, and experience with both civil society and a modern economy with broad employment. The trajectories of Japan and Germany for the last three-quarters of
a century have been nothing short of remarkable. Both have

evolved into stable, fully functioning democracies with strong private sectors; both became pillars of the U.S. alliance system, the United Nations, and the global economy. Germany (when it was still West Germany) was one of the founders of what evolved into the European Community and later the European Union.

2. Cold War

It is one of the many ironies of history that a good part of what constituted international order in the second half of the twentieth century was forged with a nondemocratic, non-market society that was an adversary of the United States, one that was dedicated to the objective of defeating it in a global competition and that sought to bring about a world made up of socialist or Communist countries that took their lead from Moscow. I am, of course, referring to the Soviet Union.

It is worth exploring both the nature of the Cold War order and what it was based on. Order of any sort was hardly guaranteed. Twice before in the century, great-power competition had led to great-power conflict on a horrendous scale. The United States and the Soviet Union had had an uneasy relationship since the Russian Revolution in 1917. The tsar may have been abhorrent to many Americans, but the ideology of Lenin and Trotsky was to most even more troubling, leading to a small American intervention in Russia's civil war on behalf of the counterrevolutionary "Whites." Twenty-five years later, the wartime alliance was often a source of friction as Stalin suspected that FDR's and Churchill's reluctance to open a second front against Nazi Germany was in no small part motivated by what Stalin saw as a desire to weaken Russia in anticipation of the postwar competition to come. More to the point, to turn the old maxim on its head, U.S.-Russian ties during the Second World War proved that the enemy of your enemy is not necessarily your friend.

no permanent allies

Actually, it was not long before the enemy of the previous enemy became an enemy. As might be expected, there is a large literature on the origins of the Cold War, some of which reflects a "revisionist" view that places the onus on the United States.[1] This is a minority view for good reason. The lion's share of the responsibility falls on the USSR, which in its approach to Germany and Korea signaled its readiness to mount a global challenge to the interests of the United States in Europe and Asia alike. But even if one disagrees, what is also fair to say is that the Cold War was to some extent inevitable given the divergent interests and ideologies represented by the two major powers of the era.

This makes it all the more remarkable that the Cold War stayed mostly cold and was conducted with a degree of responsibility that can only be judged as both uncharacteristic and impressive. Why it played out as it did is important to examine, as some of its lessons remain relevant. There was, to begin with, a balance of military power. The respective alliance systems of NATO and the Warsaw Pact made any war in Europe sure to be costly and uncertain in outcome. This was true as well of areas beyond the two formal alliances, including Asia. In addition, programs such as the Marshall Plan were put in place by the United States to strengthen—not just militarily, but economically and politically as well—potential targets of Soviet-backed challenges. The United States extended alliances and aid programs to countries on every continent, something that over time was mirrored to a considerable degree by the Soviet Union. For most of the Cold War, successive U.S. administrations paid little heed to the domestic nature of the recipient; what mattered most was foreign policy orientation and whether the government was judged to be sufficiently anti-Communist.

This balance was based not just upon orders of battle (military inventories) and the building up of locals but also on a willingness to act directly if it was determined military action was called for. (The basic bargain of membership in the NATO alliance, one enshrined in Article 5 of the North Atlantic Treaty, was that an attack on one constituted an attack on all.) The first such test arrived early, in the spring of 1948, when the Soviet Union blockaded West Berlin, which was surrounded on all sides by Soviet-controlled and -occupied East Germany. (Under the post–World War II settlement, Berlin was divided initially into four zones, overseen respectively by the United States, France, Great Britain, and the USSR. The three western zones, all part of the Federal Republic of Germany, or

West Germany, were later merged.) The answer was the Berlin airlift, which provided enough food and fuel and other basics to enable the city and its residents to survive until the Soviets backed down and lifted the blockade in the spring of 1949.

Other tests followed. In June 1950, Soviet-supported troops from the Democratic People's Republic of Korea, more commonly known as North Korea, crossed the 38th parallel and invaded South Korea (technically the Republic of Korea) in an effort to reunify the peninsula by force. North Korea's motives were nationalist and local, but the Soviets may also have wanted to score an early Cold War win in Asia as well as bring about a unified peninsula that could offset the potential emergence of a reconstituted Japan in the American strategic orbit. It is possible, too, that they believed (owing to an inadvertent public comment in early 1950 by Secretary of State Dean Acheson that South Korea fell outside the U.S. defense perimeter) that their aggression would not be directly countered. This time it took a large, sustained American-led military intervention carried out under UN auspices to frustrate Soviet and North Korean designs. The U.S. effort was successful in saving South Korea's independence and restoring the 38th parallel as the effective border, but only at enormous human and economic cost.[2]

A third major effort undertaken by the United States was in Southeast Asia, above all in Vietnam. There, starting not long after the French withdrawal from their colony in 1954 (in the wake of a military debacle near the city of Dien Bien Phu) and continuing until the mid-1970s, the United States poured in money, arms, advisers, and, when all else failed, millions of troops to shore up a regime challenged from within by an insurgency supported by North Vietnam and from the outside by North Vietnamese regular forces and, indirectly, by others. My point here is not to argue the correctness, much less the success, of all that was done, but rather to underscore that one factor that helped maintain a form of order in a world dominated by two superpower rivals was a willingness to act to maintain local balances of power where they were seen to be threatened. *trying to stabilize other countries & ignoring*

But such a willingness to act militarily was only one aspect *instability between super-powers* of what buttressed the Cold War order and quite possibly not the most critical. What most reinforced the strength of the order was the shared realization on the part of both the United *MAD—* States and the Soviet Union that any direct clash between *biggest* them could escalate into a nuclear exchange in which the *fove* costs would dwarf any conceivable gains and in which there would and could be no victor in any meaningful sense of the word. Nuclear weapons thus buttressed the traditional, conventional balance of power. In Europe, this role for nuclear weapons was explicit, in that NATO embraced a doctrine that threatened to introduce nuclear weapons first (at a tactical or theater level) in order to offset perceived conventional military shortcomings vis-à-vis the Warsaw Pact. Elsewhere, the tie between nuclear weapons and what might happen was more latent, namely, that each side could introduce them into a situation if it determined that local interests and circumstances warranted.

Expressed differently, nuclear weapons had the effect of dampening down competition between the two dominant powers of their day because leaders understood that a nuclear war would be disproportionately costly regardless of the interests at stake. Behind that was the sinister genius of mutually assured destruction (popularly known as MAD) and what was known as second-strike capability, namely, the ability to absorb a nuclear strike by the other side and still be in a position to retaliate on a scale that would deter (assuming rationality was at work) the other side from acting in the first place. Nuclear weapons, by eliminating the incentive to go first because there was little or no advantage in so doing, constituted a big innovation in the annals of order.

I should make clear that it was not nuclear weapons per se that had this effect so much as the nature of the U.S. and Soviet arsenals and the larger bilateral relationship. Nuclear weapons, like any technology or weapon, can contribute to or detract from stability and order depending on numbers, where and how they are deployed, controls instituted to prevent unauthorized use, transparency, the nature of the governments involved, and more. Indeed, and as will be discussed subsequently, nuclear weapons in other contexts are anything but stabilizing and have the potential to add significantly to prospects for disorder.

This is where arms control, in effect a specialized subset of diplomacy, made its contribution. The United States and the Soviet Union negotiated, signed, and entered into a number of agreements over the decades. The net result was to bolster deterrence and stability. The SALT (Strategic Arms Limitations Talks) and START (Strategic Arms Reduction Treaty) agreements did their part by placing limits on the number of weapons each side could deploy. Just as important were the details of the agreed-upon limits, that is, how many bombers versus submarines versus missiles and how many warheads on each, which provided a large degree of certainty that no side could strike first and be confident the other could not retaliate with devastating effect. Arms control also added a meaningful degree of predictability so that decisions premised on incorrect and "worst possible case" assumptions about what the other side was planning to do in the way of developing and fielding additional weapons could largely be avoided.³

Deterrence was reinforced, though, not just by ceilings placed on offense but by far more draconian limits set on defense. The Anti–Ballistic Missile Treaty (ABM Treaty) was signed in 1972 and remained in force for the duration of the Cold War.⁴ Under the pact, the two countries denied themselves the ability to deploy certain kinds of systems that could in principle (probably more than in practice given the state of technology not just at the time but for decades after) threaten the ability of the other side's missiles (whether launched from land-based silos or submarines) to reach their targets. This was the apogee of MAD. It is interesting to note that this near-absolute ban on defenses did not apply to efforts to defend against bombers or submarines carrying nuclear weapons (something that would have been impossible given their role in conventional, nonnuclear warfare), but nevertheless the constraints on missile defense proved to be the cornerstone of nuclear deterrence and stability.

Further adding to stability were mechanisms (both unilateral and negotiated) for monitoring the agreements so that there could be confidence the terms were being respected. Transparency was critical, something dramatically enhanced by satellites. Confidence was further bolstered by separate accords that established rules of the road for the two militaries so they could minimize the chances of incidents at sea or in space that could escalate. Also introduced were dedicated communications links (so-called hotlines) that leaders could access in times of crisis.

Diplomacy was not limited to arms control. There was normal diplomatic interaction via embassies and consulates. The respective ambassadors had access to the most senior levels of each other's governments, as did visiting ministers. There was more than a little trade, cultural exchange, and tourism. And, most dramatically, there was regular summitry involving the leaders of the two countries. In short, the United States and the Soviet Union were great-power rivals, but their rivalry was bounded and did not preclude many normal aspects of relations between two countries.

Such normalcy was in part possible because the two sides

also demonstrated a degree of restraint in their approach to each other. In the early years of the Cold War, and after the Soviet Union tested its first nuclear weapons, there was talk in the United States of "rolling back" Communism there. Rollback was in many ways the 1950s parlance for what today is often called "regime change." It was wisely rejected as both infeasible (the United States lacked the means to bring it about) and reckless, given that a threatened Soviet leadership could lash out militarily in any number of places and ways.

Perhaps more significant, the United States was quite circumspect in what it chose to do in (as opposed to say about) countries within the Soviet empire. To be sure, no U.S. administration ever formally accepted the so-called Brezhnev Doctrine (named for Leonid Brezhnev, the Soviet and Communist Party leader who first articulated the notion) by which Moscow asserted the "right" to use military force to maintain order, that is, fealty, in any of its so-called political satellites in Eastern Europe. At the same time, when there were domestic political uprisings against Soviet-backed governments in Hungary in 1956, Czechoslovakia in 1968, and Poland in 1970, the United States did not intervene in any meaningful way on behalf of those peoples trying to liberate themselves from the rule of Soviet-backed governments. Again, this was a caution born out of concern that any such intervention could lead to a direct clash with forces of the Soviet Union, which presumably would have been deployed to protect what Moscow saw as interests vital to its empire and, as a result, to itself.

This is not to say that either country ignored what was going on inside the other. The United States under Presidents Jimmy Carter and Ronald Reagan (and Congress before that) did raise human rights issues in the Soviet Union, pressing among other things to have high-profile political dissidents freed and for most Soviet Jews to be able to emigrate. And the Soviet Union would regularly point to shortcomings in American society. But these efforts were limited and did not assume a priority that threatened what was seen as a more basic stake in maintaining order either at the nuclear level or in critical regional disputes. Both fundamentally accepted and respected the classic notion that governments enjoyed the sovereign right to run their own societies as they saw fit. George Kennan's doctrine of containment, in which the United States directly and indirectly would find ways to resist Soviet efforts to expand its presence or influence around the world, held out the possibility that the Soviet Union, if sufficiently frustrated in its attempts to spread its influence, might mellow or even fade away with the passage of time, but this was more a distant hope than a policy priority.[5]

Stability during the four decades of the Cold War also benefited from the structural design of international relations at the time, namely, bipolarity. It is less difficult to manage a world of two principal centers of power than many. There are simply fewer independent actors and decision makers with real impact. This is not to say that Great Britain and France and others always did America's bidding; they most assuredly did not. And China's resentment of and late-1960s split from the Soviet Union is a matter of record. Still, the world of the Cold War was to a significant degree a stable "duopoly" in which changes tended to take place within the structure of an international system dominated by two powers. This is worth noting if only because today's world could hardly be more different in that it is neither fixed nor so concentrated in its distribution of power.

Geopolitical restraint was also a hallmark of the Cold War order. Informal rules of the road evolved between Washington and Moscow over the decades about permissible and unacceptable behaviors. One such rule involved a healthy respect for each other's backyards. The term "spheres of influence" is controversial for good reason, as such spheres suggest that the interests of some countries take precedence over the rights of their weaker neighbors. But such spheres can be and to some extent were a source of order. To a large degree each superpower acted with restraint in the affairs of those countries close (in the geographic sense) to the other. As noted above, the United States, for example, did not intervene with military force when the Hungarian people rose up against their Soviet-backed leaders in 1956 or when the people of Czechoslovakia did much the same twelve years later.

For its part, the Soviet Union did what it could to promote Communist regimes around the Western Hemisphere, and succeeded in Cuba and Nicaragua. It had the advantage of aiding individuals and movements fighting against unpopular authoritarian governments that offered little to their people. But again the Soviet help was just that—help—usually in the form of intelligence, military assistance, and subsidies. Direct Soviet military intervention for the most part did not take place in Latin America, a part of the world where the United States had declared (through the Monroe Doctrine) that it was prepared to act to protect what it judged to be important or even vital interests.

If nuclear weapons had never been developed, one could make a plausible case that the Cold War would not have stayed cold, that it might have evolved in very different ways because calculations would have been very different. Any number of confrontations might well have triggered either local military clashes or something much larger and more geographically diffuse.

This is not to say there were not close calls and difficult moments. Perhaps the most dangerous episode of the Cold War came in October 1962 when the United States discovered signs that Soviet personnel sent to Cuba were installing missiles armed with nuclear warheads that could reach the United States in just a few minutes. This move was inconsistent with showing restraint in areas close to the other power; it was also seen by some as undermining nuclear deterrence, although this concern was in fact exaggerated. The U.S. side was firm in its demand that all such missiles be removed but flexible both in how it went about pressing its case (choosing a naval "quarantine" or embargo in all but name over attack) and in quietly agreeing to remove from Turkey its own medium-range missiles that could reach the USSR. The Kennedy administration also gave a public pledge not to invade Cuba, thereby giving the Soviets a face-saving way to back down.

Order was also girded by understandings about how geopolitical competition was to be waged. These understandings tended to be more tacit than explicit. It is thus ironic that the one attempt to make the understandings formal, the 1972 "Basic Principles of Relations Between the United States of America and the Union of Soviet Socialist Republics," in which the two governments solemnly stated that they "attach major importance to preventing the development of situations capable of causing a dangerous exacerbation of their relations" and that "efforts to obtain unilateral advantage at the expense of the other, directly or indirectly, are inconsistent with these objectives," had no discernible impact. Calling for an end to seeking advantage was akin to calling for an end to geopolitical competition; it was détente's equivalent of the Kellogg-Briand Pact, an expression of high-minded aspiration (or, if you prefer, cynicism) more than anything else.

But there were meaningful understandings all the same. Both Moscow and Washington came to appreciate that when it came to supporting associates, there were limits on how much change to the status quo would be tolerable for the other. The Soviets learned this lesson in Berlin when they blockaded the Western sectors and again in Cuba a decade and a half later. The United States learned this lesson the hard way in Korea, when it was not content to restore the status quo ante and after liberating South Korea decided to press north and try to reunify the peninsula by force but under the aegis of Seoul. This outcome was too much for both the Soviets and China, and the Chinese dispatched hundreds of thousands of "volunteers" to push back against the U.S.-led, UN-authorized force. The result was an additional twenty thousand American dead and an end to the fighting two years later at the original border. And during the October 1973 Middle East war between Israel and both Syria and Egypt, when the Americans and the Soviets backed their respective allies, both superpowers also settled for an outcome that left Israel short of a complete victory and the encircled Egyptian army intact.

The region where arrangements to preserve order on terms acceptable to both superpowers were the most developed was Europe, in many ways the original and central arena of the Cold War. Already mentioned was a military balance of power. This was reinforced by a series of arms control negotiations that succeeded in limiting some theater nuclear forces and, at the end of the Cold War, by a formal agreement covering conventional (nonnuclear) military forces as well.

The two alliances also reached an understanding governing political order in Europe. The Final Act that emerged in 1975 in Helsinki from the Conference on Security and Cooperation in Europe was a remarkable document.[7] On one level it reads as a tribute to the classic Westphalian notion of order. It is a multilateral accord premised on state sovereignty, the impermissibility of the threat or use of force, the inviolability of borders, respect for the territorial integrity of all European states, a commitment to the peaceful settlement of disputes, and acceptance of the principle of nonintervention in one another's internal affairs. The one exception to this traditional approach was a commitment by all governments to respect human rights and fundamental freedoms within their own borders.

Despite this exception, the agreement came under intense criticism at the time in American political circles, as it was seen by many as locking in and legitimizing Soviet control of Eastern Europe. It was also seen as quite cynical in that governments were calling for respect for human rights at a time when every member of the Warsaw Pact was abridging them. The critics turned out to have been shortsighted; the arrangement not only helped to keep the peace in Europe, but it also bought time and space for reform efforts to emerge and gain momentum within the Soviet bloc.

Such an approach to managing competition should not be confused with peace. But it did preserve the essentials of stability in an era of nuclear weapons. The fact that the four decades are termed the Cold War counts for a great deal.

Earlier I pointed out that every war is fought at least three times, and the Cold War is no exception. There has been a debate over why it ended when and how it did. It is worth noting that the Cold War ended in a remarkably orderly fashion; it went out with a whimper, not a bang. This was anything but inevitable.

Nevertheless, there were some underlying reasons. The Soviet economic system was deeply and structurally flawed. In 1987 the historian Paul Kennedy published an influential book on why major powers rise and fall throughout history, a principal reason being that the burdens of empire often undermine prosperity and as a result stability at home.[8] The burden of its overseas role and activities surely contributed to the failure of the USSR, which had to support a large military budget, a far-flung set of allies that often needed financial help, the cost of occupation in Eastern Europe, and the economic and human price of imperial adventures such as its ill-fated 1979 intervention in Afghanistan. These costs exacerbated a difficult, inefficient reality brought about by decades of an economy ruled much more by political than by market forces.

Political decisions and diplomacy mattered too. Here much of the history derives from decisions of Mikhail Gorbachev, who led the USSR starting in 1985. Gorbachev clearly concluded that the Soviet Union could survive and compete on the world stage only if it changed in basic ways at home. But his approach to change, in which political reform came before economic restructuring, mostly resulted in a loss of control over what was happening in the streets. An attempt in the summer of 1991 by some around the Kremlin to oust Gorbachev and restore central authority fizzled; it was a classic case of too little, too late. What the failed coup did do, though, was end what little public standing Gorbachev still had, accelerate the demise of the USSR, and strengthen the position of the first president of Russia, Boris Yeltsin. Where both Gorbachev and Yeltsin deserve credit is for accepting their situation and not calling for massive internal repression or undertaking something desperate in the foreign policy realm as a last-ditch effort to alter their fate and the course of history.

But some of the credit for how history unfolded surely goes to successive U.S. presidents and, more broadly, the sustained efforts of the United States and its allies over four decades. George Kennan, the architect of containment, proved prescient when he suggested the Soviet system might not be able to withstand the prolonged frustration of being unable to expand its reach.[9] George H. W. Bush, the American president at the time the Berlin Wall came down in November 1989, deserves special praise for his handling of the Cold War's final chapter. Bush was criticized at the time and afterward for not making more of these events, but he was careful not to humiliate his opposite numbers and risk bringing about a situation that could have pressured them to take dramatic action or brought to power those who wanted to do just that. That the Cold War ended peacefully and included the breakup of the Soviet Union, the unification of Germany, and Germany's entrance into NATO is nothing short of remarkable. Again, what transpired was anything but inevitable.

Much of history is often triggered by the friction caused by epochal events, and in this case such an outcome was avoided. It demonstrates again the importance of individuals and the quality of statecraft and diplomacy.[10]

In reviewing the sweep of the four decades of the Cold War, it is hard not to conclude that it did in fact comprise a significant degree of order. There was a balance of power (and, as noted, one including nuclear weapons), a shared if limited notion of what constituted legitimacy, and a diplomatic process to maintain the balance of power and to deal with situations that challenged competing notions of what was desirable and acceptable. The result was that the third great-power struggle of the twentieth century proved to be fundamentally different from the first two.

3. The Other Order

It turns out that the managed competition that was the Cold War was not the only source of order in the aftermath of the Second World War. Indeed, there was as well what might be called a post–World War II order that operated alongside but apart from the Cold War. This second order (one sometimes referred to as the "liberal democratic order," although in fact it was both more and less than that) had multiple dimensions, including the economic, political, diplomatic, and strategic, and was both global and regional.[1] It is important to note all this because even though the order that was a function of the Cold War largely disappeared with its end and the demise of the Soviet Union, the post–World War II order lived on and continues to have an impact both in what it contributes and what it fails to.

The economic dimension of the post–World War II order was designed to promote a world (or, more accurately, a non-Communist world) that encouraged trade, development, and

1. trade
2. development
3. Markets

well-functioning monetary operations. Trade was viewed both as an engine of economic growth and as a means of creating ties between and among countries that would give them a stake in maintaining peaceful relations. Development was judged as a moral but also a political and strategic necessity so that billions of people around the world could lead productive, satisfying lives and not be tempted to opt for Communism. If they could not, many countries or colonies on a path to becoming countries would never know stability. And there needed to be a mechanism for trade and investment and tourism to work, something that required a system for managing dozens of national currencies in a fashion that would spur growth and facilitate interactions of every sort.

The result, to use the shorthand, was the Bretton Woods system, a set of arrangements along with a number of global institutions created when many of the world's finance ministers gathered in 1944 at Bretton Woods, New Hampshire. One goal was to promote the recovery of war-ravaged countries and the development of poor ones; this became the province of the International Bank for Reconstruction and Development, more commonly known as the World Bank. Another goal was to set up a functional monetary system that would reflect the desire of sovereign states to control their own fate but also to be able to trade and invest with others. The dollar became the effective world currency given the size and strength of the U.S. economy; all currencies were "fixed" in relation to the dollar, which in turn was backed by gold. In principle, anyone could exchange excess dollars for gold. The International Monetary Fund (IMF) was established to provide loans on a temporary basis to governments running a net deficit so that they could meet their short-term spending needs and reach a point of fiscal balance.[2]

A related but distinct set of issues concerning trade was formally taken up not at the Bretton Woods gathering but separately by trade ministers. The intent was to create an entity called the International Trade Organization, but differences between countries (and the politics within them) precluded it at the time. Instead, a series of major meetings over the decades developed rules for global trade and led to a number of important pacts that reduced tariff barriers. (These all came under the rubric of the General Agreement on Tariffs and Trade, or GATT.) It took no fewer than fifty years for the World Trade Organization (WTO), with the ability to adjudicate disputes as well as provide a forum for global negotiations, to be born.

The second dimension of the post–World War II order was diplomatic. The United Nations was the centerpiece. The idea was to create a global body, a standing forum that could prevent or, if prevention failed, resolve international disputes. The UN Charter instructs parties to any dispute that threatens international peace and security to "seek a solution by negotiation, enquiry, mediation, conciliation, arbitration, judicial settlement, resort of regional agencies or arrangements, or other peaceful means of their own choice." It could also be a force for peace in the literal sense, as under Chapter VII of its charter members can take measures ranging from blockades to whatever action is needed using air, land, and sea forces "to maintain or restore international peace and security." But the bias was clearly one of discouraging the use of force as the means of settling disagreements between states.[3]

chpt [7]

The responsibility for operationalizing all this was to be vested in the Security Council, the body of five permanent members (the United States, the Soviet Union, China, Great Britain, and France) and originally six and later ten rotating members serving two-year terms. Only the five permanent members (which at the time the UN was created were considered the dominant powers of the post–World War II era) were given a veto. The Chinese seat passed from the Republic of China, or Taiwan, to the People's Republic of China (PRC), or mainland China, in 1971. The Soviet seat was inherited by Russia in late 1991. The Security Council was given the "primary responsibility for the maintenance of international peace and security." In principle, it was to be the "concert" that would orchestrate international relations and maintain order between and among states in the post–World War II era.

The UN also both reflected and reinforced existing thinking about order. Article 51, for example, famously declares, "Nothing in the present Charter shall impair the inherent right of individual or collective self-defense if an armed attack occurs against a Member of the United Nations." Implicit in this and explicit elsewhere in the charter was that member-

right to self-defense

ship in the UN was limited to sovereign states (Article 4, clause 1) and that all such entities enjoyed "sovereign equality," that is, were equal in standing (Article 2, clause 1). This principle is manifested most sharply in the General Assembly, which has a "one country, one vote" premise that gives the United States or China no more of a role than the weakest or least populous country anywhere in the world. The charter also specifies that "nothing . . . shall authorize the United Nations to intervene in matters which are essentially within the domestic jurisdiction of any state" (Article 2, clause 7). What all this adds up to is a Westphalian order, in which the rights of sovereign entities, that is, states, are recognized and protected.

create collective interests by commitments w/o infringing on sovereignty

The third pillar of the postwar order was strategic. The goal here was to forestall risks to peace that would be difficult to manage and ruinous if management failed. Here the UN was largely limited by the realities of great-power relations, and above all U.S.-Soviet relations, in that both (along with the United Kingdom, France, and China) possessed permanent vetoes in the Security Council. Implicit in this design was that the UN was not to be used as an instrument by one great power against another; rather, it was meant to be preserved as a venue the major powers could and would turn to even when they disagreed. Also understood in principle if not in practice was that uses of military force for purposes other than self-defense were to be avoided.

Relevant too in this context was the Treaty on the Non-

Proliferation of Nuclear Weapons, or NPT.[4] It was based on the premise that a world of additional nuclear states (there were five when it was signed in 1968) would be more dangerous and potentially disorderly for any number of reasons. Danger could come from the complexity of establishing deterrence relationships among multiple parties. There was also the risk that nuclear weapons in more hands could lead to those weapons or materials falling into the wrong hands. And of course there was the concern that the existence of such weapons meant that the possibility of their use could not be ruled out.

The NPT is a series of bargains. It asks the five countries allowed to possess nuclear weapons (the United States, the Soviet Union [subsequently Russia], China, Great Britain, and France, all of which are essentially grandfathered) not to transfer nuclear weapons or to assist, encourage, or induce any state without them to acquire them. It also sets forth the principle that these states will avoid a nuclear arms race and move toward ridding themselves of the nuclear weapons they do have. It asks those states without nuclear weapons not to acquire such devices or related assistance and not to produce such weapons themselves. It guarantees access to nuclear energy for peaceful purposes. And it asks the nonnuclear-weapon states to accept "safeguards" (essentially inspections) that would verify that they are acting consistently with the treaty.

Parallel efforts were undertaken in other realms. The Biological Weapons Convention, signed in 1972 and entering

how we need this sort of regulation on cyber warfare

into force three years later, <u>makes it illegal for any state party</u> <u>to the accord (and all the parties to it were states) to acquire,</u> <u>develop, or transfer biological weapons of any kind.</u>[5] Those who possessed such weapons at the time the agreement entered into force in 1975 were responsible for destroying them. A global accord (the Chemical Weapons Convention) that banned the production and use of chemical weapons finally came into effect in 1997.[6]

Although regional bodies were formed in every part of the world, the most significant process by far took root in Europe. The motivating idea (one normally attributed to the then foreign minister of France, Robert Schuman) was to knit Germany and France so closely together that the notion of yet another war between them would become unthinkable. This objective was meant as well to reinforce the political project of remaking West Germany's economy, society, and political institutions so as to prevent the rise of another authoritarian regime that would be a threat to its own people and its neighbors. The European Coal and Steel Community, consisting of France, West Germany, Italy, and the three Benelux countries of Belgium, the Netherlands, and Luxembourg, was the beginning of the European project, one that over the following decades evolved into the European Community and later still the European Union, in the process broadening its membership and deepening the areas of domestic and foreign policy it affected.

There was also the matter of bringing the colonial era to

an end. At the close of World War II, much of the world, including most of the Middle East, Africa, and Asia, was ruled by the countries of Europe. Decolonization was founded on the idea that peoples had the right to establish independent nation-states; this was the concept of self-determination. Independence was sought by virtually all the populations living under colonial rule. Interestingly, it was also supported by both the Soviet Union and the United States: the former saw it as an opportunity to win converts, while the latter feared that absent independence these societies would turn to the Soviets for support against the Western colonialists. With time, the populations of the mostly European colonial powers themselves grew weary of the costs of maintaining rule in faraway places that wanted to be on their own.

By then, decolonization was viewed as a prerequisite to order, as otherwise it was feared that conflicts would develop in many of these places. That was an understandable concern, although it is one of the tragic ironies of history that the end of the colonial era, rather than promoting order, in many instances created disorder on a large scale. This was certainly the case when the British gave up responsibility in 1947 in South Asia, which triggered a violent war that led to the partition of the subcontinent between India and Pakistan. Partition was also the approach for Palestine, where the British departure a year later was followed by the establishment of the state of Israel and an immediate invasion of the new state by its Arab neighbors. France tired of trying to maintain control of Indochina and conceded defeat in 1954, leaving behind a divided country that would continue to be at war with itself for another two decades. France walked away from Tunisia and Morocco in 1956 and was effectively driven out of Algeria in 1962 after a bloody civil war.

Perhaps the turning point in the decolonization process came in 1956 following the takeover of the Suez Canal by Egypt's nationalist leader, Gamal Abdel Nasser. A coordinated British, French, and Israeli invasion of Egypt only managed to strengthen Nasser's position and to infuriate the U.S. administration of the day, which wanted to keep the world's focus on the brutal Soviet repression of the people of Hungary that was being carried out at the same time. The British government fell; the country's appetite for an imperial role waned, as did its capacity to maintain one. Most of the remaining British holdings in the Middle East, Africa, and Asia broke away and established their independence in the ensuing decade. Other European powers such as Belgium and Portugal experienced similar fates in Africa in the 1960s and 1970s. The colonial era was over, replaced by an uneasy mixture of local nationalism and Cold War competition.[7]

Another aspect of the post–World War II order was political, but in a different sense. The Universal Declaration of Human Rights, adopted by the UN General Assembly in 1948, notes that every person on the planet without exception possesses a broad and extensive range of rights, including equal standing before the law; freedom of movement and residence within his country's borders; the right to own property; freedom of thought, conscience, and religion; freedom of expression and opinion; the right to peaceful assembly; and much more. To be sure, the declaration lacked any enforcement provisions and was cynically ignored from the start by most of the governments that signed it. Still, it is noteworthy in expressing the position that states are not the only ones with rights.[8]

Around the same time most of the world's governments also approved the Convention on the Prevention and Punishment of the Crime of Genocide. The impetus was to make sure that the experience of the Holocaust would never again occur. The Genocide Convention, though, provided few mechanisms for prevention. The emphasis was on bringing anyone responsible for carrying out a genocide to justice; ideally, the certainty of punishment would deter individuals and governments from undertaking a genocide in the first place. Even so, it took another fifty years, until 1998, for a standing International Criminal Court to be established to try individuals charged with crimes relating to genocide.[9]

A final element of the post–World War II order was legal in nature. To some extent, just about every aspect of order already noted had a legal dimension. But there was as well an explicit legal order composed of rules and procedures to facilitate commerce, travel, communication, and other day-to-day

[handwritten margin notes: "significant in that it recognized individual rights beyond state sovereignty" and "fighting human rights abuses"]

forms of interaction between and among people, corporations, and/or countries. There were also norms meant to facilitate diplomacy, from the obligations of governments to
provide protection to foreign embassies, consulates, and diplomats to principles for recognizing governments and entering
into and sustaining treaties and other forms of international
agreements.

What can be said about the post–World War II order?
Global economic performance was impressive even though
the gains to some extent reflected population increases. The
world economy increased fivefold between 1950 and 1990.
Trade volume grew even more rapidly, from approximately
$125 billion in 1950 to $7 trillion forty years later. As for
development, the number of people on the earth living in
extreme poverty (about 1.3 billion) stayed roughly constant
over those years even though global population doubled,
from 2.5 billion to more than 5 billion.[10]

But to note this accomplishment is not the same as attrib-
uting it to global machinery or giving that machinery high
marks. A good deal of what was accomplished represented
national economic policies. The World Bank's impact on development, for example, was modest. The trade regime (the
GATT) deserves credit for reducing tariffs and other barriers to trade in manufacturing. But it did less well at promoting trade in agriculture or services and failed to get a handle
on government subsidies.

The monetary order had its own shortcomings. The system set up could not contend either with the chronic deficits run by the United States or with the chronic surpluses (resulting in enormous pools of dollars) maintained by such countries as export-oriented Japan. This reality led the Nixon administration in 1971 to end the convertibility of dollars into gold, as there was no way the United States could continue the practice given the massive dollar holdings of others. There was tension due to the dollar's being the de facto global currency as well as the national currency of the United States. Policies introduced for domestic reasons—say, to accelerate economic growth at home—would invariably have consequences elsewhere. The IMF for its part did not have the authority, tools, or resources required to impose discipline on most of its members.

The Universal Declaration of Human Rights both reflected and contributed to the growing salience accorded human rights concerns. In many ways it was the forerunner of other efforts to protect individuals from the actions of government and to hold governments and those who acted on their behalf responsible for such actions. But as will be seen, there was little in the way of international consensus on these issues and no enforcement mechanism. Much the same was the case with the Genocide Convention, which had no impact on preventing a genocide in Cambodia, where between one and a half and two million men, women, and children were killed by the Khmer Rouge in the late 1970s. And it took

Cambodian genocide
late 1970's

three decades for any of those responsible to be tried and sent to prison.

The United Nations never fulfilled the hopes of its most ardent proponents, but these hopes were never realistic to begin with. It could not provide the machinery for managing the Cold War given the gaps on many issues between the United States and the Soviet Union. The Security Council became as much an arena of the Cold War as anything else. The two superpowers chose to use it as a stage in the effort to win over public opinion around the world. It did, however, offer a venue for useful venting, and the UN's back rooms provided a place where diplomats could meet out of the glare of cameras.

All this began to change only toward the closing act of the Cold War. The Security Council did play an important role in coordinating the international response to Saddam Hussein's aggression against Kuwait. But what this highlighted was not just that the Cold War had lost most of its intensity but also that the issue at hand—the violation of the territorial integrity and sovereign status of a UN member state—was one of the few around which consensus could be generated. This was the bedrock of the traditional approach to world order. The Security Council did not generate this consensus so much as reflect it.

Nor did the UN do much to advance the post–World War II order. Decolonization was a messy business, often determined by the domestic politics of the colonial power, the often violent situation on the ground, or both. Elsewhere, and as was the case with the 1990 Kuwait crisis, the UN was able to contribute only when consensus existed; its ability to forge international agreement was largely absent. For its part, the General Assembly showed itself to be ideological and inefficient and hence largely irrelevant except for the occasion early on when it authorized the international response to North Korea's invasion of the South in June 1950.

The Non-Proliferation Treaty likewise has had a mixed record. Much of one's assessment depends on one's expectations. President John F. Kennedy spoke in 1963 of a world that could see a number of additional countries acquire nuclear weapons by the mid-1970s.[11] Fortunately, nothing like that came to pass. But in its first three decades the NPT could not prevent the emergence of four additional nuclear-armed states: Israel, India, Pakistan, and North Korea.

Much of this mixed record stemmed from limits to the NPT itself. To begin with, no country is required to join. Second, the treaty makes clear that nothing in it is meant to stand in the way of a member country's developing or importing what is needed to produce nuclear energy for peaceful purposes. Unfortunately, much of what is needed to produce a weapon can be developed or acquired under the cover of producing nuclear energy. Third, the entire inspections process is designed to be cooperative; it is a gentleman's agreement in a world in which some governments are led by individuals who are anything but gentlemen and who are prepared to lie about or conceal relevant activities. Fourth, there are no automatic penalties or sanctions built into the agreement for violations. And fifth, states retain the option to withdraw from the treaty with no more than three months' notice. In short, it is a pact among sovereign entities not to violate the norm of proliferation unless they determine it is in their interest to do so.

The record for biological and chemical weapons has been similarly mixed. In the case of the former, it is difficult and at times impossible to be confident that the ban is being observed. Verification was and remains a problem. To name one example, Iraq (which was a signatory of the Biological Weapons Convention) under Saddam Hussein built a serious capability that escaped detection for years. The challenge was (and is) even greater with chemical weapons, which are less difficult to fabricate (all it takes is a simple level of manufacturing know-how) and to conceal. As noted previously, a global convention that banned the production and use of chemical weapons did not come into effect until 1997; more significant, chemical weapons were used on several occasions (by Egypt in Yemen in the 1960s, by Iraq against Iran in the 1980s, by Syria in 2013) without any serious consequences for the side using them.

Europe was one of the post–World War II era's signature

successes. The region that had been at the core of so much destructive history experienced its most peaceful and successful decades in centuries. Some of this was due to stability that had its roots in the balance of power and deterrence stemming from the Cold War, but much of what was accomplished also reflected Western Europe's rapid economic recovery (in no small part because of the Marshall Plan), the successful democratization of Germany, and the progress of European construction.

Other regions had a more mixed record. One reason is that regional bodies in Latin America, Africa, East and South Asia, and the Middle East counted for little owing to a lack of universal membership, a requirement of consensus that could rarely if ever be met, a lack of capacity, or some combination of the above. Asia was the locus of two of the major conflicts of the Cold War era: the Korean War and the Vietnam War. The former took place before the implicit rules that would structure Cold War competition had fully emerged. Vietnam for its part can be seen both as a failure to maintain order and as something of a success in that the competition was restrained. Soviet and Chinese support for Vietnam was indirect and U.S. military intervention was kept relatively localized. South Asia witnessed several limited conflicts between India and Pakistan, the crisis within East Pakistan that (with India acting as midwife) led to the creation of an independent Bangladesh, and the conflict in Afghanistan that by the time it ended in 1989 had contributed to the demise of the Soviet Union. The Middle East was in many ways the most violent of regions in terms of number of conflicts. One fault line associated with recurring conflicts was that between Israel and its Arab neighbors. There was the 1948 war at the time of Israel's independence, the 1956 Suez Crisis, the 1967 Six-Day War, the 1973 October or Yom Kippur War, and the intifadas that brought Palestinians and Israelis into direct conflict. Elsewhere in the region numerous other conflicts took place, from the civil war that began in Lebanon in the mid-1970s to the eight-year war between Iran and Iraq that ended only in 1988. Latin America and Africa also experienced conflict, almost all of it within states (civil wars of one sort or another) or fought by armed groups that were based in one country and intervened in another. Largely missing from both continents were wars of scale fought between states.

Decolonization was in many ways unique and essentially completed in a matter of just a few decades. Unfortunately, the process, undertaken in the name of building a more just and stable order, often resulted in just the opposite. Promoting independence may have avoided one set of disorders, but if so, it quickly replaced them with another, many of which linger in one form or another to the present. Self-determination proved to be no panacea. Many of the countries were not ready for self-governance; many of these same countries found themselves embroiled in disputes or conflicts with their neighbors.

International law had its greatest effect in areas in which

the political stakes were the most modest—and, as one would expect, the least impact where the stakes were greatest. The law was useful in facilitating the operations of the international system but did not take precedence over what governments considered to be their national interests. International courts operated in technical areas but for the most part not in the diplomatic, especially where major issues were contested.

Overall, the post–World War II order was predicated on familiar, traditional approaches to international relations, as state sovereignty was for the most part at its core. This was the impetus behind decolonization and the philosophy and structure of the United Nations. There were exceptions, including in the realm of human rights, but these were more in form than in fact. The bigger exception in many ways was the rise of supranational bodies in Europe, reflecting a willingness on the part of its member states to cede some of their autonomy and authority to regional bodies.

It thus comes as little surprise that the post–World War II order—effectively World Order 1.0—provided only a degree of structure for the international system once the overlay and discipline of the Cold War order disappeared. Just as important, the world was not well positioned to deal with the diffusion of power that was to come, with the emergence of nonstate actors, or with the many challenges of globalization. There was little in the way of thinking about, much less agreement on, what would constitute a legitimate order and the global architecture and machinery that would be needed to create and sustain it. This would call for a new and different approach, World Order 2.0. Thus when the Cold War ended it was as if the tide had gone out, leaving a world that had been expecting something of a respite from history mostly exposed and unprepared for what was to follow.

PART II

4. The Post–Cold War World

A large part of history over the past three centuries arose from the interaction between and among the major powers of the day. Competition and disagreement often led to conflict, at times on a scale and at a cost that dwarfed all else. This was certainly the case during the twentieth century, which was defined by two world wars and the Cold War, which arguably stayed cold mostly because of the stabilizing effect of nuclear weapons.

I say all this because by the measure of major-power politics, the quarter century that is the post–Cold War world appears to have gone quite well. Relations among the major powers of this era—the United States, China, Russia, Japan, Europe, and India—while far from harmonious, have been by historical standards pretty good. Direct conflict between one or more major powers has been absent from international relations over the past twenty-five years. Indeed, it is hard to point to a case where major conflict (as opposed to an armed incident) was even a serious possibility. This as much as anything else distinguishes these few decades from most others in the modern (post-1648) era. Yet, as the title of this book makes clear, ours is a world in disarray. All of which raises the fundamental question: How is it that the world is not doing better, if what has been the principal source of history's problems is by most measures relatively absent?

Answering this question requires an examination not just of great-power relations but also of global and regional dynamics. But first it is essential to focus on why major-power ties have been better than history's pattern. One factor is that U.S. primacy has been so pronounced that it would have been difficult and unwise for any power to directly challenge the United States militarily. It is also true that while other powers have often disagreed with particular U.S. policies, they did not for the most part see the United States as pursuing a course of action in the world that threatened their own vital national interests. All of this highlights a related factor, namely, that today's powers have been more concerned with internal economic and social development than with external conquest, and internal development requires not just external stability but relationships that contribute to economic development. Interdependence—the degree to which the fate, economic and otherwise, of one country is tied to and directly correlated with that of another—has proved to be a bulwark against conflict.

Great-power relations have also been relatively good because three of the powers (the United States, Europe, and Japan) are not just market-oriented democracies but are tied by alliances. India likewise is democratic and, with the exception of Pakistan, has not been overly preoccupied with geopolitics. The governments of both China and Russia, while concerned with maintaining control over their populations and territory, also evolved in ways that made them less closed than they were during the Cold War. China in particular focused on economic development; Russia for its part rode the wave of higher oil prices. Neither was in a position to carry out a foreign policy premised on confrontation and expansion on a global scale. Nevertheless, great-power relations were most complex when they involved the United States and either China or Russia or when they involved either of the latter and one or more of their immediate neighbors. More important, these relations have taken a turn for the worse, especially between the United States and Russia. The question is whether this is a temporary blip or a prelude to a secular decline in the quality of the relationships and, as a result, a return to something closer to history's norm.

No relationship has been more important than the one between the United States, the dominant power of the era, and China, the country widely seen as posing the biggest challenge to American primacy. It is also true that no relationship was likely to experience more difficulties. Much of history is the result of friction leading to conflict between existing and rising powers, reflecting the difficulty in peacefully

[margin note: to think evolved to be part of LISO]

[margin note: power-transition theory]

accommodating the changing power balance and relationship between the two. This pattern often goes by the shorthand of the "Thucydides Trap," named for the ancient Greek historian who two and a half millennia ago chronicled the competition between a rising Athens and the established but suspicious power of Sparta, which resulted in the Peloponnesian War.[1] The realist school of international relations, which is mostly about power and the unavoidable struggle for absolute and relative shares thereof, would have predicted that the Sino-American relationship would inevitably deteriorate.

Adding to this pessimism was that with the end of the Cold War and the demise of the Soviet Union came the disappearance of what had been the glue of the U.S.-China rapprochement that developed in the early 1970s under Richard Nixon and Henry Kissinger on the U.S. side and Mao Tsetung and Chou En-lai for the Chinese. A shared adversary was enough for the two countries to get over their hostile past and their ideological differences, but it was not at all clear what would take its place if Sino-American cooperation was to survive the removal of what had brought them together in the first place.

Nevertheless, the relationship between the two remained surprisingly good in the aftermath of the Cold War. Growing economic ties filled much of the space that had been taken up by shared concern about the Soviet Union. Two-way merchandise trade alone grew from $20 billion in 1990 to nearly

$600 billion twenty-five years later.[2] Investment likewise grew from negligible to truly substantial amounts. Meanwhile, diplomatic interaction both increased and expanded as top-level summits came to be supplemented by frequent meetings involving both governments' bureaucracies discussing the full range of bilateral, regional, and increasingly global issues.

But the congruence was broader. The underlying premise of China's national security following the chaos of Mao's Cultural Revolution was that the country needed several decades of economic development if it was to be stable and secure, that the rate of development needed to be rapid, and that such growth could take place only amid regional stability and decent relations with the world's largest and most innovative economy. All of this provided a rationale from China's perspective for behaving with restraint and maintaining good relations with the United States so that trade would grow and technology transfers would be forthcoming.

The United States also had reasons to continue to maintain a working relationship with China. Again, economics was at the core: there was plenty of incentive to gain access to a burgeoning middle class in a country of well over one billion people. Over time, the imbalance between exports to and imports from China turned China into a massive holder of U.S. debt. This reality actually tied the two countries' fates to each other: the last thing Washington wanted was for China to stop buying or, worse yet, start unloading U.S. debt, which could have forced the Federal Reserve Bank to raise interest rates and slow an economy that didn't need slowing; the last thing Chinese officials wanted to see was their sizable dollar holdings lose value. Even more important to China was access to the wealthy U.S. market and to U.S. investment. The core bargain between China's ruling Communist Party and the country's people was that the party would deliver ever-improving living standards and employment, something that required the ability to export ever-increasing amounts of manufactured goods to the United States (representing as it did one-fourth of the world's economy) and to tap U.S. technology and investment so that China could expand its ability to produce in a competitive fashion. In return, the Chinese people were mostly prepared to accept that their political and personal choices would be heavily influenced and constrained by the party.

None of this is meant to suggest that the Sino-American relationship was not without major problems. The first and arguably most dramatic took place just as the Cold War was winding down, in the spring of 1989, when Chinese students and others gathered in Beijing's Tiananmen Square to mourn the death of Hu Yaobang, a former general secretary of the Communist Party and someone associated with a reformist orientation. The protests grew in size and intensity, and after much internal debate over how to respond, the government declared martial law and subsequently moved to clear the square with force. Thousands of students and some police were killed or injured.

For U.S. officials, these events brought into sharp relief a question that had long been at the center of the American foreign policy debate: To what extent should U.S. ties with other countries be based upon matters of state and foreign policy, and to what extent should U.S. attitudes and policies be shaped by what other countries did within their borders, by their domestic nature as much as or more than anything else?

The administration of President George H. W. Bush, who among other things had been the de facto U.S. ambassador to China for just over a year (from late 1974 through the end of 1975) after the United States opened up a liaison office in Beijing in 1973, leaned heavily in the direction of foreign policy realism and opted for maintaining the core of the relationship despite the Chinese government's harsh repression of the students and others. There was some public criticism, and limited sanctions were put into effect, but the Bush administration went to considerable lengths to protect the core relationship and maintain a dialogue.[3]

Some on the left and right alike saw this as unprincipled, but actually it was realpolitik. It was the right choice for a number of reasons. First, the United States had many interests involving China; it did not have the luxury of allowing the entire relationship to rise and fall on how China treated its own citizens. Second, it is anything but clear that a U.S. policy of greater censure and sanction would have brought about a China that accorded its people more political and economic freedom. Isolating China might have had precisely the opposite effect. Indeed, there is every reason to believe that China's leaders would have used more force against their own people if they had determined that such a course was required to maintain an intact country and the primacy of the Communist Party.

Another interest at stake with China was Taiwan. Again, the United States opted for what might be termed realism as opposed to idealism. This is an issue with a long story attached to it, one that goes back to the 1930s and 1940s and the Chinese Civil War. The United States was a longtime ally of the Republic of China (led by the Nationalist government of Chiang Kai-shek), which fought alongside the United States during World War II against Japan. But fours year after the end of the war, China's Communists, led by Mao Tse-tung, defeated the Nationalists, who fled to the island of Formosa (now Taiwan). The People's Republic of China came into being in 1949 and ruled the mainland; the Republic of China ruled just Taiwan and a few surrounding islands. Both claimed to be the only government of all China; both held firmly to the proposition that there was and could be only one China.

The United States refused to recognize what was informally known as Communist or mainland (or "Red") China after its victory in the civil war. This policy was consistent with the anti-Communism that animated U.S. policy during the Cold War. National concerns and nationalism often received less weight in U.S. assessments than professed ideology. But all this began to change in the late 1960s and early

1970s amid evidence of a serious split between Communist China and the Soviet Union. Richard Nixon and his national security adviser, Henry Kissinger, saw this growing rivalry as an opportunity to coordinate with China to contain Soviet power. Ping-pong diplomacy and secret consultations with Chinese leaders ensued. In 1971, the mainland took up China's place in the United Nations and its permanent chair (along with its veto) in the Security Council.

What remained, though, was the question of the status and fate of the Republic of China or Taiwan. The government in Beijing insisted that it alone was the government of China, that Taiwan was a province of China, and that Taiwan could never be independent. The United States for its part agreed that "there is but one China and that Taiwan is a part of China." But the United States also stated its interest that there be a peaceful settlement of the Taiwan question worked out by the Chinese themselves. The U.S. side declared as an "ultimate objective" the withdrawal of all U.S. forces and bases from Taiwan, and committed itself to a gradual reduction in its military presence "as the tension in the area diminishes." All this and more was spelled out in the 1972 Shanghai Communiqué, the defining document of the new relationship between the United States and the People's Republic of China, issued when Nixon and Kissinger visited China in early 1972.[4]

Subsequent decades and communiqués saw efforts to make good on these pledges, or at least to finesse them.[5] In late 1978, the U.S. and (mainland) Chinese governments agreed to establish diplomatic relations as of January 1, 1979. On that same date, the United States terminated both diplomatic relations and its security treaty with Taiwan. All U.S. military forces (which had been stationed there since 1955) were withdrawn. Months later, though, Congress passed and President Jimmy Carter signed the Taiwan Relations Act (TRA), which established offices in each other's capitals (in place of formal embassies) and committed the United States to make available to Taiwan "such defense articles and defense services in such quantity as may be necessary to enable Taiwan to maintain a sufficient self-defense capability." The United States also expressed its commitment to carry out appropriate action in response to any threat to Taiwan. However hedged this comment was, it signaled to the government in Beijing that it could not assume it had a free hand to coerce Taiwan or use force to affect its status.[6]

As was the case before, relations among Beijing, Washington, and Taipei became an exercise in managing the tensions if not contradictions among pledges made in the three communiqués and those incorporated into the Taiwan Relations Act. In reality, both the PRC and Taiwan have avoided significant changes to the status quo: the mainland has not used force to bring about reunification, something that would likely trigger a U.S. defense of Taiwan and deal a serious blow to China's economy; Taiwan for its part has not unilaterally declared independence, something likely to trigger a Chinese armed response and cause massive disruption to Taiwan's

a delicate balance

economy, which is heavily dependent on trade with the mainland. In short, both deterrence and economic interdependence appear to be working as designed here. The issue has been handled sufficiently well that it has not interfered with the ability of the United States and the PRC to carry out a largely mutually beneficial relationship. In foreign policy, managing a situation in a manner that fails to address core or what are sometimes described as final status issues can be preferable to attempting to bring about a solution sure to be unacceptable to one or more of the parties and that could as a result provoke a dangerous response.

Economics, cited earlier as a source of interdependence and hence some ballast for the United States and China, also became a recurring source of friction between the two countries. The imbalance in merchandise trade was a source of considerable resentment within the United States. China replaced Japan in the eyes of many Americans as the poster child for unfair foreign trade practices that were viewed as eliminating American jobs. To some extent this was true, in that China, like other countries, often kept its currency at artificially low levels to decrease the cost (and increase the attractiveness) of its exports and to increase the cost of (thereby reducing demand for) imports. It also heavily subsidized some industries, kept wages low, and gave short shrift to environmental concerns. ·

Regional issues were similarly occasions of cooperation and disagreement. China was mostly supportive of U.S. efforts to reverse Saddam Hussein's invasion of Kuwait in 1990 given its views on sovereignty and its desire to cultivate good ties with the only remaining superpower. It similarly was sympathetic to U.S. actions in the immediate aftermath of 9/11 given its own concerns about terrorism and its desire to see Afghanistan (a neighbor) stable. The same cannot be said of the war with Serbia in the 1990s, which China mostly opposed, consistent with its expansive view of sovereignty. Adding insult to injury was the accidental U.S. bombing of the Chinese embassy in Belgrade, which not all Chinese were prepared to view as unintentional.

From the American perspective, one particularly frustrating dimension of Chinese regional policy involved North Korea. China was unhappy with the North's nuclear program, and relations between them deteriorated across the board, hardly a unique outcome for a relationship between unequals. But China was unwilling to use most of the leverage it derived from all it did to buttress the North's economy, including allowing goods to pass though China as they headed to or from North Korea. China clearly feared that too much pressure would trigger instability in the North, which could create a refugee crisis or, more seriously, lead the North to do something desperate with its conventional armed forces, its nuclear weapons, or both. And there was the concern that any such crisis could lead to a war that would end with a unified country on China's border with its capital in Seoul and in the American strategic orbit. The result was that the United

States and China could often find common ground on UN resolutions and sanctions aimed at North Korea, but not on a policy that would actually lead to its denuclearization, fundamental reform, or demise.

On other issues there was a similar mix of overlap and disagreement. Like most other countries, China opposed the U.S. decision to attack Iraq in 2003, believing it was unwarranted. China went along with what it thought was a limited humanitarian intervention in Libya in 2011, but, like Russia, it was critical when the effort expanded into one of regime change. China also was more supportive than not of sanctions to curb Iran's nuclear ambitions and, as will be discussed in greater detail below, committed itself to take steps to reduce its own carbon emissions starting in 2030.

There has been some deterioration in U.S.-Chinese relations in recent years. From the U.S. perspective, the reasons include more assertive Chinese behavior in the region, such as the unilateral declaration of a large "air defense identification zone," the staking out of expanded claims to territorial seas, and the physical expansion of islands in the South China Sea; a Chinese military buildup across the board; widespread theft of intellectual property; a persistent large trade imbalance in China's favor that many in the United States judge to result at least in part from unfair trading practices; and an increase in Chinese political repression at home. There are as well American observers concerned that China will embrace a more nationalist foreign policy in order to compensate for a

diminution in support for the government and the Communist Party brought about by lower levels of economic growth.[7]

China for its part has its own bill of particulars. Chinese
officials regularly express their frustrations with export regulations that limit its access to advanced American technology.
They argue that U.S. military support of Taiwan contravenes
U.S. commitments to China. They also view U.S. criticisms
of their behavior in the South China Sea as constituting a
double standard, as other countries they judge as acting similarly (including Vietnam and the Philippines) are not singled
out for criticism by U.S. officials.[8] The Chinese also see the
United States rallying to Japan's side in their dispute over islands in the East China Sea. Widespread is the belief that
the United States stands in the way of China's emergence as
a regional and global power of the first rank. One relatively
minor episode was telling in this regard. In late 2013, Chinese
president Xi Jinping announced a plan to build the Asian
Infrastructure Investment Bank, or AIIB. As the name suggests, it would gather international funds to finance major
transportation, energy, telecommunications, and other projects in that part of the world. China itself promised to provide
a substantial amount of the initial funding. The United States
resisted the project from the outset, fearing it would undercut
the work of other institutions (such as the World Bank and
the Asian Development Bank), which had a record of insist-
ing on higher standards for everything from environmental
protection to limiting corruption. Also motivating the U.S.

stance was a desire to push back against this latest bid by China for a larger regional role.

The Obama administration went so far as to lobby friends and allies not to join the Chinese-sponsored institution. This effort failed miserably, as more than fifty countries, including such close friends and allies as the United Kingdom, South Korea, Israel, and Australia, opted to become founding members of the AIIB. Why the United States did not choose to join from the outset if certain conditions were met is a mystery. The result was that Washington lost influence over the effort, looked impotent, and persuaded many in China that the United States sought to prevent China from assuming a leading role in the world.[9]

Overall, Sino-American relations a quarter of a century after the end of the Cold War are difficult to describe or categorize. In many ways, the two are still searching for a rationale to take the place of the anti-Sovietism that informed their relationship prior to 1989. The Chinese speak of a new model of a major-country relationship, but the two governments have not for the most part been able to fill in the blanks and move past generalities.[10] Adding to the uncertainty is the vulnerability of the relationship to a crisis growing out of competing claims in the South China Sea, Sino-Japanese tensions, or Taiwan.

Still, for all this, the durability of the Sino-American relationship is striking, something worth commenting on given the changing strategic context and power balance between the two countries as China has grown in both absolute and relative terms. The relationship has done fairly well under Democrats and Republicans alike and under a number of Chinese leaders. Again, history would have predicted far more friction, and while it is still possible that something approximating a new cold war could materialize, it is by no means inevitable. Indeed, how to prevent that from happening while protecting U.S. interests and even expanding U.S.-Chinese cooperation is one subject of the last section of this book.

The post–Cold War relationship with the Soviet Union and then Russia was problematic from the start. This may well have been inevitable given that the USSR lost the Cold War, saw its external empire in Eastern Europe break free, and then experienced its own internal breakup. Russia represented roughly half the population and three-fourths the land area of the former Soviet Union. It retained a seat on the UN Security Council and a vast nuclear arsenal, but it was a superpower in name only. In reality it had become a much-diminished country with an economy heavily dependent on oil and gas, a situation typically associated with a developing country. Its population declined steadily for some two decades; male life expectancy was only around sixty, the result of alcoholism, drugs, crime, and a poor public health system. The country had suffered a humiliating and costly military defeat in Afghanistan, with the last Soviet troops departing that country in February 1989 just as the administration of George H. W. Bush was getting under way. All this created a large gap between Russian realities and how many Russians viewed themselves and their country.

U.S. actions, though, contributed to Russia's problems and humiliation. The United States did not do all it could and should have done to help the Soviet Union and then Russia make the transition from a controlled political and economic system to something more democratic and market oriented, and what "help" some Americans provided turned out to be more of a burden.[11] U.S. officials also did not give Russia the respect it sought; the United States elected, for example, to downgrade the importance of formal arms control (where Russia still could appear to be something of an equal) when it just as easily could have gone through the motions of according it more priority.

More significant, though, was the decision to enlarge NATO, which started in the late 1990s under the Clinton administration and was continued by its successors. This policy has proved to be one of the most consequential and controversial of the post–Cold War era. That NATO would continue, much less enlarge, was hardly a foregone conclusion. It is rare in history for an alliance born in one strategic context (in NATO's case, the Cold War, to deter and if need be defend against a Soviet/Warsaw Pact invasion of Europe) to remain in place once the context has changed and the mission has become obsolete. The question was whether NATO could and should endure—or whether its success would prove to be its undoing.[12]

NATO did survive in a new and much changed strategic context, mostly by taking on new missions. One was "out of area"—that is, NATO would become something of an interventionary force for problems outside the traditional treaty area (much but not all of continental Europe), including the Balkans, Afghanistan, and parts of the Middle East. It also became a body that would consolidate and anchor newly liberated (and, in the case of Germany, newly unified) countries. The Czech Republic, Hungary, and Poland all joined in 1999, motivated in part by a hope that NATO would provide something of an insurance policy against the possibility that Russia might one day reassert itself and resume its traditional custom of pressuring its neighbors.

Meanwhile, Russia was getting increasingly uneasy with this process. First, Russia and NATO were on opposite sides of the Serbian crisis, as it was NATO that provided the political backing and military means for air assaults on Serbia, something Russia (which was sympathetic to Serbia for political, historical, and cultural reasons) opposed and blocked in the UN Security Council. Second, many of its neighbors were joining an alliance Moscow had long viewed with suspicion. Seven more countries (Bulgaria, Latvia, Lithuania, Estonia, Romania, Slovakia, and Slovenia) became NATO members in 2004, while talks were initiated that could lead to NATO membership for still others, including Georgia and Ukraine. Vladimir Putin, among other Russians, also felt that enlargement was inconsistent with pledges Russian officials had received from the German government and the administration of George H. W. Bush at the time Russia went along with not just German unification but also its joining NATO. As to be expected, U.S. officials deny ever making such pledges. Mixed signals and ambiguity can often facilitate reaching agreements, but at the cost of sowing the seeds of disputes and ill will down the road.[13]

There was no consensus in the United States or the West as to the wisdom of NATO enlargement. Some defended it on the grounds that it stabilized former Soviet satellites and republics and discouraged the sort of aggression against them that was visited upon Georgia and Ukraine, neither of which was a NATO member. Others, echoing Winston Churchill's dictum calling for magnanimity in victory, viewed NATO enlargement as an unnecessary provocation, one that all but guaranteed that relations with Russia would sour. Enlargement for those of this perspective was also unnecessary, as many of its positives were available through the "Partnership for Peace," an arrangement created in 1994 to promote security cooperation among all European countries, including Russia. But Russia's membership in the partnership and the failure of the commitments made under its rubric to match the sort of alliance commitment at the heart of NATO devalued its appeal for some Europeans and Americans.

Historians will debate the wisdom of NATO enlargement for decades to come. There is no way of knowing whether the trajectory of relations with Russia would have been better had there been no NATO enlargement—and no way to know whether the trajectory of European security and stability would have been worse without it. Even with hindsight, history is not always 20/20.[14]

My own preference was to make more of the Partnership for Peace—or, more radically, to consider bringing Russia into NATO as a way of integrating it into the status quo. (I wrote a memo along these lines when I was the head of the Policy Planning Staff at the State Department between 2001 and 2003. As was the case with many of my proposals at that time, the idea went nowhere.) There are always "what ifs" when it comes to history, and this is one of many; all that can be known for sure is that NATO enlargement contributed to the alienation of Russia.

A more specific crisis in U.S. relations with Russia emerged in Georgia in 2008. It arose against a backdrop of some two decades of friction between Russia and Georgia (a former Soviet republic that achieved independence in 1991) centering on the desires of two ethnic groups and regions within Georgia (Abkhazia and South Ossetia) for countries of their own. Russia was supportive of those aims and intervened both indirectly (with money, arms, and, according to some reports, small numbers of soldiers) and, in the summer of 2008, directly with a significant number of troops. The fighting was short-lived, but a cease-fire failed to bring about either complete Russian military withdrawal from Georgia or a political settlement; to the contrary, Russia recognized the independence of both Georgian regions, putting itself at odds with the United States and the rest of Europe. Russian forces remain in Georgia to this day.[15]

It was over Ukraine and Crimea, however, that the United States (along with much of Europe) had its greatest differences with Vladimir Putin's Russia. The background to the crisis can be readily summarized. Ukraine and the European Union had long been in negotiations about their relationship. (Ukraine, a republic in the old Soviet Union, became independent in 1991.) Russia was uneasy about close EU-Ukraine ties, especially if they came at the expense of Russia's ties with and influence over Ukraine and if closer ties with the EU could pave the way for Ukraine's entering NATO. Matters reached a full boil in late 2013, when Ukraine's president, Viktor Yanukovych, rejected a trade deal with the EU in favor of closer economic ties with Moscow. Hundreds of thousands of protesters took to the streets in Kiev. Violence ensued, demands escalated, and before the end of February, Yanukovych had been chased out of the presidential palace.

None of this sat well with Putin, who was unhappy with the reality that the world was watching events in Ukraine more than the expensive Olympics he was staging in Sochi. There was also the likelihood that he did not react well to the precedent of a mob ousting an authoritarian leader in a country so close to his own. In any event, what happened next was the outbreak of clashes in Crimea, a region of Ukraine with a Russian majority. (Crimea had in fact been part of the Russian

Republic in the former USSR, becoming part of the Republic of Ukraine only in 1954.) The fighting quickly escalated, as locals of Russian ethnicity and armed with Russian-origin and presumably -supplied equipment gained control of the area. Within weeks Crimea was part of Russia, following a referendum passed by an overwhelming majority of Crimea's population. The reaction of the United States and much of Europe was to dismiss the referendum as a sham (conducted as it was in an area mostly controlled by Russian-backed rebels) and to impose political and economic sanctions against Russia. A military response was ruled out; not only was Ukraine not a member of NATO, but it would have been equal parts difficult and risky to try to defend territory of a weak country on Russia's border.

The instability was by no means confined to Crimea. Russian equipment and soldiers (not wearing formal uniforms so as to mask their nationality) also made their way into eastern Ukraine, a region that bordered on Russia and that included significant numbers (but not a majority) of ethnic Russians. Indeed, in early March 2014, Putin articulated a security doctrine that essentially declared it was Russia's right to intervene on behalf of ethnic Russians where they were under threat.[16] Low-level fighting between Ukraine government forces on one side and local militias supported by Russia on the other continued in eastern Ukraine. A cease-fire and political agreement was signed by Russia, Ukraine, France, and Germany in early 2015 (the Minsk Accord), but it has never been fully implemented, with each side blaming the other for not observing one or more of its parts.[17]

All this is relevant for reasons that transcend the importance of Ukraine, a country of some forty-five million people. What happened broadly affected perceptions of and relations with Russia. It also reintroduced a military dimension to Europe that many observers thought had vanished with the end of the Cold War. And it weakened the global norm that military force should not be used to change borders. Russia paid a political and economic price for its actions, but not one high enough to reverse a policy that enjoyed the support of most of its people.

Russian assertiveness has not been limited to its near neighbors. It also intervened militarily in Syria starting in 2015. The goal may have been to demonstrate its willingness and ability to act decisively, to maintain access to a military facility there, or something else. Whatever the motive or motives, hopes that the Russian intervention would be limited, carefully targeted, and short-lived proved unfounded. Instead, Russia elected to use airpower in large doses but not against terrorists so much as against groups (many backed by either the United States or its partners) opposing the government of Bashar al-Assad. It also seems that the Russian intent was not to prevent the collapse of the Assad regime before a political transition could be planned and carried out but to keep the regime in place. There was no attempt to pacify or politically transform the country.

The result of these past two and half decades is that U.S. relations with Russia (and relations between much of Europe and Russia) have sharply deteriorated.[18] It is telling that Russian prime minister Dmitry Medvedev, speaking at a conference in Munich in February 2016, stated that the world was sliding into a new cold war.[19] Adding to the tension is that Russia itself is far from the democratic, market-oriented partner that many hoped for. To the contrary, it is an illiberal, authoritarian political entity in which Vladimir Putin enjoys tremendous power. It is no exaggeration to say that he is less constrained by bureaucracy and colleagues than were his predecessors who oversaw the Soviet Union. Putin has "deinstitutionalized" Russia and introduced a worrisome degree of personal rule.

Russia's economy for its part is heavily dependent on oil and gas and thus closely tied to the price of energy. As the price in oil collapsed in 2015, the Russian economy shrank along with it. The question is whether Putin will decide to do what it takes to improve his country's relations with the outside world (so as to ease sanctions) and even introduce some reform, or instead turn to an even more confrontational foreign policy in an effort to tap into the population's nationalism and distract from multiple problems at home. Options for dealing with Putin's Russia are discussed in the final part of the book.

Other major-power relationships, for example those between the United States and Europe, Japan, and India, were far more cooperative than not, while those between, say, China and Japan or Russia and Europe (which are discussed in a subsequent chapter focusing on regional developments) were more scratchy but still more orderly than not. The point is that relations between and among the major powers were relatively good or at least not all that bad by historical standards. That said, a break in the historical pattern of great-power conflict in and of itself does not make for an orderly world. There is a fundamental difference between the absence of major-power conflict and the presence of major-power cooperation. Or to return to the themes that have informed this book, there were bulwarks that worked against direct conflict, including a balance of power (reinforced by nuclear and nonnuclear deterrence) and economic interdependence. But missing was anything approximating a shared definition of legitimacy as applied to determining how best to deal with either global or regional challenges. What all this means, though, is that the causes of the world's increased disarray lie elsewhere, beyond the dynamics of direct major-power competition. Identifying those causes is the subject of what follows.

5. A Global Gap

A theme that ran through the early part of this book was
that of order and its centrality to understanding international relations. Three criteria are central to the degree or
quality of order: the extent to which there is a widely shared
definition of the rules and principles by which the world is to
operate; the existence of a broadly accepted process for setting, adjusting, and applying these rules and principles; and a
balance of power. There was as well the judgment that international order at the end of the Cold War in 1989 was both
incomplete and fragile, with the loss of the constraints, discipline, and structure of a world dominated by two nuclear-
armed superpowers and the relative weakness of the remaining
post–World War II arrangements.

This was not the way it looked at the time, though. To the
contrary, it appeared as if the divided world of the Cold War
had given way to one more united in its outlook and structure.
Almost all the world's governments came together to oppose

in practice as well as in principle Saddam Hussein's 1990 invasion of Kuwait, underscoring the breadth and depth of support for the notion that state sovereignty constituted the fundamental building block of international order. The UN Security Council passed more than a dozen resolutions not just reiterating this principle but putting in place sanctions (along with the green light to enforce them) and, after the mix of sanctions and diplomacy failed to persuade Saddam Hussein to rethink his behavior, authorizing the use of "all necessary means," UN-speak for military force, to liberate Kuwait.[1] An American-led international coalition accomplished the mission in short order, demonstrating the existence of a balance of power in the Middle East upheld by the United States and that strongly favored those preferring a version of the status quo to far-reaching change.

It also appeared that the world had gone from being led by two countries to one, from bipolarity to unipolarity. It is true that with the Soviet Union no longer in existence, no other country possessed both the means and the desire to counter or balance the United States. But any unipolarity was short-lived. Indeed, it is probably more accurate to say that it never really existed and that the ability of the United States to translate its clear advantages in wealth and military power into influence was limited at the global and local levels alike. The Gulf War, it turns out, was misleading in two ways: not only was there uncharacteristic global consensus surrounding the issue at stake, but virtually nothing about Operation Desert Storm was a template for subsequent military interventions.

Indeed, developments over the ensuing quarter century have revealed a far more complex reality, one of much less international consensus on what constitutes legitimacy in principles, policies, and process and not much in the way of a balance of power in practice. This more uneven, complex order has been quite disorderly, a conclusion that emerges clearly through an examination of the major historical events of this period, the gap between global challenges and re-sponses, and regional developments. The bottom line is that we live in a world far less rosy than that imagined by Presi-dent George H. W. Bush when he articulated his vision of a new world order.

This more sober picture emerged quickly, beginning with the Soviet Union. The USSR was in fact two empires: an in-ternal empire, dominated by Russia but consisting of fourteen other republics and an even larger number of nationalities, and an external empire, dominated by the USSR and includ-ing a half-dozen countries in Eastern Europe. What ensued following the Cold War's end was a series of protests and con-flicts that might be called the wars of Soviet succession. The division and weakness in Moscow removed much of the glue that had kept nationalist forces in check inside the USSR's internal and external empires alike. By the end of 1991, the USSR no longer existed. Instead there were fifteen independent countries, including Russia. In addition, by then the countries of Eastern Europe had become independent in fact as well as in name.

In many cases the path to independence was relatively smooth. This was so even in Czechoslovakia, where tensions between the Slovak south and Czech north of the country intensified as the Soviet grip eased. Nevertheless, in 1992, leaders of the two regions managed a political process that in 1993 culminated in the peaceful emergence of two separate independent countries. The contrast with the violence that characterized the political transition in Yugoslavia could not have been more stark. Yugoslavia—more specifically, the Socialist Federal Republic of Yugoslavia—existed for nearly three-quarters of a century, coming into being as World War I ended and lasting until 1992. It was a patchwork quilt of six republics—Slovenia, Croatia, Bosnia and Herzegovina, Montenegro, Macedonia, and Serbia—with Serbia also including within its territory a number of autonomous regions, the most important being Kosovo. The country was multiethnic and multireligious within and across regions and anything but integrated either socially or geographically. Serbs were a plurality but even then made up only just over a third of the total population. What kept the country intact for so long was less the rule of Moscow than a wariness of it and its reach, deftly exploited and managed by Yugoslavia's longtime nationalist ruler, Josip Broz Tito, who kept order through a mix of authoritarianism tinged with administrative decentralization and modest elements of economic reform.

What changed the internal dynamics of the country was the death of Tito in 1980, followed by the emergence of Gorbachev and a Soviet Union that no longer provided grounds for fear. These changes were further reinforced by moves toward independence in and around the soon-to-be former Soviet Union. Latent frictions between and among the nationalities of Yugoslavia boiled up. In 1991, Slovenia declared its independence; the army of federal Yugoslavia invaded but withdrew after some ten days, making Slovenia effectively a separate country. Croatia followed suit, and it too came under attack from federal forces. But these federal forces were not just fighting for their country; they were agents of an extreme form of Serbian nationalism, something that became all too apparent when the federal government forces attacked the republic of Bosnia and Herzegovina in the aftermath of its declaration of independence. Bosnia had a Muslim plurality, but also areas of significant Serbian population.

The push for independence created difficult political dilemmas for outsiders. One of the widely shared principles of the post–World War II era was the notion of self-determination, that people living in colonies had the right to have sovereign, independent countries of their own. The principle was so broadly embraced that it often included sympathy and even outright support for the use of violence in its pursuit.

Self-determination was thus a fundamental tenet of the post–World War II order.

But less clear and certainly less broadly embraced was the notion of a right of self-determination for peoples living within established nation-states. Unlike those seeking to get out from under colonial rule, self-determination broadly applied would not be a one-time affair. To the contrary, it could be potentially unlimited in its application. What is more, if it applied to groups living within countries, it threatened the idea and the ideal of state sovereignty, in that sovereignty could be attacked and undermined not just from the outside but from within. It was thus a potential threat to the integrity of many countries as well as to the basis of international order.

self-determination – to a degree – not universal

It was one thing when a society decided through a widely accepted political process to divorce amicably, as with Czechoslovakia. But it was something very different when the desire to break free was not consensual. Still, the bias of outsiders was to respect assertions of independence when those seeking it had a basis in history, ill treatment at the hands of the existing central government, and potential viability as an independent state. For these and other reasons, both the European Community and the United States moved to recognize the newly established countries that had been part of Yugoslavia. This diplomatic step did nothing to douse the fire; if anything, it added to it and contributed to a dynamic of secession and violent intervention.

The United States for its part found itself caught between

competing considerations, which goes some way toward explaining why U.S. policy was as inconsistent as it was. The administration of George H. W. Bush was reluctant to get involved in what it tended to see as a messy civil war. There was also no strong agreement as to what extent a central government had the right to push back against those who would secede and how it applied in this instance. The successor Clinton administration, too, was reluctant to get heavily involved militarily, which explained its choice of airpower over ground forces when it did finally decide to employ military force. What influenced its decision, though, was not support for any right of self-determination but rather humanitarian concerns along with pressures from European allies demanding that the United States act on behalf of those seeking separation or refuge from what remained of the central government in Belgrade.

What ensued over three years, from 1991 to 1994, was a pattern of declarations of independence by portions of the former Yugoslavia, diplomatic recognition by outsiders, vicious fighting, efforts undertaken by the United Nations to promote cease-fires and political settlements, and the dispatch of peacekeeping forces that often proved feckless in the face of ethnic cleansing, that is, the forced transfer and separation of Croats and Muslims, and attacks by Serbian forces of one sort or another on areas that had been declared safe for civilians but in fact were not. Matters came to a head in the spring and summer of 1995. Hundreds of European peacekeepers were taken hostage by Bosnian Serb forces. The so-called safe area of Srebrenica was attacked and taken by mid-July; weeks later, the Serbs shelled the marketplace in Sarajevo, the capital of Bosnia and Herzegovina. Within days, NATO launched a sustained bombing campaign designed to weaken Serbian forces and change the calculus in Belgrade. Airpower accomplished what peacekeepers, diplomacy, and economic and political sanctions could not, as within months a political settlement was reached (at a military base in Dayton, Ohio, in November 1995) that has mostly kept an uneasy peace among independent countries and autonomous areas and large numbers of peacekeepers.[2]

Before long it became clear that the problem of civil conflict was hardly limited to one section of Europe. Nor was it limited to populations seeking to break free of their existing bonds and form a state of their own. The driving force in many cases around the world was less a push for self-determination and the creation of a new state than it was some version of score settling or a winner-take-all effort to establish a new political, social, and economic hierarchy.

It is only a slight exaggeration to suggest that the dominant foreign policy challenges confronting the United States and the world for much of the 1990s stemmed from internal conflicts of this variety and from weak rather than strong states.[3] Strong states need no definition, but weak states arguably do. What makes a state weak is not an inability to project military power or fight wars beyond its borders so much as its inability to control what takes place within its borders. It is a lack of capacity, one that often leads to large swaths of territory (often termed "ungoverned spaces") being outside the writ of the government. A failed state is simply the extreme version of a weak state, one in which governmental authority effectively collapses, leading to chaos, the rise of local gangs and militias ruling over parts of the country, or both.

failed state

The first such example came in Iraq in the aftermath of Operation Desert Storm and the liberation of Kuwait. Rebellions (intifadas in Arabic) against the harsh rule of the central government broke out in the Shia-dominated south and the Kurdish-dominated north of Iraq. For a number of reasons—principally uncertainty as to the political goals and consequences of the rebellions and concern over the difficulties of designing and implementing a military intervention in such confused circumstances—the United States held back. But as the humanitarian situation in the north deteriorated and waves of civilians headed toward the Turkish border, U.S. military forces established a no-fly zone (so that Iraqi government aircraft could not attack civilians) and provided food and other necessities, saving hundreds of thousands if not millions of lives in the process. The Bush administration was motivated by the humanitarian plight, but also because it was under pressure from its partner and ally Turkey to do so. The administration also felt a special obligation given that the war that it had just pursued had ended without the expected resolution of the political situation inside Iraq. It is important to

Iraq - Kurdistan

underscore, though, that the U.S. involvement was strictly humanitarian, as it did not attempt to bring about a separate Kurdish state in the north of Iraq (or a separate Shia state in the south) or to overthrow the existing political authority in Baghdad.[4]

Somalia followed soon after. The country at the time lacked a functioning central government; it was a nation in name only, more a territory where rival warlords fought and competed for local power while the people suffered. UN efforts to provide food and other basics accomplished little as rival militias often stole the supplies and sold them, using the proceeds to purchase arms. By mid-1992, mass starvation was a real danger. This was the context in late 1992 when in the final months of the administration of George H. W. Bush, the United States stepped in with military forces (roughly twenty-five thousand soldiers, constituting the bulk of a UN force) to create an environment in which food and other humanitarian aid could be safely delivered.

The intervention worked, but only in the narrow sense of delivering food and keeping the warring groups apart. The mission did not create a capable government or a peace that was not reliant on external forces. There was no obvious way it could come to an end without triggering a resumption of the humanitarian conditions that had brought it about. A successor UN force in May 1993 (with the support of the new American administration of Bill Clinton) attempted to do just that—to transform a narrow humanitarian undertaking into a

broader political one that would seek to put into place a responsible political authority and defeat anyone who stood in
the way. The result was calamitous, leading to the deaths of
eighteen U.S. soldiers and the subsequent withdrawal of all
U.S. and ultimately UN forces without having brought about
any lasting improvement in the situation on the ground.

The Somalia experience had a ripple effect, which limited what the United States was initially willing to do in Haiti
when order was threatened there that same summer. Months
after the U.S. withdrawal from Somalia, a ship carrying some
two hundred U.S. and Canadian soldiers being sent to train
Haitian forces under a UN authorization was literally chased
away by an angry mob that gathered by the dock. The United
States regrouped, and by the summer of 1994 had secured the
passage of a new UN Security Council resolution authorizing the use of armed force to oust the military leaders ruling
Haiti and to facilitate the return of the elected government. A
significant military force was readied to do just this, which
provided the necessary backdrop for a successful diplomatic
effort led by former U.S. president Jimmy Carter to persuade
the illegitimate government to step down.[5]

More profound was the impact of Somalia on U.S. behavior in Rwanda. This turns out to have been critical, as, more
than any other crisis, it was Rwanda that affected subsequent
views around the world about sovereignty and humanitarian
intervention. Rwanda is a small country in Africa with a population that was predominantly (on the order of 80–90 percent)

ethnically Hutu, but with a minority of Tutsis. The Tutsis, as is often the case with minorities, enjoyed many economic, social, and political advantages during the time Rwanda was a Belgian colony and UN trusteeship. Gradually, however, the majority Hutus gained the upper hand. Fighting became increasingly common; many Tutsis sought refuge in neighboring Uganda. Hutus dominated Rwanda by the time it became an independent republic in 1962.

Fighting and polarization between Hutus and those Tutsis still living in Rwanda increased after Tutsi refugees in neighboring Uganda founded the Rwandan Patriotic Front (RPF) in 1988. Uganda did much to support the RPF, not for humanitarian reasons but to set the stage for overthrowing the Hutu regime, which would allow Tutsis to return home. The situation seemed to have stabilized some five years later when a peace agreement was signed calling for a cease-fire and local power sharing among the Hutu-dominated government, Hutu oppositionists, and Tutsis living in Rwanda. A small UN peacekeeping force was created and dispatched to buttress the agreement. Within months, though, the cease-fire broke down completely, and close to one million Tutsis were murdered by extremist Hutu militias and the Hutu-dominated army. Only after the mass killings was the RPF able to take control of the country and establish a broad-based successor government. The small UN force posted there had proved unable (some would argue unwilling) to act. The world essentially sat on its hands, doing little or nothing when it is quite possible that even modest action early on might have saved hundreds of thousands of lives at little cost.[6] It was neither the first nor the last time that a decision not to act proved every bit as consequential as any action that might have been undertaken. Interestingly, several of the Americans most influenced by this history were in government two decades later when the question of whether and how to intervene in Libya arose. As will be discussed, once again a lesson was overlearned, in this case in the opposite direction. Learning from history is easier said than done.

What these crises had in common was that they involved governments that either attacked elements of their own population or failed to protect their own people from attacks. The crises tended to have stakes and consequences more humanitarian than strategic, although in some cases the population flows that resulted posed problems for the stability of neighboring states. But the issue contained within it a major challenge to governments everywhere, in that it raised the question of what if anything was to be done if local governments were unable or unwilling to provide basic security to their own citizens.

What gradually emerged from this conundrum was the notion of "Responsibility to Protect," or R2P, as it became widely known. The idea was enshrined in a 2005 statement of a "World Summit" convened by the United Nations. "Each individual state has the responsibility to protect its populations from genocide, war crimes, ethnic cleansing and crimes

2005 World Summit

against humanity." Such a statement of sovereign responsibility was significant. But what made R2P even more significant was an associated notion, namely, that the "international community" also had the responsibility to help to protect populations from the same four threats, including through the use of military force if need be, regardless of whether the government of the country involved asked for it or even if it opposed outside involvement. The world's governments expressed their preparedness to take "collective action in a timely and decisive manner" on a case-by-case basis, acting in concert with the relevant regional organization or the UN itself.[7]

It seemed as if the concept of world order had taken a major turn, now embracing not just the external behavior of states but their internal actions as well. In so doing, it was stipulated that under certain circumstances other governments had not just the right but the responsibility to act to protect innocent people when a particular government would not or could not. This represented something far more consequential than the Universal Declaration of Human Rights, which contained no mechanism for addressing situations in which fundamental human rights were violated. In many ways, R2P provided an authority to make good on the prevention component of the Genocide Convention.

Yet beneath this apparent unity was significant disunity. It was as if several of the major powers, including China, Russia, and India, had been swept along by the strength of the American and more broadly international reaction after Rwanda, by the widespread view that the world had failed to act when it could and should have to avert a calamity. But their instincts and their interests were opposed, as they worried that the concept of R2P and what might be described as diluted sovereignty could be turned against them if they ever felt compelled to do things at home that outsiders found objectionable. Later (in the aftermath of the 2011 Libyan intervention) they became even more concerned when they saw what began as a humanitarian intervention quickly evolve into something much more, that is, regime change. This experience reinforced their deepest fear that R2P represented the thin end of the wedge of a new, dangerous approach to sovereignty that could all too easily be turned not just against their interests but against them.

There was also another problem when it came to R2P. It was one thing to enshrine it as a norm, as was done in 2005. It was quite another to implement it in practice. The difficulty here reflected not just fears about precedents or local interests but also concerns over military and economic costs. Protecting citizens amid civil conflict had the potential to become extraordinarily difficult and demanding.

Syria has become the depressing and dangerous case study par excellence of this reality. Syria had long been a typical Middle Eastern authoritarian regime; what made it different was that it was dominated by an ethnic minority and by one family. For forty-five years—well over half of its life as an independent country—Syria has been led by either Hafez al-Assad or his son Bashar, both Alawites, a small Muslim sect that constitutes only 10–15 percent of Syria's overall Sunni-majority population.

Syria was stable for decades, in no small part because of the regime's brutality, exhibited most starkly in 1982 when an estimated ten thousand to twenty-five thousand Sunnis in the city of Hama were killed. Hama was a hotbed of Muslim Brotherhood political activity, and Assad the father put down the rebellion both to nip any broader movement in the bud and to discourage others from challenging him and his regime.

Events played out differently in 2011, when the Syrian version of the Arab Spring broke out. Troops were sent to quell antigovernment protesters; some protesters were killed, causing others to take up arms. A political challenge was fast morphing into a civil war. Early diplomatic efforts (backed by sanctions against the regime) to end the fighting came to naught, as did calls from inside and outside the country for Bashar al-Assad to step down.

Things went from bad to worse over the ensuing years. The government received economic and military support from Iran and Russia but still lost control of considerable territory to various armed groups, most notably the al-Nusra Front (an al-Qaeda offshoot) and the Islamic State, variously called ISIS, ISIL, or (from the Arabic) Daesh. Other armed groups emerged, in some cases with backing from Saudi Arabia, other Sunni Arab countries, Turkey, and/or the United States. Hundreds of thousands of Syrians lost their lives amid the prolonged fighting; roughly half the population (some eleven to twelve million out of a population of approximately twenty-two million at the war's start) was displaced and forced to find a place to live elsewhere in the country or as refugees beyond its borders. Despite this disruption and loss of civilian life, R2P never kicked in, in part because of how difficult it would have been to make the country safe, in part because outsiders could not agree on who was to blame for events and what any intervention would try to leave in its wake. The result was to leave Syria a battleground (and a humanitarian nightmare) and to leave R2P in tatters.

An additional problem associated with weak states emerged alongside that of widespread harm to local civilians: terrorism. The response to the September 11, 2001, attacks were about many things, but high among them was the obligation of states not to permit their territory to be used by terrorists. A government could choose to allow a terrorist group to operate out of its territory or it could simply be so weak as to be unable to prevent a group from doing so. In the case of Afghanistan, it was a government (controlled by the Taliban) that chose to provide sanctuary to al-Qaeda.

In the immediate aftermath of the attacks, the United States presented the Taliban government with a stark choice: either end its relationship with al-Qaeda (and hand al-Qaeda's leaders over to U.S. or international authorities) or face the consequences. The Taliban government refused to take these steps, and the United States committed to ousting the government, something accomplished over the next few months as U.S. intelligence personnel and military forces cooperated with members of the so-called Northern Alliance, a loose collection of anti-Taliban tribes with roots in those parts of Afghanistan not dominated by the Pashtuns, the ethnic group mostly located in the south of the country that constituted a plurality of its population and the core of the Taliban's support. Soon after, the United States, meeting in Bonn with prominent Afghans and most of Afghanistan's neighbors, helped forge a new government led by Hamid Karzai, a prominent Pashtun who was nonetheless acceptable to representatives of many of the country's other ethnic groups.

There was broad international backing for these actions. Such a stance was not entirely predictable despite the awfulness of what took place on 9/11 and the fact that it claimed the lives of individuals from some eighty countries besides the United States. The reason it was not predictable is that for decades governments had been unable to reach a common position on what constituted terrorism. The cliché that "one man's terrorist is another man's freedom fighter" was representative of the political reality in that many supported or were tolerant of terrorism if they were sympathetic to the stated cause of those carrying out the acts. Beginning to take its place (a process substantially accelerated by the 9/11 attacks) was a new and less subjective definition of terrorism, which could be summarized as the intentional killing of innocent men, women, and children by actors other than states for political purposes. Also gaining ground was the related notion that governments that harbored or otherwise aided terrorists were no better than the terrorists themselves and as a result were liable to sanctions or worse.

What had changed was a number of things. Al-Qaeda represented a new and more dangerous form of terrorism, one with global reach and real potential to cause damage and harm. Not just that, but its goals appeared to be essentially unlimited, unlike "traditional" terrorists who more often than not had relatively local and narrow aims, such as a small state of their own. In addition, many of the world's governments found themselves vulnerable to terrorism of one sort or another. Europe had long contended with homegrown radical terrorists or with various Palestinian groups mounting attacks on its soil. China, for its part, was increasingly worried about Muslim terrorists in the western part of the country; Russia was concerned with Chechnyan terrorists. Years of civil war in Afghanistan in which Muslims from all over the world had gone to help fight the Soviet occupation had produced a new generation of terrorists schooled in the most modern means. Terrorism had, like so much else, gone global.

I had my own small window on this shift in attitude. In 2001 I was working in the State Department as the head of its

Policy Planning Staff, and one of the additional hats I wore was that of the U.S. envoy to the Northern Ireland peace process. More than three thousand people had died over the previous four decades in Northern Ireland as a result of politically inspired violence. I was in Dublin meeting with the Irish prime minister at the precise time when the planes flew into the twin towers, and as I could not return home given the grounding of all aircraft, I went on as planned to Belfast that same day. I made clear to the parties (and in particular to leaders of the Catholic nationalist party Sinn Fein, the political wing of the Provisional Irish Republican Army, or IRA, which had long used violence to further its political agenda) that any American tolerance of, much less support for, terrorism of any kind had evaporated when the twin towers fell. This message was later echoed by many of the group's traditional supporters in the U.S. Congress and beyond. This change in attitude imparted new momentum to the peace process, eventually leading the group to give up its weapons and to work with local Protestants (Unionists) in the local political assembly.

If there was the appearance of global consensus on not allowing governments to practice or allow genocide on their territory and something much closer to an actual consensus on not tolerating terrorism, there was even more agreement that the United States was wrong and unjustified in the spring of 2003 when it went to war with Iraq. Unlike the case in the

1990–91 Gulf War, when Iraq invaded and took over what had been a sovereign country, this time there was no Iraqi breach of a widely shared norm. Rather, the administration of George W. Bush determined that in the wake of 9/11 the possibility that Iraq possessed weapons of mass destruction posed an unacceptable risk.

There were of course other motivations for the war, including the belief that Iraq was ripe for democracy and that the precedent of a democratic Iraq would be one the other countries of the region would be unable to resist. The outcome, it was believed, would result in nothing less than the democratic transformation of the Middle East, which in turn would pave the way to a regional peace. This view, while deeply and widely held in the administration of George W. Bush, was not the argument that was mostly used to explain U.S. policy to the world. Again, the argument was much more security-related, linked to the unacceptable risk of Saddam Hussein's possessing weapons of mass destruction, which was widely believed to be the case given the available intelligence. Saddam's refusal to cooperate fully with UN weapons inspectors further reinforced the prevailing view that he had something to hide.[8]

The experience of the 2003 Iraq War demonstrated, though, that no such international support for a norm of "preventive" intervention existed. Often the word "preemptive" is used to describe what the United States did—indeed, it was the word used by the Bush administration in its 2002 national security document—but this is to confuse two terms that mean very different things and have very different standing and acceptance.[9] To be clear, what the United States did in 2003 was to launch a *preventive* action, one aimed at stopping a *gathering* threat, in this case what was thought to be Iraq's development of a nuclear weapon. Such an action is for good reason controversial, as governments inevitably see threats gathering from many sources, and a world of frequent preventive military actions against perceived gathering threats would soon degenerate into a world of frequent conflict.

By contrast, *preemption*—defined as military action taken to stop an *imminent* military threat—is widely accepted. Indeed, one of the principal legal authorities in the field goes so far as to label such actions "legitimate anticipation."[10] What is critical is that the side taking the action be able to demonstrate that the threat was in fact imminent. Iraq in 2003 did not qualify, even though it was widely thought at the time to have been accumulating the prerequisites of a nuclear weapon.

Adding to the isolation of the United States was its unwillingness to hold off acting until it had received specific blessing or authorization from the United Nations or any other body with meaningful international standing. As a result, the United States acted against Iraq in 2003 without adequate legitimacy in the eyes of much of the world.

This was not surprising. Support for the norm that the further spread of weapons of mass destruction and nuclear weapons in particular was to be avoided was strong in principle but much less so in practice. Israel became the first exception to limiting such weapons to the five countries "allowed" to have them in the NPT. This became a reality as early as the late 1960s, although it was never more than implicit as Israel avoided acknowledging that it possessed nuclear weapons lest it find itself even more isolated internationally and provide Arab states with a rationale for pursuing nuclear arms of their own. There was a willingness in the United States and much of Europe to look the other way given that the Arab governments did not accept Israel's right to exist much less live in peace, and nuclear weapons were widely seen as the ultimate protector of the Jewish state, one in a unique position due to the Holocaust. It was also thought that the possession of such weapons might give Israel the confidence to take risks for peace. The optimists went even further, suggesting that nuclear arms might actually facilitate diplomacy to bring about conditions in which Israel might no longer feel it needed to possess them to guarantee its security.[11]

India also developed nuclear weapons. Here the principal motive was its larger neighbor, China.[12] Again, there was a history of conflict and unsettled borders between the two states, including a limited war fought in 1962. India refused to sign the NPT, arguing that it was discriminatory in that it allowed a small number of countries (five, in fact) the "right" to possess nuclear weapons while denying that same right to all others. Consistent with this position, in 1974 India conducted its first test of a nuclear device. It was more than prepared to pay the price in economic and military sanctions introduced by the United States and several others, in part because it knew it could expect support from its patron in Moscow. Over the decades India gradually amassed a substantial inventory of weapons. The world came to accommodate itself to this situation. Indeed, in 2008 the United States effectively accepted the Indian nuclear program when the two countries entered into a pact for civil nuclear cooperation, something that had been precluded by U.S. sanctions. Washington had made the strategic decision that further opposition to what a stable, democratic India had done would have no effect other than to continue to be a drag on a relationship that had become far more important and promising both economically and strategically in a post–Cold War world.

North Korea was a very different case. (The official name of North Korea is the Democratic People's Republic of Korea, or DPRK, reinforcing the rule of thumb that a country that includes the word "Democratic" in its formal name tends to be anything but.) It was a closed country led by the most repressive of regimes. It was also one of the world's most militarized societies. It thus became a case study of the world's ability—or, more accurately, inability—to come together to prevent new countries (especially those with a history of acting aggressively and/or supporting terrorism) from acquiring nuclear weapons.

The United States was caught in a difficult situation. It understood the importance of not allowing a regime such as the one running North Korea to gain nuclear weapons. But that would most likely require a preventive military strike, a military action designed to destroy much of the North Korean nuclear establishment before it could field a weapon. The problem with acting was less one of feasibility or a lack of international support for preventive strikes than it was the strong possibility that such an attack could lead to a war on the peninsula, something very much opposed by the two U.S. allies that would bear the brunt of any North Korean military retaliation, namely, South Korea and Japan. Such a war would also have required a costly U.S. military response given U.S. alliance commitments and North Korean military capabilities.

All this came to a head in 1994. Although North Korea had joined the NPT a decade earlier, it had never given up pursuing nuclear weapons. Indeed, in 1993 the International Atomic Energy Agency (IAEA), the watchdog agency tasked with the job of monitoring compliance with the NPT, accused the North Koreans of violating their treaty obligations.[13] Inspections were never conclusive, in part because the IAEA was often denied the access it required to fulfill its mandate. Articles were written, one by Brent Scowcroft and Arnold Kanter in the *Washington Post*, another by me in the *New York Times*, arguing that the United States ought to carry out preventive strikes to stop North Korea from producing nuclear weapons unless it allowed the sort of continuous, intrusive inspections required to assure the outside world that it had not crossed relevant lines.[14]

The Clinton administration was not prepared to press this demand. Instead it entered into talks and signed an agreement with North Korea that limited what Pyongyang was permitted to do while establishing a new inspections regime.[15] Here and elsewhere, the option not to act decisively had real and lasting consequences. North Korea effectively exploited the time it took to negotiate, mostly using it as a cover under which to pursue a nuclear weapons capability. It is impossible to pinpoint when exactly North Korea came to possess nuclear weapons, although it is likely to have been around that time or at most a few years later. Decades of negotiations failed to alter this fundamental reality. North Korea has conducted at least four nuclear tests (detonations) since 2006. It now possesses as many as a dozen nuclear devices and is developing missiles capable of carrying warheads thousands of miles. A moment for a preventive military strike that could have destroyed much of North Korea's existing nuclear capacity was allowed to pass.

North Korea was not alone in crossing the nuclear threshold. In the case of Pakistan, practical geopolitical concerns again took precedence over the principle that nuclear proliferation was to be avoided at all costs. China saw Pakistan as something of a strategic hedge against India, and was therefore willing to assist with its nuclear efforts. The United States for its part was working closely with Pakistan in Afghanistan ever since the December 1979 Soviet-engineered coup; it was through Pakistan that anti-Soviet forces (the mujahideen) were organized and armed.

Pakistan had long sought a nuclear weapons capability, seeing such a weapon as essential to match its larger and stronger neighbor India, with which it had fought wars and contested territory. India's testing of a nuclear device in 1974 surely accelerated Pakistani preparations. Through stealth and help from China, Pakistan reached the threshold of such a capability by the mid-1980s; a decade later, in 1998, it openly tested nuclear devices in the wake of India's having done the same. Pakistan had achieved overt nuclear weapons status.

The United States tried and in the end failed to square the circle between close cooperation with Pakistan in pursuit of one goal (fighting the Soviet occupation of Afghanistan) and opposition on another (nuclear proliferation). The answer was to turn to economic and military sanctions to discourage Pakistan from realizing its nuclear ambitions. In reality, sanctions turned out to be the worst possible compromise. They were not strong enough to dissuade Pakistan from developing nuclear weapons—there is scant evidence that sanctions can ever be made strong enough to dissuade a country from pursuing what it believes to be a vital national interest—but they did help to alienate the country and the military leadership that plays so large a political role there. The sanctions also reinforced the narrative that outsiders and the United States in particular could not be trusted to be there for Pakistan in difficult times, which only reinforced the view that it needed to take control of its own security needs, which in turn argued for acquiring nuclear weapons. Today, Pakistan has more than one hundred nuclear weapons and the world's fastest-growing nuclear arsenal. Adding to the concern is that it is a weak state—civilian authority is mostly a veneer—and is home to some of the world's most dangerous terrorist organizations. Pakistan has a history of aiding the nuclear weapons programs of other countries. It is also in a confrontational relationship with nuclear-armed India. All this leads to the possibility that nuclear weapons may be introduced into a conflict or lost to a terrorist group.

What is also worth noting here is that Israel, Pakistan, and India never signed the Non-Proliferation Treaty, the document representing what global consensus there was that nuclear weapons ought not to spread beyond the five original nuclear weapon states. The treaty contains no penalty for remaining outside it, and no penalty for resigning, which is what North Korea did. It is not that the opposition to the spread of nuclear weapons is not real; it is. But no less real is the limit to the price governments of the major powers are prepared to pay to see proliferation stopped.

Iran is a very different example. It is a signatory of the NPT, and originally received assistance from the West with its nuclear energy program when the country was still ruled by the shah. The world came to see Iran's nuclear activities in a very different light, however, when they were continued and expanded by the Islamic regime that came to power via revolution in 1979.

A three-and-a-half-decade-long struggle ensued between an Iranian program that was often inconsistent with its NPT commitments and designed to undermine the work of the IAEA and efforts by the United States and others to frustrate that program through sanctions or other means, such as employing malware to interfere with the software instructing the centrifuges central to the process of enriching uranium. Iran continued to advance, however, and the choice facing the United States and the world several years into Barack Obama's presidency boiled down to undertaking a preventive strike against Iranian facilities, accepting an Iranian nuclear weapons program, or entering into an agreement that would place a ceiling on the Iranian program short of its fielding nuclear weapons.

The Obama administration rejected the first two options. Determined to reduce U.S. involvement in the Middle East, it had little stomach for another conflict. Indeed, reducing the U.S. military footprint in the region was a defining objective for this president and many of those around him. Moreover, it was not at all clear what military force could accomplish; a preventive attack might set the Iranian program back several years but at the price of triggering a broader war, strengthening the hands of Iranian hard-liners, and destroying international support for sanctions that had raised the direct and indirect cost to Iran of pursuing nuclear weapons. Yes, it would take some time for Iran to rebuild the equipment and factories needed to produce nuclear weapons, but it would do so, presumably in a place too far underground for either U.S. or Israeli weapons to reach.

At the same time, simply permitting Iran to cross the nuclear weapons threshold, as the world had essentially done in the cases of Israel, India, Pakistan, and North Korea, was also rejected. Such a development would likely trigger a race to acquire nuclear arms throughout the Middle East, which could make what was already the most unstable part of the world that much more so. Nuclear weapons would allow Iran to pursue its regional ambitions with that much more impunity, as it would have little to fear from Israel or the United States. Also, a nuclear-armed Iran would pose what many Israelis and others considered to be an existential threat to the Jewish state given the many statements by Iranian leaders rejecting Israel's right to exist.

All of which led the Obama administration to embrace the diplomatic option. What was and remains controversial was not this choice but rather the decision to embrace a diplomatic option of limited ambition, seeking, in the words of one participant involved in U.S. decision making at the time, a goal of constraining, not eliminating, relevant Iranian capabilities.[16] My own view (admittedly impossible to prove) is that the United States committed the cardinal negotiating sin of wanting an agreement too much, and therefore compromising too much. In particular, I believe the U.S. side would have been wise to demand constraints of much longer duration, especially because the drop in world oil prices and the strength of the sanctions combined to give considerable leverage to the United States and other countries negotiating with Iran.

The adoption of more modest aims may well have reflected a desire to go the extra mile so as not to have to use military force. It may also have reflected the hope in some quarters that a diplomatic settlement of the nuclear issue could pave the way for broader cooperation between the United States and Iran as well as bring about a more moderate Iran. There is no way of knowing whether such hopes will be borne out; what is known is that diplomatic efforts culminated in the summer of 2015 when the United States, the four other permanent members of the UN Security Council, Germany, and Iran signed the "Joint Comprehensive Plan of Action," an accord that provided Iran relief from economic sanctions (and access to large amounts of capital) in exchange for its accepting significant limits for ten years on its centrifuges and for fifteen years on the quantity and quality of enriched uranium it would be allowed to possess.[17] These limits and inspections had the desirable effect of markedly increasing the likely warning time (from an estimated several months to as much as a year during the decade and a half the agreement's principal limits would remain in force) the world would have if Iran made a decision to violate the agreement and try to produce nuclear weapons.

Iran also agreed to accept a more intrusive set of international inspections in order to verify that it was living up to its commitments under the accord. The result was a more stable situation in the short run, in that the world would have a high degree of confidence it would discover and have time to act against any Iranian attempt to develop nuclear weapons during those fifteen years. But this confidence came at a steep price, as Iran gained access to financial resources on a scale (estimated to be in the range of $50 to $100 billion) that gave it a much greater ability to carry out an aggressive regional foreign policy over that same time. It would also be in a position to develop a large number of nuclear weapons in short order and with little warning time after the periods of ten years (in the case of centrifuges) and fifteen (in the case of enriched uranium) had elapsed. (What would remain in place at that point would just be Iran's agreement to submit to intrusive inspections and honor its NPT commitments.) And as will be discussed below, the agreement contributed to the emergence of a major diplomatic challenge; namely, how to dissuade several of Iran's neighbors from following suit and putting into place many of the prerequisites of nuclear weapons programs of their own.

At least four and possibly all five of these cases—Israel, India, North Korea, Pakistan, and Iran—resulted in outcomes that represented a partial erosion of the global regime of resisting the proliferation of nuclear weapons. This is not intended to be a glib criticism of American foreign policy over the decades. U.S. influence was limited by the commitment of the target country to pursue its nuclear-related goals and, partly as a result, to resist U.S. pressures. U.S. influence was also undercut by the actions of other governments that did not share U.S. preferences or priorities. Influence is not the same as control, especially when confronted by a determined nationalism that views nuclear weapons as an existential need rather than (as was the case with the U.S. support for nonproliferation) a policy preference.

In addition, all five cases involved difficult realities and choices alike. The interest in opposing the spread of nuclear weapons had to coexist with other interests, be they to safeguard an ally in a unique security environment (Israel); avoid triggering a war that the United States and two of its closest allies were anxious to avoid (North Korea); build ties with a major emerging power (India); protect cooperation with a valued partner in the struggle against the Soviet Union (Pakistan); or avoid a conflict with all the uncertainty of what would follow (Iran).

The norm against the proliferation of nuclear weapons was also weakened in a practical sense by decisions taken in isolation but that had a perverse cumulative effect. Just because an outcome is unintended doesn't make it any less significant. Ukraine, soon after it became independent, voluntarily gave up its nuclear weapons in the early 1990s at the urging of the

United States. Two decades later, it was invaded by Russian-backed forces and lost Crimea and forfeited significant control over its eastern provinces. Iraq for its part was forced to abandon its nuclear weapons program in the aftermath of the 1991 Gulf War—and just over a decade later the country was invaded by the United States and the government of Saddam Hussein ousted. The third example was Libya, which after 2003 gained credit as the country that after years of significant pressure decided to give up its nuclear program and submit to the most intrusive inspections. Less than a decade later, the country was invaded by a joint U.S.-European force, resulting in the removal of the government of Muammar Gadhafi. Meanwhile, the North Korean government remained in place, apparently shielded from military attack by its nuclear program. All this added up to a powerful lesson that nuclear weapons can offer protection against foreign intervention—and the lack of them can increase the odds of a country being attacked and its government ousted. Presumably this lesson was not lost on either North Korea or Iran.

There is as well an international norm (and formal conventions or treaties signed by most but not all governments) against the production, possession, and use of both chemical and biological weapons. The norm operates on what might be described as a cooperative basis—governments choose to subscribe to specified policies, report on related activities, and, in the case of the Chemical Weapons Convention, agree to inspections of those facilities they declare to be relevant.

The Syrian government's uses of chemical weapons amid its civil war is noteworthy here. Preventing the spread of chemical weapons is virtually impossible, as producing them is something most countries can do if they choose. It is also nearly impossible to determine that such weapons are being produced, as there would be little or nothing that would distinguish their production from normal industrial activity. No inspections regime can ever be sufficiently intrusive and comprehensive to unearth chemical weapons production or storage. The clear line when it comes to chemical weapons is to discourage use, which, unlike production and possession, can normally be verified. Use can be deterred by threatening penalties against those who use chemical weapons and implementing these penalties if deterrence fails. Penalties could include severe sanctions, the initiation of war crimes proceedings, and military action of significant scale and for purposes that range from inflicting pain to altering the course of an ongoing conflict to ousting the regime. The purpose of after-the-fact action is to discourage additional use by the government in question as well as to set a precedent that would presumably discourage others from following suit.

The bottom line is that global efforts to prevent the spread of nuclear, biological, and chemical weapons are more supported in principle than in practice. The problem with making opposition to proliferation a priority in practice is that it often comes into conflict with other policies, relationships, and objectives, many of which are priorities as well. As a result, proliferation tends to be opposed, but with a degree of restraint that makes some WMD spread inevitable. Adding to this inevitability is the fact that a capable, determined country can advance despite direct and indirect efforts by outsiders to frustrate its progress and alter its calculus.

Another domain of international life beyond those already discussed—sovereignty, self-determination, humanitarian intervention, combating terrorism, and frustrating the proliferation of weapons of mass destruction—involves climate change. This issue hardly figured when the Cold War came to a close. Indeed, it was not until 1995 that the first global gathering of governments under the UN Framework Convention for Climate Change (UNFCCC) was convened. Although there are some who question the science, a broad international consensus has emerged that climate change is real, that it is largely caused by human activity, and that it constitutes a threat that will affect not just populations in low-lying areas but also societies and economies everywhere given the potential impact on weather, health, agriculture, water, and food security.

This consensus notwithstanding, annual gatherings of government leaders and their representatives accomplished little, as poor or developing countries resisted signing on to constraints that they feared would slow economic growth and in effect asked them to pay a price for a problem (climate change) that had mostly been created by the behavior of others, that is, the wealthier, developed countries of North America, Europe, and Asia. Wealthier countries, and the United States in particular, were loath to sign on to binding pacts that they feared could slow their own economic growth, require major transfers of resources to either poorer countries or those most vulnerable to climate change, or both. The result was little agreement on what needed to be done or on who was to do it.

One such gathering (the twenty-first Conference of Parties, or COP21) was held in Paris in late 2015. The approach adopted in Paris to the climate challenge was much more modest in means and ends than had been the case at previous and largely unsuccessful international gatherings. There was no attempt to create a new international agreement that would either place a price (effectively a tax) on carbon emissions or establish a global market in which permits to emit carbon could be traded for a price, thereby creating incentive to reduce output. Rather, the Paris gathering asked individual countries (including less-wealthy developing countries) to produce and commit to individually tailored trajectories (so-called nationally determined contributions, or NDCs) that over time would reduce their carbon output. The articulated goal was to keep the total increase this century in average global temperature to 2 degrees Celsius or some 3.5 degrees

Fahrenheit, although this aim was mostly aspirational as the commitments announced, even if implemented, would not achieve the stated goal.[18]

National commitments were not legally binding and in some cases lacked specificity as to when they would be reached or what the target would actually be. What could prove critical are the assessments to be made of national programs and their effects at five-year intervals and the reactions to them. The implicit thinking is that pressures will grow within countries to "do the right thing" and adopt policies that increasingly delink economic growth and desired activities from the increased use of fossil fuels (and coal in particular) or risk being "named and shamed." The language agreed to on the transfer of funds and technologies from developed to developing and at-risk countries was similarly hortatory and directional rather than specific and binding in nature. The result, even if it represented a degree of progress, fell far short of what was needed.

Cyberspace is the newest international domain to emerge. The experience with nuclear technology in the 1940s and 1950s comes to mind. Then, as now, a new technology with multiple uses, malign and benign, had emerged, and the question then, as now, was how governments could encourage what was viewed as desirable and discourage what was not. In the case of nuclear weapons, this meant trying to limit the number of countries possessing such weapons, placing (through diplomacy and arms control) quantitative and qualitative limits on the arsenals of those countries in possession of such systems, and allowing countries to develop nuclear energy programs for peaceful purposes under conditions meant to provide confidence that they were not a stealth means of producing nuclear weapons.

Managing cyberspace poses an even more difficult challenge. Building and operating nuclear weapons and nuclear power plants are demanding undertakings that require significant resources, access to technology, advanced manufacturing skills, and space. Only a few governments are capable of doing such things on their own; most require assistance from another government. Nuclear programs (or indications of them) tend to be observable from the outside. Confidence is high that attacks using nuclear weapons could be traced back to their origin, something that would invite retaliation and, as a result, discourage an attack in the first place.

In cyberspace, by contrast, there are now billions of actors, as it takes no more than access to a cell phone or tablet or computer connected to the Internet. Much of what is needed can be purchased easily. The Internet plays an incomparably larger global role in the civilian or commercial economy than does nuclear energy, a reality that make restricting the spread of technologies all but impossible. States do not dominate; to the contrary, groups of a few talented individuals can have real impact. Attacks can often be carried out in a manner that disguises those responsible, which makes retaliation and hence deterrence far more difficult.

The Internet grew up with little government role, even though it had its origins in a precursor invented in the late 1960s by the Advanced Research Projects Agency of the U.S. Department of Defense. Rules, to the extent they exist, have been set from the bottom up, by the efforts of and interactions among individuals, civil society, corporations, and governments. This "multistakeholder" process is the closest thing there is to a governing example of Adam Smith's "invisible hand."

This era seems to have run its course, or at least run into strong headwinds. Cyberspace increasingly resembles nothing so much as the old American Wild West with no real sheriff. The Internet is more important to economies, societies, and militaries than ever, but there are few if any rules preventing or even limiting disruptive operations, the theft of intellectual property, violations of privacy, and government censorship—and even when there are rules, there are few or no means for enforcing them.[19]

This is not to suggest an absence of global governance and multilateral arrangements. ICANN, the Internet Corporation for Assigned Names and Numbers, was established in 1998 and has essentially acted as the Internet's traffic cop. Two years later, the United States and the EU reached a so-called Safe Harbor agreement that allowed businesses to transfer data concerning EU citizens to the United States, something close to essential for a corporation doing business on both sides of the Atlantic.[20] And there were any number of international gatherings convened to combat cybercrime, facilitate commerce, advance human rights, and protect privacy over the Internet. The U.S. government, for its part, in 2011 issued a strategy for cyberspace in which it called for the Internet to be "open, interoperable, secure, and reliable."[21] China and the United States agreed in September 2015 not to steal intellectual property, something China had been doing extensively.[22]

But there were at least as many steps backward as forward. Attacks to deny service and disrupt specific activities and operations were carried out with increasing frequency. Espionage and intellectual property theft became common. The World Conference on International Telecommunications, held in Dubai in December 2012, ended with no consensus as to whether the International Telecommunication Union (ITU), established in 1947 for different purposes, would gain oversight over the Internet, something that would bring about a larger role for governments. What little consensus there was on how to handle data in a manner that protected privacy broke down in the wake of the revelations by the disgruntled former CIA employee Edward Snowden; the EU Court of Justice voided the 2000 Safe Harbor accord, causing frictions across the Atlantic until a U.S.-EU pact was reached in 2016 that addressed EU concerns.[23] Overall, the governance gap over all things cyber expanded, the result of rapid technological innovation and an absence of much in the way of consensus as to what the rules ought to be. The U.S. goals for a cyberspace that is open, interoperable, reliable, and secure appear to be in jeopardy.

Global health is another realm of international relations involving a confusing array of actors and arrangements. The UN's World Health Organization (WHO) is the principal governing body, but it is widely seen to be ill prepared and underfunded to meet global health challenges, be they infectious diseases, pandemics, or noncommunicable (noninfectious) diseases. All this matters not simply because of the economic and human cost of disease (and its ability to weaken states) but because of globalization. An outbreak of disease in one country can easily spread around the world.

The most important set of arrangements in this realm is the International Health Regulations, first adopted in 1969 and amended in 2005.[24] The original guidelines require governments to notify the WHO of outbreaks of certain highly communicable diseases, such as cholera, yellow fever, and smallpox. The 2005 revisions to the guidelines require countries to monitor any major public health risks and to put in place capabilities to prevent and respond to them. These undertakings are meant to be legally binding, but compliance has fallen far short owing to a lack of commitment and resources. Recognition of this shortfall explains the introduction in February 2014 of the Global Health Security Agenda, essentially an international monitoring mechanism designed to add some momentum to efforts to encourage governments to meet the obligations they signed on to a decade before.[25] Reactions to the 2014–15 Ebola crisis and the poor performance of the WHO further underscored the gap between the capacity and arrangements that existed and what was needed to prevent and cope with outbreaks of highly infectious diseases.

Economics arguably constitutes one of the more developed areas of global governance. Two areas stand out. The first is trade. As noted earlier, global trade arrangements have been in place since the beginning of the post–World War II era, although the mechanism (the General Agreement on Tariffs and Trade, or GATT) fell short of the international trade organization that many envisioned would coexist alongside the International Monetary Fund and the World Bank. Nevertheless, trade grew in volume as successive rounds of multilateral trade talks had the effect of reducing tariffs and some of the other barriers to trade in manufactured goods in particular.

What has occurred over the last quarter century has been somewhat contradictory. On one hand, there has been great progress on the trade front. The Uruguay Round of global trade talks, launched in the mid-1980s, came to fruition in late 1993, reducing barriers to trade and establishing the

World Trade Organization.[26] The WTO has grown to over 160 members and has reduced obstacles to trade as well as provided a venue where disputes between members can be adjudicated. The last quarter century was as well an era of proliferation of regional and bilateral trade accords. Some of the most prominent included Mercosur (the Southern Common Market), the ASEAN Free Trade Area (AFTA), and NAFTA (the North America Free Trade Agreement involving Mexico, Canada, and the United States). The net result is that world trade volume increased more than fivefold over this period, from a total of $3.5 trillion in 1990 to $19 trillion twenty-five years later.[27] Trade became an important vehicle for integrating developing countries such as China into the world economy, contributing significantly to their economic growth and development in the process. Trade also became a force for stability, as it not only bolstered the economic position of U.S. allies but also gave many countries a stake in avoiding actions that would jeopardize economic arrangements that worked to their benefit.

But as noted just above, it was also an era filled with contradictions. Efforts to facilitate the expansion of trade at the global level ran into many difficulties; indeed, this is a principal reason for the large number of regional and bilateral agreements, which are second best given the issues and participants inevitably left out. The so-called Doha or Development Round of global trade talks, launched in 2001, failed to reach agreement as differences over such issues as government subsidies, nontariff barriers, and how to treat trade in agricultural goods and services (as opposed to manufacturing) could not be bridged. Efforts to reach consensus were not helped by the large number of participants. In recent years, the rate of growth in world trade has slowed significantly. What also occurred was a falling off of domestic political support for trade pacts in the United States and many other countries, casting uncertainty over future efforts to promote a more open world trading system.

There was arguably less formal governance but still significant coordination on the monetary side. The principal characteristics of the era were floating exchange rates, central bank independence, and dollar dominance. The IMF assessed ("surveilled") economies and gave them public report cards but had no power to insist on reforms other than when it was involved in extending loans to governments in financial difficulty. In the banking arena, the so-called Basel Committee established standards (for example, for the amount of capital required to be kept on hand) that banks were encouraged to follow. Its work was reinforced and complemented by the Financial Stability Forum, a group created in 1999 by a dozen or so governments representing many of the world's largest open economies. A decade later, in the wake of the 2008 financial crisis, the forum became the Financial Stability Board, involving finance ministries and central banks of the G-20 countries and a few others. Again, the purpose was to develop and promote policies and "best practices" that would, if adopted by governments, help them prevent and mange risks to their economies and to the world financial system.[28] The idea was to set in motion a race to the top that would encourage responsible behaviors, allowing a country to compete successfully in a world in which capital and investment would find their way not just to countries and institutions of high return but also to those of safety. In addition, the realities of globalization and the potential for contagion gave all governments a stake in one another's adopting responsible practices.[29]

This is not meant to paint too positive a picture, as in some areas coordination was lacking. Central banks could take actions to stimulate growth that would also affect currencies, in the process lowering the prices of exports and raising those of imports. Certain countries (China, Japan) built up enormous dollar holdings; others, notably the United States, ran enormous deficits. To some extent this U.S. deficit was necessary, as it provided liquidity to the world; at the same time, it raised questions as to the future value of the dollar. Indeed, no progress was made on the tension arising from the U.S. dollar's status as both the national currency of the United States and the global reserve currency, that is, the currency used for most international transactions, which required most countries to keep a store of it on hand. The U.S. Federal Reserve thus acted as both the country's and the world's central bank; the problem in the eyes of many resulted from the

A GLOBAL GAP | 149

fact that the world had no oversight or control over the U.S. central bank or U.S. economic policy more broadly. Attempts to strengthen the role of other currencies or to create a new global currency (so-called special drawing rights, or SDRs, issued by the IMF came the closest) amounted to little. The 2008 financial crisis and the recession that followed made clear the system's vulnerability to U.S. mismanagement. There was in effect no global central bank or financial regulator.

This survey of global cooperation adds up to a mixed picture of significant global cooperation in some areas, limited cooperation in others, and some significant gaps. The same holds true for other areas of global cooperation, including refugees and migrants, energy, the Arctic, oceans and the seabed, and outer space. Respect for sovereignty remains a central component of what order there is, but even this principle is being challenged by Russian behavior in Ukraine along with disagreements over when some or even all of sovereignty's privileges are to be forfeited. In many domains of international life there is a pattern of agreement in principle that translates into little agreement in practice. In still other domains there is not even much in the way of agreement in principle. Such differences cannot for the most part be resolved through negotiation; process cannot overcome policy given the large number of governments in the world and the reality that nongovernmental entities that often matter a great deal never get invited into the room.

The result is that the phrase "international community" is far more aspirational than actual. Much less international community exists than anyone could be forgiven for thinking given how often the phrase is invoked. In principle, a community (or "society" in Hedley Bull's lexicon) would agree on both the means and the ends of international relations, on what was to be done and how that was to be determined. But the cold reality is that no such broad and deep consensus exists as to what is to be done, who is to do it, and how to decide. There is a substantial gap between what is desirable when it comes to meeting the challenges of globalization and what has proven possible. This gap is one of the principal reasons for the disarray that exists in the world.

6. Regional Realities

The world can be viewed and understood through several prisms. We have already looked at two: great-power relations and global governance. A third is the regional. Many of the most important economic, military, and diplomatic interactions take place at this level for the simple reason that proximity matters. Many countries that count for little at the global level, because of a lack of either reach or relative weight, have a much greater impact on their neighbors. At the same time, they are affected significantly by those same neighbors. To this I would add only that the range of outcomes between regions could hardly be greater; just as order varies at the global level from issue to issue, so too does it vary from region to region.

The post–Cold War era had its first major test in the Middle East, and with the United States taking the lead, order was restored by a broad international coalition acting pursuant to a number of UN Security Council resolutions to deny

Iraq in its bid to take Kuwait by force. Order in this case meant a region of nearly two dozen Arab states led by authoritarian rulers with borders that were mostly accepted in fact, if not always formally agreed on. The countries ranged from relatively poor and populous Egypt to several small city-states of enormous wealth in the Persian Gulf. One outlier was Israel, the Jewish state established in 1948. It by then had a de jure peace with Egypt, a de facto peace with Jordan, and a state of nonwar with Syria. What was unresolved and a source of regular friction was Israel's relationship with the Palestinians, in particular those living in lands ruled by Israel since the 1967 war. Israel was by far the strongest local state and the only country with nuclear weapons. A second outlier was Iran, a Persian and mostly Shia country in an Arab- and Sunni-dominated region. Since its 1979 revolution, Iran had been ruled by a political-religious regime committed to expanding its influence throughout the region, often through direct support of proxies and Shia communities. Iran, though, was much weakened by its decade-long war in the 1980s with Iraq and in no position to mount a serious challenge to regional stability. In addition, it was effectively balanced by Iraq; indeed, in 1991, the United States made the decision during Operation Desert Storm to leave the bulk of Iraq's army and air force intact so that it could continue in this role.

The United States was the principal external influence on the region, demonstrated by its successful leadership of the coalition that liberated Kuwait, its substantial economic and military support of Israel and Arab states such as Egypt and Jordan, and a residual military presence in the region, most of which was aimed at making sure Saddam Hussein complied with various international sanctions still in effect and that he did not again threaten or attack a neighbor. U.S. policy was shaped mostly by existing and projected American dependence on the region's oil and by its support for Israel and the more moderate Arab governments. No longer a factor in the region was the sort of great-power jockeying for comparative position that had characterized the United States and Europe in the first decade after World War II and the United States and the Soviet Union over the next three decades.

This order largely continued to dominate the region until 2003, when the United States attacked Iraq. Unlike the 1990–91 Gulf War, a conflict undertaken for the limited purpose of reversing Iraq's aggression and its hold over Kuwait, the 2003 Iraq War sought to bring about a change of regime in Baghdad. The ostensible reason was that the Saddam Hussein regime refused to comply fully with UN demands prohibiting Iraq's possession of weapons of mass destruction. This was part of what led to the war, especially because after 9/11 there was little willingness to tolerate any possibility that Iraq might develop and either use or make available to terrorists nuclear or biological weapons.[1] The motive that most captured the imaginations of the upper reaches of the George W. Bush administration, though, was the belief that a post-Saddam Iraq would become democratic, setting an example and a precedent that the other Arab states and Iran would have great difficulty resisting. The road to a transformed Middle East, it was widely believed, ran through Baghdad. I did not share this view, but I had little opportunity to challenge those who did, given the structure of decision making in the George W. Bush administration. Even if I had, I would not have prevailed.

As is so often the case, things didn't work out as planned. Iraq proved far less ripe for democratic change than had been anticipated by the war's proponents. To the contrary, the removal of the regime, coupled with subsequent misguided decisions by the U.S.-led occupying authority that ran Iraq from May 2003 through June 2004 to dismantle much of the army and to ostracize many members of the ruling Ba'ath (Renaissance) Party, fueled a civil war between the long-discriminated-against Shia plurality and minority Sunnis who had lost their advantaged status with the fall of the Saddam Hussein regime. It also provided both cause and opportunity for the rise of al-Qaeda in Iraq, a terrorist group mostly manned by disgruntled Iraqi Sunnis opposed to the new Shia-dominated political order.

The war and its aftermath had numerous consequences beyond Iraq's borders. Contrary to what was hoped for, democracy was dealt a major setback throughout the region as the ideal of democracy had come to be associated in the eyes of many in the Arab world with chaos. National identity in Iraq had been superseded by subnational identities tied to sect, tribe, and ethnicity; people saw themselves far more as a Sunni or Shia or Kurd than as an Iraqi. Sunni anger and humiliation stoked recruiting for both al-Qaeda and subsequently ISIS. Images of Iraq broadcast throughout the region reinforced subnational identities in other countries, creating and reinforcing frictions between local Shia and Sunni. Iran, long since recovered from its decade-long war with Iraq and no longer tied down, much less balanced by a strong hostile Arab regime, was in many ways the principal strategic beneficiary of the war, as it was freed up to promote the interests of the Iranian state and Shia populations. The 2003 Iraq War violated any number of strategic tenets, beginning with the Hippocratic oath: First do no harm.

Despite these and other changes brought on in part or in whole by the 2003 conflict, the Middle East of 2010, two decades after the Iraqi invasion of Kuwait, was still more recognizable and similar than not. What set in motion events that changed the region beyond recognition was the humiliation and subsequent self-immolation of a Tunisian fruit and vegetable vendor that December. People took to the streets in Tunis and beyond, protesting against a heavy-handed leadership that had been in place for more than two decades. The Arab Spring was born.

What led to the Arab Spring remains a subject of conjecture and debate. On one hand, there was nothing new or fundamentally different to point to. The region was dominated by authoritarian governments that demonstrated little or no commitment to political or economic reform. Islamists could claim much more political energy, but were eyed with suspicion and targeted by internal security forces. Civil society was thin, the quality of education terrible, the so-called Israeli-Palestinian peace process stalled.

Yet as we know, political protest gained a foothold throughout much of the region in 2011. It is possible that cell phones and social media made it easier for people inclined to protest to communicate with one another, but this hardly explains why it happened then. The same holds for the suggestion that it was the removal of Saddam Hussein that sent the message that no despot was permanent.[2] My own view is that the region was ripe for political challenge and even upheaval, that the pressures had been building for some time, and that if the Tunisian vendor had not immolated himself, some other person or development would have provided the spark leading to widespread challenge to political authority.

It is instructive in this regard to look at the *Arab Human Development Report 2009*, written by a group of independent Arab scholars, analysts, and practitioners from the region. Its assessment was nothing short of devastating. It detailed the pressures resulting from a backdrop of large and rapid population increases, a youth bulge, fast urban growth, a lack of civic consciousness, weak constitutions, the prevalence of prolonged martial law, widespread violence against women, high unemployment, poverty, water scarcity, expanding desertification, and widespread air and water pollution. As if all this were not enough, the report went on to say, "The majority of states failed to introduce democratic governance and institutions of representation that ensure inclusion, the equal distribution of wealth among various groups, and respect for cultural diversity."[3] Upheaval in such circumstances was highly likely if not inevitable.

But regardless of the general or specific causes, what soon materialized were protests or uprisings against authoritarian rulers in much of the Arab world, including Egypt, Bahrain, Syria, and Libya. Each situation played out differently, as did events in Iraq.

Egypt saw protests come to the main square in the capital soon after Tunisia. Thousands protested against the regime of Hosni Mubarak, a typical Arab strongman who had introduced a degree of economic reform and little political change. Making matters worse, corruption was considerable and Mubarak and many of those around him seemed determined not just to get rich but to pass power on to his son Gamal. As the protests mounted, belated offers by Mubarak to step down later in 2011 fanned rather than doused the flames. A succession of transitional governments likewise failed to maintain order, and parliamentary and then presidential elections ushered into office a government led by Mohammed Morsi and dominated by the Muslim Brotherhood and other Islamists.

The Islamists won because they were the best organized and because most Egyptians were alienated from traditional politics and wanted to see order restored. Elections, however, are not to be equated or confused with democracy, which is about constitutional restraints, checks and balances, and the sharing of power, not its concentration. The honeymoon lasted about a year, until the summer of 2013, when the Egyptian military (led by General Abdel Fattah el-Sisi) responded to public pressure and stepped in to oust a government many Egyptians feared would change not just the nature of the society (Egypt had been a largely secular country) but also the political system to ensure that Islamists would continue to rule. "One man, one vote, one time" had to many become an all too real possibility. The result was that more than five years after the Arab Spring, Egypt resembled nothing so much as Egypt before the Arab Spring.

The United States paid a substantial price in both Egypt and the region for its actual and perceived role during these upheavals. In early 2011, in the opening weeks of the Arab Spring, the Obama administration promoted a delayed transition of power in Egypt, only to change its mind amid growing violence in the streets and call for Mubarak to step down right away.[4] The public call for Mubarak's departure was gratuitous. It would have been far wiser to stand by the proposed departure in a few months and allow events to play out. It may have been that Mubarak could not have survived. But there was no need for an American push, which was taken as a sign in Riyadh and elsewhere that the United States could not be expected to back its friends of long standing. It also played into the narrative that the United States secretly preferred the Muslim Brotherhood, a belief that gained credence when U.S. criticism of the short-lived regime of Mohammed Morsi was widely viewed as relatively muted. This perception of American bias was then further reinforced by the protracted friction between the Obama administration and the successor Egyptian government, friction that manifested itself not just in verbal criticism but with denial of certain military support. For many in Washington, General Sisi had come to power by a coup and then lost further legitimacy by his government's harsh treatment of many Egyptians. The Obama administration was right to be concerned—it is quite possible that the Egyptian government's "you are either entirely with us or you will be seen as against us" policies will prove counterproductive—but it arguably would have been wiser to opt to support the new government in the short run and press for reform over time only once it was established and the relationship reaffirmed.

Another early challenge arose in Bahrain, a tiny country with a population of just over one million and consisting of one main island (as well as many small ones) connected by a causeway to Saudi Arabia. It functions as something of a financial center and a place for Saudis and others to blow off steam on weekends. Bahrain is of particular importance to the United States, as U.S. warships have operated out of it since the late 1940s. The country is overwhelmingly made up of Shia Muslims, but the ruling al-Khalifa family and the elites are predominantly Sunni.

Not surprisingly, the Arab Spring triggered protests in the capital of Manama. Protests grew in size and demands in response to heavy-handed police and army tactics. The monarchy put forward certain concessions, but as often happens in such circumstances, compromise was judged by many of the protesters to be too little, too late and only added fuel to the proverbial fire. The leadership in Saudi Arabia and the United Arab Emirates quickly became alarmed over the prospect of a Shia overthrow of the regime, one that if successful would lead to a Shia-dominated government that would likely align with Iran. So in March 2011 the Saudis and the UAE (under the aegis of the Sunni-led regional security organization, the Gulf Cooperation Council) dispatched some fifteen hundred troops to back up the Bahrain government and crush the protests. Ever since, Bahrain has been the venue of a low-level civil conflict between lightly armed Shia protesters and the government. Allegations of human rights abuses are numerous. Dialogue and attempts at reconciliation have failed. In effect, there is a standoff. The United States, in an embrace of foreign policy realism, said little and did less given its military use of Bahrain and its desire not to alienate the Saudis.

Libya proved to be a textbook case of where the United States and the world got it wrong (and contributed significantly to disorder), first by doing too much, then by doing too little. The story is well known. In February 2011, in the early weeks of the Arab Spring, protests began to surface calling for the removal of the regime of Muammar Gadhafi, the all-powerful ruler of Libya since 1969. The Libyan government pushed back and was gaining the upper hand, creating fears in some quarters that this would lead to widespread killing of civilians, especially in the city of Benghazi, the principal locus of antiregime protests and violence. Calls for Western military intervention mounted, motivated by a desire both to prevent any massacres and to oust a regime correctly viewed as a serial abuser of human rights. On March 17, 2011, the UN Security Council passed Resolution 1973, authorizing member states to both "take all necessary measures . . . to protect civilians and civilian populated areas under threat of attack" and establish a no-fly zone over the whole of the country.[5] Soon after, a "humanitarian intervention" was carried out by a coalition of NATO members led by the Europeans, with the United States "leading from behind."[6]

There were any number of problems with all this. First, it is far from certain that the situation on the ground warranted a humanitarian intervention. The protests against the government were violent from the outset, and any government, even an authoritarian one, has the right to counter armed opponents. This is, after all, what civil wars are all about. What is more, there is reason to believe that the civil conflict was petering out on the eve of the NATO intervention. There was also no hard evidence that Gadhafi planned an indiscriminate attack on civilians.[7]

Second, that the intervention quickly went beyond a narrowly designed effort to protect civilian lives (the thrust of the UN mandate) and expanded to regime change introduced important new costs. Russia and China complained bitterly that they had not signed on to any such broader undertaking. What they came to see as a diplomatic bait and switch served mostly to reinforce their view that the Responsibility to Protect doctrine was a dangerous concept that could be used to violate sovereignty and overthrow governments. Not only would gaining international support for humanitarian intervention in the future be more difficult, but Russia would use humanitarian intervention as the cynical pretext for its intervention in Ukraine.

The ouster of Gadhafi also sent the unfortunate message that giving up nuclear weapons could be dangerous to your political health. In a matter of months the Libyan leader went from the poster child of responsibility in the proliferation realm to war criminal.

The other problem with the intervention, whether one thinks it was warranted or not, was that it was not followed up. None other than Barack Obama described this failure to prepare for the day after in Libya as his biggest foreign policy mistake.[8] Colin Powell is often cited for quoting the so-called Pottery Barn rule: "You break it, you own it." The United States and several NATO countries did a great deal to help break Libya but then refused to take any ownership of the ensuing situation. To the contrary, they avoided anything that smacked of nation building, partly out of naïve hopes that

Libyans would come together on their own, but more out of a concern about the cost of putting the country back together. The result is a civil conflict that has claimed far more lives and uprooted far more people than even the worse estimates of what Gadhafi might have unleashed. Another result is the existence of not just one but multiple failed states in the territory that was once the country of Libya. Not surprisingly, the Islamic State is making growing use of this largely ungoverned territory.

The Syrian case is if anything even more consequential. Indeed, it is as strong an argument as exists that when it comes to foreign policy, what you choose not to do can be every bit as consequential as what you do. Syria in the years since 2011 is the bookend to the 2003 decision to go to war with Iraq. One was an act of commission, the other largely one of omission, and each in its own way proved costly beyond imagination.

The background was already described earlier, namely, that the so-called Arab Spring arrived in Syria in March 2011. Anti-Assad protests were put down violently by troops, which led elements of the opposition to take up arms. In August President Obama first called for Bashar al-Assad to step down.[9] Little was done, however, to increase the odds that he would depart, much less that he would be replaced by something and someone better. Peace plans and cease-fires, along with both Arab League and UN monitors, came and went to little effect as the violence escalated. Here and elsewhere, policymaking under the Obama administration was plagued by a gap between pronouncements and policies. Anytime such a gap emerges it is dangerous, as it raises questions about credibility and competence alike. It can disillusion friends, in the process forcing them to reevaluate their relationship in ways that make them less friendly, more independent, or both.

The stakes grew in the summer of 2012 amid reports the Syrian government might be employing chemical weapons against opposition forces. President Obama went public with the statement that were the Assad government to do so, it would cross a "red line" that would significantly alter the calculus of U.S. military intervention.[10] Roughly a year later, in August 2013, the Syrian government did just that, using sarin gas and killing an estimated fifteen hundred civilians near Damascus. Expectations were high that the United States would intervene directly, although the details of what it would actually do remained a matter of speculation.

U.S. determination to act began to fade when, on August 29, the British Parliament refused to authorize the government of Prime Minster David Cameron to join a multilateral air campaign that would destroy targets associated with chemical weapons and/or targets of political or military value to the Syrian government. At that point President Obama clearly began to have second thoughts about his warning as to what would follow if Syria crossed the red line of chemical weapons use. My sense at the time was that these doubts reflected his own qualms about what a limited use of force would trigger in the way of pressures to do more, something that would cut across the principal strategic thrust of the administration, which was to reduce U.S. military involvement in the greater Middle East.

I had something of a strange window on all this. The night before the president chose to announce his decision not to use military force, I was at a wedding when I received a call from what the media would describe as a very senior administration source. The individual wanted to know what I thought of the idea of the president not taking military action but instead asking Congress for authorization to act. I responded that I thought it would be a terrible decision that would raise questions in the region and beyond as to American reliability, and that would empower the Assad regime and sap the morale of the Syrian opposition. I also argued that the president had no need to get additional authority from Congress, that under the American system the executive enjoyed great latitude when it came to limited uses of military force. I was also anything but certain that Congress would provide such authorization given opposition in both parties to renewed U.S. military involvement in the region and the reflexive opposition of some Republicans to supporting anything this president sought to do. (Some of that opposition reflected concern that any use of force would be token.) The last thing the United States needed to signal to the world was that it was so divided that its words and commitments could no longer be relied on. The senior official thanked me for my views without revealing where matters stood.

I had no idea that the hypothetical presented to me would in a matter of hours become U.S. policy, as President Obama announced that he would consult with Congress before ordering any military retaliation for the Syrian use of chemicals.[11] It was in this context that the United States and Russia agreed to work together on an initiative by which Syria could avoid being attacked if it agreed to give up all of its remaining chemical weapons.[12] Secretary of State John Kerry's Russian counterpart ran with this idea, and in a matter of weeks Syria had agreed to destroy all of its chemical weapons in cooperation with the United Nations.

That Syria agreed to give up its chemical weapons was a plus, but in no way did it offset the costs of the United States not following through on its warning to the Assad regime. Any suggestion to the contrary is political spin or an avoidance of reality.[13] Granted, it is impossible to know what would have happened had the United States followed through on its threat. War inevitably surprises. Much would have depended on what the United States actually did. A symbolic "pinprick" of an attack—for example, launching a few cruise missiles at a single target—would likely have accomplished little. But a meaningful strike against important military and political targets over several days involving both aircraft and cruise missiles would have bolstered the morale of the opposition and shifted the military momentum in its favor. Any such strikes could have been punitive, leaving the United States and its European partners in a position to judge when enough punishment had been meted out. Alternatively, the strikes could have been coercive and continued until the Syrian government gave up its chemical stocks. Air attacks might also have set in motion political dynamics within the regime that could have weakened the position of Bashar al-Assad or even led to his ouster. They certainly would have strengthened the norm that no weapon of mass destruction could be used with impunity. For all these reasons I would argue that President Obama was right to set a red line of no chemical weapons use but wrong not to have responded to its violation.

All that we know for sure is what followed in the wake of the United States deciding not to act. Saudi Arabia, already unhappy with the United States over what it saw as a lack of steadfastness in the U.S. treatment of Hosni Mubarak in Egypt, seems to have determined that henceforth it would defer less to Washington and act more independently. Subsequent Saudi decisions, from its invasion of Yemen in 2015 to its actions in Syria, bear this out. I know from personal conversations that the U.S. inconsistency rattled senior officials and leaders of allied and friendly countries as far away as Asia. Within Syria, the U.S. decision forfeited an opportunity to weaken the regime. What also followed was a strengthening of the more radical elements of the Syrian opposition, including ISIS and al-Nusra, the local branch of al-Qaeda.

At several points in this book I have underscored the

potential costs of inaction. I am reminded here of the Yom Kippur service, the Jewish Day of Atonement, during which no fewer than ten times each member of the congregation recites a prayer in which he or she asks forgiveness for specific transgressions committed during the year about to end. Some forty sins, reflecting the full range of improper thoughts, words, and behaviors, are noted. The last sin, however, often translated from the Hebrew as the sin of having "a confused heart," is the sin of inaction when action is warranted.

As President John F. Kennedy once warned, "There are risks and costs to a program of action. But they are far less than the long-range risks and costs of comfortable inaction."[14] The lesson to be derived is not that acting is always right—in the case of the 2003 Iraq War, to name just one example, it most surely was not—but rather that *not* acting can be every bit as consequential as acting and, as a result, needs to be assessed with equal rigor. In my experience this is rarely done. What is more, every action that is examined always entails drawbacks, and as the cliché goes, analysis can lead to paralysis. The hope that imperfect options become less imperfect with the passage of time is almost always illusory. Red wine may improve with age, but policy choices rarely do. The default bias thus becomes the status quo. This was all too often the case with U.S. policy toward Syria.

The next two years, 2014 and 2015, saw the intensification of civil war within Syria. But like many civil wars, it was heavily influenced by the direct and indirect involvement of outsiders. Indeed, Syria became one of the principal venues of the Sunni-Shia and Saudi-Iran rivalries that have come to characterize much of the region. Iran provided significant economic and military aid to the government; in addition, Iranian Revolutionary Guard forces and Iran-backed Hezbollah forces fought with and for the Syrian government.

Major powers were also in evidence. Russia intervened directly in Syria in late 2015. The result was heavy air attacks designed to shore up the Assad regime. This was not entirely a bad thing, as the rapid collapse of the Assad regime without careful preparation for what would take its place would likely have paved the way for ISIS to establish a caliphate in Damascus, something to be resisted at all costs. The Russian strategy appeared to succeed, although at a considerable price of numerous civilian deaths and the weakening of groups backed by the United States and its erstwhile partners (such as Saudi Arabia) rather than, say, terrorists including ISIS and al-Nusra. More than anything else, Russian policy seemed to be motivated by a desire to show that it remained a major power able to make a difference on the world stage. There was as well a Russian interest in bolstering a long-term ally where it had a military base; also possible is that Russian leaders hoped that their actions in Syria (which could in principle reduce the flow of refugees to Europe) might win the country favor and increase the chance that sanctions introduced because of Ukraine would be reduced or rescinded.[15]

As for the United States, its involvement remained limited. The goal seemed to be to avoid a major military commitment as much as to achieve a particular outcome. Some twenty years ago I wrote a book about American foreign policy titled *The Reluctant Sheriff*. It referred to foreign policy during the presidency of Bill Clinton, but with the passage of time I believe the description fits Barack Obama even better.[16] There is no denying that the raid that killed Osama bin Laden was a courageous decision, but this was something of an exception that may well have reflected the narrow nature of the mission. Far more often than not, Barack Obama proved wary of contemplating or continuing military interventions of potential scale and duration. Thus in Syria, even as conditions worsened, U.S. policy did not change meaningfully. There was some bombing of ISIS positions but no ground element. The United States opposed the creation of a humanitarian zone or safe area for Syrian civilians, something that would have required the commitment of considerable air assets as well as ground forces from either the United States or another country such as Turkey. Attempts to build a "moderate" Syrian opposition from scratch were jettisoned in 2015 after several years of fruitless but costly effort. Only by 2016 did a somewhat more promising strategy begin to emerge, one of arming local Kurdish and Sunni groups, aerial attacks on ISIS positions, and emplacement of a small number of U.S. special operations forces alongside the Kurdish and Sunni fighters. But the United States backed off providing Sunni groups with more capable arms (such as surface-to-air missiles) or attacking Syrian military assets directly, possibly because it might risk a confrontation with Russia, whose planes were already flying.

The result was that by early 2016 the situation on the ground had become something of a dynamic stalemate, with the government stabilized thanks to Russian and Iranian support, both ISIS and al-Nusra controlling shrinking but still sizable pieces of the country, the Kurds controlling a narrow strip of land in the north along the Turkish border, and other Sunni groups holding on to small pieces of territory. The biggest losers were the people of Syria, hundreds of thousands of whom lost their lives, and more than ten million of whom lost their homes and became either internally displaced or refugees. That said, there were many other losers as well, from the neighboring countries and Europe that came to bear the burden of refugees to the United States, which because of Syria found its reputation and standing diminished.

Some signs of diplomatic possibility came at the end of 2015, in a UN Security Council resolution (2254) proposing some of the principles that would necessarily inform a peace agreement for Syria.[17] There were also several announcements by the United States and Russia of local "cessations of hostilities."[18] But it would be wrong to exaggerate the significance of any of this. As a rule of thumb, diplomacy and negotiations tend to reflect realities on the ground, not change them. Consistent with this principle, the resolution made no mention of the departure of the Syrian leader, the principal priority for Saudi Arabia, Turkey, and many Syrian opposition groups. Nor was there evidence that the principal backers of the regime, including Russia and Iran, were prepared to sign on to any timetable for Assad's departure. Also missing was even a modicum of unity among the many opposition groups. And of course there was no role for extremist groups such as ISIS and al-Nusra, the al-Qaeda affiliate that controlled territory. Meanwhile, the fighting raged in many areas of the country, with the civilian population of Syria continuing to pay an enormous price and the country effectively divided into zones or cantons controlled by the government or one or another organization.

Adding to the turmoil in the region were events in Yemen. That country, too, was affected by the Arab Spring. Protests, armed attacks, and some regional diplomacy combined to bring about a new government led by the former vice president in early 2012, but it was a government atop a country in which both the Houthis (a Shia-based rebel movement) and al-Qaeda undermined the government's authority and the country's stability. By 2015, the ability of the Sunni-dominated government to survive was in doubt, at which point Saudi Arabia began attacking Houthi forces (which the government in Riyadh saw as little more than Iranian proxies) from the air. Yemen thus joined the ranks of countries in the Middle East paying the enormous humanitarian price for wars that were at one and the same time civil, proxy, and regional.

The Saudi intervention was a costly distraction for a country much weakened by low energy prices and infighting over the line of royal succession. The Saudi foreign minister described the intervention as a war of necessity, but in actuality it was a war of choice.[19] Saudi Arabia had more modest options to protect itself, options more in line with its limited military abilities and constrained financial position. The net result was that Saudi Arabia, the ostensible "Islamic state" overseeing the faith's holiest cities and shrines, may well have made itself more vulnerable to ISIS, which could pose as a reform movement to the large number of young, digitally savvy Saudis with few prospects for meaningful jobs and alienated by the pervasive corruption and inequality.

One more country merits mention here: Iraq. Turmoil there was not a function of the Arab Spring. To the contrary, critical events predated its advent by several years. Conditions inside Iraq had gone from bad to worse in 2005 and 2006. Much of the foreign policy establishment in the United States favored reducing the U.S. role in what was turning out to be a fiasco.[20] Beginning in early 2007, however, President George W. Bush opted for a new and different tack, one that sought to provide security to the inhabitants of the western-most, predominantly Sunni part of Iraq. The policy had two dimensions: extending financial and military support to select Sunni tribes (sometimes dubbed the Sunni Awakening) and increasing the U.S. troop presence by some thirty thousand soldiers, often described as the "surge." The effort seemed largely to succeed, and by the end of 2008 al-Qaeda in Iraq had been put on the defensive and significant parts of the country had achieved at least some stability.[21] As one of his last major foreign policy acts, President Bush signed a status-of-forces accord with Iraqi prime minister Nouri al-Maliki in which the two agreed that all U.S. combat forces would be withdrawn from Iraq by the end of 2011.[22]

Barack Obama, soon after entering the Oval Office in January 2009, announced and began to implement an accelerated drawdown of U.S. troops.[23] It soon became apparent, however, that Iraq lacked the political cohesion and military capacity to maintain order absent a continuing American military role. It was in this context that the United States made two fateful decisions. First, it went ahead with the planned troop withdrawal rather than find a way to renegotiate the status-of-forces agreement that would have allowed for a limited number of U.S. forces to remain. Second, it threw its political support behind the incumbent prime minister (Maliki) even though he failed to gain a plurality in the 2010 elections and was known to be a narrow sectarian who favored Shia interests over national ones.[24] Against this backdrop of political infighting and mounting sectarian violence al-Qaeda in Iraq regained its strength and spread into Syria, in the process becoming ISIS. By 2014, the United States was again bombing targets in Iraq and some thirty-five hundred U.S. troops had been sent back to assist government forces in their war against the Islamic State.

It is not central to this book to do a detailed assessment of the decisions and events relating to Iraq. I have already written one book on Iraq and do not intend to make this a second. What I will say, though, is that the principal errors of policy were the decisions to launch the war in 2003 and the decisions made afterward to disband the army and ban far too many of those associated with what had been the ruling party. The 2007 and 2008 surge and Sunni Awakening provided something of a second chance to stabilize Iraq, but what chance there existed was undermined by the premature withdrawal of all U.S. forces, which left the United States less able to influence either local security or politics. I do believe a way could have been found to keep U.S. forces in Iraq after 2011 along lines used several years later when more than three thousand U.S. troops returned to the country without the Iraqi parliament having approved a formal agreement granting full immunity. That said, it is impossible to know for sure whether any level of U.S. involvement could have saved Iraqis from themselves and their deeply flawed political culture. Indeed, this last point reinforces doubts about the wisdom of invading Iraq in 2003.

This combination of local realities, along with a mixture of American acts of commission and omission, of action and inaction, has made the Middle East what it is: the most unstable part of the world. Earlier, in the context of the 2003 Iraq War, I referred to the violation of the Hippocratic oath, to first do no harm. Here another medical analogy comes to mind. The Middle East is akin to a sick patient, one with all sorts of life-threatening maladies. But the patient's terrible physical condition is also attributable to negligence on the part of doctors and medical staff. There is a term for illness that is treatment-induced: iatrogenic. Today's Middle East is the result of local pathologies made worse by foreign policy action and inaction alike. "Iatrogenic disorder" is not a term of art when it comes to foreign policy, but it should be.

The historical comparison that comes to mind when looking at the contemporary Middle East is that of the Thirty Years War, the political and religious struggle fought by local forces and outsiders alike within and across borders that decimated Europe in the first half of the seventeenth century. Such struggles tend to end only when one or another protagonist wins, when order is imposed from the outside, or when exhaustion overwhelms all involved, akin to a fire deprived of wood or oxygen. Missing from this list is compromise. On the other hand, what is plentiful now are recruits, dollars, arms, proxies, militias, and a willingness to fight. The next section of this book will focus on what can be done here and elsewhere, but I say this here to underscore that a quarter century after the end of the Cold War, a quarter century after the American-led and internationally supported effort to push Saddam Hussein out of Kuwait, the Middle East is more unstable than ever, with dire consequences for the region and the world.

I don't want to leave this discussion of U.S. Middle East

policy over the past twenty-five years without making one more point. How foreign policy is made counts for a great deal. It is no accident that the highly disciplined and relatively formal national security decision-making process of the George H. W. Bush administration tended to yield effective policies for the most part. What also helped was that the most senior people involved were experienced, had independent standing apart from their relationship with this president and their position, and were comfortable with both one another and with disagreement. There was as well a balance between the influence of the National Security Council and the various departments and agencies. Some of these same characteristics existed in the successor Clinton administration. But the presidency of George W. Bush introduced an unfortunate degree of informality in decision making—there was no structured meeting, for example, to review the decision to initiate war with Iraq in 2003—and poor oversight of planning for the war's aftermath. Policymaking arguably deteriorated further under the Obama administration. Informality again became the order of the day, the most notorious example being the decision not to make good on the threat to Syria if it used chemical weapons. The White House staff became much too large in size, function, and influence. Process is no panacea, but it can protect presidents, who too often opt for the decision-making process and staff they feel comfortable with and want, not the ones they need.[25]

The history of the Asia-Pacific region over the same time could hardly be more different from that of the Middle East. The region remained remarkably stable throughout this period. I use the word "remarkably" with clear intent, as there was little reason to assume this would be the case. To begin with, there were a large number of unresolved territorial disputes in the region, many going back to the end of the Second World War or before. Even a short list would include China and India over their border, Japan and Russia over the so-called Northern Territories, China and Japan over islands in the East China Sea, and China and just about everyone else over islands as well as air- and sea-space in the South China Sea. Alongside all this is the fact that the Korean Peninsula remains divided at the 38th parallel; still missing more than seventy years after the end of the Korean War is a formal peace treaty.

A second reason the region's stability is remarkable is that it survived amid significant change and dynamism. The economic rise of the Asia-Pacific is nothing short of extraordinary. Economic output, whether by country or per capita, increased by over 300 percent over this two-and-a-half-decade period. And again, what makes this so remarkable is that stability held despite this economic transformation and with sharp increases in spending on national military forces.

A third reason the history is something of a pleasant surprise is the relative lack of regional architecture. There was nothing in this part of the world comparable to what existed in Europe during the Cold War or what exists even now. This may seem to be an odd claim in a part of the world that at first glance appears to be an alphabet soup of regional structures, including ASEAN (the Association of Southeast Asian Nations) and APEC (Asia-Pacific Economic Cooperation), but these multilateral regional structures are mostly to promote economic interaction, not to discourage arms races or to prevent or limit conflicts.

The question obviously arises as to why the Asia-Pacific region remained relatively stable in these circumstances. One reason is economic. Many governments focused on their economic development, something that required external stability so that they could trade with their neighbors and not see resources siphoned off by preparing for or fighting wars. This high degree of economic interaction resulted in a degree of interdependence that constituted something of a collective bulwark against any conflict that would jeopardize a situation that worked to everyone's advantage.

A second reason is structural. Unlike the Middle East, where many loyalties are to tribe or religion and many borders lack deep historical roots, in Asia most of the countries have strong national identities and strong governments. China, Japan, Korea—all have long and proud traditions. All are also countries with a considerable degree of demographic and linguistic homogeneity.

A third reason for the region's stability is the United States. The United States departed South Vietnam ignominiously in 1975, but it did not leave either Asia or the Pacific more broadly. To the contrary, it maintained a substantial military, economic, and diplomatic presence, and maintained alliances with such countries as Japan, South Korea, the Philippines, Thailand, Australia, and New Zealand. This mixture of close relationships and physical presence worked both to deter would-be adventurists or aggressors and to dampen down pressures and incentives for governments to become self-sufficient in the security sphere, something that would have led to more frequent conflict, much larger standing militaries, and quite possibly the proliferation of nuclear weapons.

This is not to say that U.S. policy toward Asia was always ideal. To the contrary, U.S. national security policy over the past quarter century has been guilty of a geographic bias that constitutes a strategic distortion. That so much of American diplomatic attention and military effort over the twenty-five years was devoted to the greater Middle East, including two wars in Iraq, a lengthy conflict in Afghanistan, attempts to negotiate peace between Israelis and Palestinians, an agreement limiting Iran's nuclear program, and dealing with the aftermath of the Arab Spring, was not lost on those living in the Asia-Pacific region. What developed among friends and foes alike was a perception that the United States no longer saw their part of the world as a priority. This view gained strength when contrasted with China's increased effort to play a large role in regional economic organizations, its greater military activity, and above all its staking claims to various airspace and island areas in the South and East China seas.

The United States pushed back to some extent. Early in its tenure the Obama administration articulated the notion of a pivot (later recast as a rebalancing) to Asia, a posture meant to signal that the period of exaggerated emphasis on the Middle East was over.[26] The concept was sound even if the presentation further unsettled traditional partners in the Middle East and Europe without necessarily reassuring those in Asia. Also, to borrow from Woody Allen, if 80 percent of life is showing up, in foreign policy 80 percent of life is following up. Here the record was uneven. High-level trips to the region by the president were canceled, and in the second term of the Obama presidency neither the secretary of state nor the national security adviser made the region a priority. Increased naval and air presence was slow to materialize, but it did eventually come about in the form of periodic air and naval challenges to Chinese claims. Most important, the Obama administration completed (in 2015) the negotiation of a regional trade accord, the Trans-Pacific Partnership (TPP).[27] The positive impact of this accomplishment was diluted, however, as its fate remained uncertain given domestic politics inside the United States. The net result of the region's own dynamics and inconsistent U.S. policy was to leave the Asia-Pacific in a sort of limbo, stable on the surface but unsure of its future.

What emerged as the most significant local relationship was that between China and Japan, the world's second- and third-largest economies. (Indeed, it was during this period that the two exchanged places, with China surpassing Japan in overall economic output.) What made the relationship uneasy was the legacy of history and above all Japan's often brutal treatment of the Chinese people before and during World War II when the two countries were at war and Japan occupied large parts of China. Various statements by Japanese politicians went some way toward assuaging Chinese bitterness, but they were undercut by what appeared in Japanese textbooks and by symbolic visits of Japanese leaders to shrines associated with war criminals. Adding to the tension were mutual military buildups, signs that Japan was moving beyond its limited post–World War II military missions, and evidence that China's "peaceful rise" might not be all that peaceful.[28] Many of these tensions coalesced around competing claims to fisheries, offshore resources, and disputed islands in the East China Sea that go by the name Diaoyu in Chinese and Senkaku in Japanese.[29] There were a few incidents, but none that escalated, despite the lack of dedicated emergency communications links and confidence-building measures. Two things kept events in check: uncertainty as to how any military confrontation would play out given the large capabilities of each as well as the U.S.-Japan alliance, and economic interdependence. Two-way trade had increased tenfold since the end of the Cold War, leaving the fate of each closely tied to the other.[30]

South Asia is relatively close geographically to East Asia but distant in its geopolitics. It is dominated by two countries, India and Pakistan, which have had a friction-filled and often violence-defined relationship since their mutual births in 1947. Indeed, for many in India, Pakistan's existence was something of an affront, as they saw no need for a Muslim-defined country given that India itself had and has an enormous Muslim minority population that for the most part lives a relatively integrated life there. Wars erupted over the disputed territory of Kashmir in both 1965 and 1971; as discussed earlier, both countries developed nuclear weapons, India to ward off China, Pakistan to keep India at bay.

The end of the Cold War might have been expected to usher in an improved era in Indo-Pakistani ties, in the sense that India was more often than not aligned with the Soviet Union and Pakistan with the United States, China, or both. But it turned out that the Cold War's end inaugurated an .era in which the two protagonists were largely left to their own devices. Indeed, the two nearly went to war in the spring of 1990 when the eyes of the world were focused on events in Europe and just months before they turned to Kuwait and Iraq.

Making matters worse was the lack of virtually any regular

interaction between the two. One way to underscore this reality is to note that at the height of the Cold War there was incomparably more diplomatic, economic, and cultural exchange between the United States and the Soviet Union than existed between the two South Asian states. There was little interdependence, economic or otherwise, to raise the costs of going to war.

Today, the situation is brittle and precarious. Relations between India and Pakistan remain thin. Pakistan is a weak state in the political sense but a strong one when it comes to things nuclear. Elected civilian politicians are in charge of the country only in name; real power lies with the military officers who head up the armed forces and the intelligence machinery. Pakistan is also weak in the sense that the government is unable to assert its authority over terrorist groups while the military and intelligence services that exercise real power may be unwilling to take on terrorists given their perceived utility versus India and in Afghanistan. Indeed, it was terrorist actions carried out by groups based in Pakistan against India in both 2001 and 2008 that again brought the region to the brink of war.

U.S. policy over this era has been a delicate balancing act. The United States did what it could to help the two countries avoid sliding into war. What this amounted to was regular encouragement that the two develop a more normal relationship and emergency diplomatic activism when it looked as if war might erupt. (I was involved in one such trip in May

1990, when Bob Gates, then the deputy national security adviser, and I visited both countries in what proved a successful effort to interrupt what appeared to be a slide into conflict.) The United States also sought to build a deeper and broader relationship with India, something that made great sense given India's economic and strategic potential. Trade and investment increased significantly. A critical breakthrough came in 2005, when the two countries first announced their commitment to cooperate in peaceful uses of nuclear energy. Several years later just such an accord was signed, in the process ending U.S. sanctions and putting to rest differences stemming from India's nuclear weapons program.[31] High-level meetings, including two visits to India by President Obama, both reflected and contributed to the deepening of ties.

Progress with Pakistan proved to be more elusive. This was less because of its nuclear weapons program (which Washington had long since reluctantly accepted as a reality) than because of Pakistan's tolerance of and outright support for terrorism and its destabilizing role in Afghanistan through its providing sanctuary and support to the Afghan Taliban. What made it all so complicated was the difficulty of holding Pakistan's elected leaders accountable in that they were not in charge of the policy. Even more of a problem was Pakistan's very weakness: sanctions and the like could further destabilize a country with a large nuclear arsenal and thousands of terrorists. Dealing with adversaries may be dangerous, but it tends to be relatively straightforward; there is a familiar set of tools, including among other things negotiations, sanctions, and the use of armed force. Managing ties with partners and friends where there are disagreements is much more complicated, as what tools to use and how to use them is unclear. Anyone doubting this need only think of U.S. relations with Turkey, Saudi Arabia, and Israel. And more complicated yet is dealing with weak friends such as Pakistan and Afghanistan, as the alternatives could easily be worse.[32]

The other country of South Asia that merits discussion is Afghanistan. It was noted earlier that the United States helped bring about a new national government in 2002 after the Taliban leadership was ousted from power. But this development did not bring about anything resembling peace or a normal country. Civil war continued, with remnants of the Taliban receiving sanctuary and support in and from neighboring Pakistan. The George W. Bush administration (as part of a larger UN military effort) increased troop numbers to some twenty-five thousand, but never quite settled on a policy. The troops were more than enough to carry out a narrow counterterrorist mission but not nearly enough to attempt to pacify the country and make it strong enough to stand on its own. There was little appetite for nation building in Afghanistan, where, as opposed to Iraq, the prospects for success were judged to be poor and the consequences (if it were somehow achieved) to be limited to that country rather than triggering similar changes in others. Interestingly, this was similar to the thinking that affected U.S. policy toward Afghanistan in the years after the Soviet troop withdrawal in 1989, a stance that contributed to the situation in which the Taliban first came to power. I know this from firsthand experience, as on both occasions I was involved in the making and implementation of the policies, neither of which could be described as a success.[33]

By the time Barack Obama became president in 2009, the security situation in Afghanistan had deteriorated even further. This president, like his predecessor, was also caught between competing priorities, in Obama's case between a desire to prevent Afghanistan from going back to what it was prior to 9/11 and a pledge to bring U.S. soldiers home. The result was a decision, announced in December 2009, to increase U.S. troop levels by some 50 percent (to one hundred thousand) but to begin the process of drawing them down in eighteen months.[34] In so doing, the Obama administration made the serious error of basing policy on the calendar (which is inherently arbitrary) rather than local conditions. The announced schedule, along with the drawdowns and limits on what soldiers could actually do, worked against the goal of stabilizing the country, as it signaled a lack of commitment that undermined U.S. ability to shape subsequent events. The effects of this policy were only partially offset by a decision announced in late 2015 to delay the full withdrawal of U.S. troops and to keep several thousand in country and by a subsequent announcement in July 2016 that eighty-four hundred U.S. troops would be kept in Afghanistan indefinitely.[35] The reality was that by 2016 the Taliban were estimated to control as much as 20 percent of the country. ISIS, too, was making inroads.

Europe's evolution has been markedly different. As noted previously, the history of post–World War II Europe marked a break with much of what had occurred during preceding centuries. The structure and discipline of the Cold War had a good deal to do with this outcome, but in some ways even more basic was the successful project that was Western Europe and the European Union. This undertaking not only created an economic powerhouse on the scale of the United States but also helped make Western Europe the most stable region of the world.

With the end of the Cold War, the question for many European governments was what degree of integration was desirable and politically feasible with their citizens. In some ways the debate can be summarized as that between two visions for Europe. The first is best captured by the phrase "the United States of Europe." What this suggests is a Europe in which authority is increasingly transferred from national capitals to Brussels and to supranational authority granted the EU.

Several steps were taken in this direction. The most significant development was the signing of the Maastricht Treaty in early 1992 by the leaders of the twelve countries of the

European Community, in so doing creating the successor European Union.[36] One difference between the EC and the EU was that the latter included the "pillar" of a common foreign and security policy in addition to the economic and other dimensions long a part of the European project. A decade later, the EU assumed responsibility for peacekeeping (taking over from NATO) in parts of the Balkans. On the economic side, Maastricht introduced the idea of a central banking system and a common currency, all of which materialized by the end of the decade. By 1993, a single EU market came into being, one that ensured the free movement of goods, services, people, and capital across national lines. Years earlier, the so-called Schengen area (named for the city in Luxembourg where it was negotiated) had been established, essentially erasing national borders when it came to the movement of people and the use of passports. At the same time, the EU was not just getting deeper in the sense of becoming more integrated; it was also getting broader, expanding to fifteen countries in 1995 and to twenty-five a decade later, standing in 2016 at twenty-eight.

The project was never to the liking of many, who feared the loss of national identity and sovereign authority, as well as the consequences of coming under the sway of a large bureaucracy. This alternative vision is best captured by the phrase "a United Europe of States." In this alternative Europe, the balance between national capitals and Brussels is much more weighted toward the former. In 2005, publics in several countries rejected a new European constitution, one that would have further shifted the balance of authority away from governments to what was widely seen as an impersonal and unaccountable bureaucracy in Brussels. Some but not all of this was dealt with by the substitute Lisbon Treaty that entered into force in 2009 and strengthened the hand of the directly elected European Parliament.[37]

But the reality of Europe over the last decade is one in which what came about did not conform to visions. The EU was hamstrung by a succession of weak leaders and an unwillingness on the part of governments to devote significant resources to defense or to make the most of those that were spent. To the contrary, national governments kept control of foreign and defense policy; coordination in the realm of intelligence and law enforcement was no better. When it came to Europe, the whole was often less than its parts.

Even more significant were economic problems resulting from a lack of real structural reform. The result was prolonged low growth and problems stemming from the mismatch between a common monetary policy for the nineteen countries in the Eurozone and the fact that fiscal (tax and spending) policy was and is determined by national governments. There is as well no European banking mechanism in which deposits up to a specified level are guaranteed, as is the case for individuals in the United States; instead, each country is effectively on its own. Demographic challenges ranging from aging (and a worsening of the ratio of those of working age and those too young or too old to work) to the crisis of how to absorb and integrate the influx of refugees from Syria and elsewhere in the Middle East added to the burden.

The results of what at best could be called European drift have been several and sharp. There has been an increase in the number and strength of populist parties on both left and right. One consequence is that the choice for many Europeans is not so much between that of a more centralized "United States of Europe" and a more decentralized "United Europe of States" as between the latter and an even less integrated, more national version of the continent. As demonstrated most dramatically by the June 2016 vote in favor of Brexit, there has been a measurable loss of popular support in many European countries for the European project. And as if this was not enough, adding to Europe's difficulties in recent years has been the return of geopolitics. I am not referring to the problems associated with the breakup of the former Yugoslavia, which were mostly a product of that event rather than something much more enduring. Nor am I alluding to terrorism, although this too has increased. Rather, what is most relevant here is the Russian conquest of Crimea, its blatant interference in eastern Ukraine, and the potential threat it poses to several of its small neighbors. In a span of little more than two years, Europe has gone from being the most integrated and stable region in the world, the region most resembling an "end of history" ideal, to one that appears to risk being overwhelmed by history returning with a vengeance.

Latin America in many ways deserves the award for the part of the world that most changed for the better in the twenty-five years following the end of the Cold War. This has less to do with the Cold War's end—the region was with a few notable exceptions not a significant venue of East-West competition—than with changes in the region itself. Several countries made the successful transition from authoritarianism to democracy with increasingly robust market economies. Chile and Mexico stand out among these. Colombia, with considerable U.S. assistance, overcame a large guerrilla movement that by 2016 appeared defeated militarily and about to agree to peace terms. Brazil made important strides in bringing millions out of poverty. Regional economic output increased by more than 400 percent. Argentina by the end of 2015 began to emerge from years of misrule. Even holdouts such as Cuba looked somewhat more open than they had been; the end of the Cold War deprived Cuba of backing from its long-term patron.

This is not to suggest a region without its challenges. Venezuela is suffering from more than a decade of authoritarian rule and overdependence on oil. Central America is coping with the interwoven problems posed by criminality, drugs, and weak, often corrupt governments. Mexico likewise faces challenges related to drugs, crime, a poor judicial system, inequality, and a central government that lacks the means to provide order throughout the country. Brazil is suffering under the weight of endemic corruption, a bloated public sector, high debt, and a shrinking economy. But what is striking about the region as a whole is the near absence of geopolitics. There is little spending on the sorts of arms that fight wars rather than maintain internal security. There is no threat of nuclear proliferation: what nuclear programs there were, in Argentina and Brazil, were abandoned long ago, and the Treaty of Tlatelolco bans nuclear weapons from the region.[38] Contested borders are few; the threat of conflict between countries is small. This is a good thing for many reasons, one of which is the weakness of Latin America's regional organization, the Organization of American States (OAS), which requires unanimity to act, something that all but guarantees inaction. The problems and challenges facing the region are real, but almost all are a function of governance, economics, and building state capacity.

Africa, with its more than fifty countries, shares characteristics of both Latin America and the Middle East. Again, there have been impressive strides in the case of many African states. The peaceful end to apartheid in South Africa was a major accomplishment, even if many developments since have been disappointing. Rwanda is for the most part a positive example of a country coming together in the wake of a national calamity. Countries such as Botswana, Cape Verde,

Kenya, Namibia, and Senegal regularly score high on measures of governance and economic competitiveness. Overall
economic growth over the last twenty-five years was some
500 percent, although this number reflects the low level at
the beginning of the period and the distorting effects of com-
modities, and masks enormous inequalities within and between countries.

As in Latin America, most at issue in Africa have been
questions of political governance and economic and social
development. Corruption is widespread. But largely absent
are classic geopolitics. China has made some economic inroads, but in the process is also learning the limits of what
outsiders can accomplish.[39] There are few examples of stronger states threating the independence of weaker neighbors;
many of the most pressing challenges have been and are
intra- rather than interstate. There is no threat of nuclear proliferation. What threats to order there are have come mostly
from minorities with separatist agendas, from majorities re-
pressing minorities, from tribal and religious clashes, from
refugee flows, and from terrorist organizations. This is not
intended to sugarcoat a history that has included multiple
prolonged civil wars, genocides, and numerous examples of
repressive rule, but rather to say that the continent has not for
the most part been a venue of either major-power competition or classical war.

7. Pieces of Process

When I taught at Harvard's Kennedy School of Government, a common theme was that 90 percent of life in the public sector was implementation. Policy design of course mattered, and agreement in principle was of course desirable, but what counted most was what actually got done. I emphasize this here because legitimacy and order are a function of process as well as policy. The post–Cold War era seemed to begin with broad agreement on both as much of the world came together in the UN Security Council to rebuff Saddam Hussein's invasion and annexation of Kuwait. But this success in large part was made possible because there was broad support for the traditional notion of sovereignty and because of the starkness of what Saddam had done. Indeed, the United States would not have gone to the Security Council as it did throughout the crisis if any of the other four permanent members had viewed things differently and was prepared to use its veto to frustrate American designs. Put differently, the legitimacy bestowed by the support of the UN Security Council was judged by Washington to be desirable rather than essential.

The very same issue arose amid efforts to galvanize an international response to what was widely viewed in the United States and Europe as unwarranted, immoral behavior by Serbia. When it became clear that Russia would use its veto to block UN endorsement of armed attacks on Serbia, the United States, along with Great Britain and France, took the issue to NATO. Such "forum shopping" is a practical way to generate multilateral support and a degree of legitimacy for an endeavor, but it is resented by those who disagree with the policy at issue or who see it as an end run around those organizations they believe are unique in their ability to confer legitimacy.

In the case of what became the 2003 Iraq War, the United States began by working with the UN Security Council but in the end abandoned it and essentially went to war with little international backing, formal or informal. Just over a decade later, Russia intervened in Crimea, again without resort to the Security Council. The UN did meet about Crimea, but that was in response to what took place, not to provide any authorization for what Russia was doing.

There are several conclusions to draw here. The first is that no country, much less a major power, is prepared to forgo the opportunity to act on behalf of what it perceives as its national interest simply because it lacks a blessing from the

legitimation by the UN is desirable but not essential

United Nations. The Balkans situation just alluded to is a case in point. One can argue that what the government of Serbia was doing was illegitimate in terms of international law or values and that what the United States and Europe sought to do was inherently legitimate. But the refusal of Russia to go along meant the action could not receive the legitimacy stemming from approval by the authority that traditionally bestows it. A dilemma to be sure.

legitimacy dilemma

What this shows is that it is impossible to define legitimacy in terms of process alone if there is no consensus on norms and rules. There is an obvious tension here, one between what might be termed legitimacy based on principle and legitimacy based on process. The United States tends to favor the former; weaker states tend to favor the latter, if only because it provides them a means to constrain what major powers might do.

A related issue is that the UN Security Council itself does not deserve the mantle of dispenser of legitimacy given that its own legitimacy is in question. The problem with the Security Council as currently configured is that it is not representative of today's world. Not surprisingly, it reflects what those decision makers who gathered during World War II imagined the postwar world would look like—and what they wanted it to look like. Europe is arguably overrepresented with the United Kingdom and France as permanent members. At the same time it could be said that Europe is under- or poorly represented in that Germany and the EU are not to be found.

Neither Japan (excluded originally, as was Germany, for being a defeated foe in World War II) nor India (then a colony) has a permanent seat. Attempts to reform the Security Council have come to naught, as proposal after proposal was shot down. Explaining this outcome is not very hard, as any conceivable proposal would advantage some existing permanent members or disadvantage others as they see things. Not surprisingly, those who saw proposed changes as disadvantageous made clear they would block them. The result was a growing tendency to do work-arounds.

One such work-around was already noted: during the Serbian conflict, the United States and Western Europe, frustrated by Russian resistance in the UN, took the issue to NATO. Other multilateral groups grew up to contend with specific countries (one for the Iran nuclear issue, another for North Korea) or problems, most notably the Proliferation Security Initiative, which was designed to buttress efforts to stem the spread of nuclear weapons and that now includes more than one hundred countries working in various ways toward that end. I have described such approaches as constituting multilateralism à la carte; others have called the phenomenon designer multilateralism. All these arrangements were helpful in their own ways, but even collectively they should not be mistaken for a modern-day concert given their narrow focus and limited, shifting memberships.

Other work-arounds were less reactions to particular circumstances than attempts to create new institutions that better reflected the distribution of power and influence in the world as it has evolved. These efforts also reflected a desire to contend not just with issues of war and peace but also with a broader agenda that included a range of economic and other global issues. There was some updating of long-standing institutions such as the World Bank and the IMF to reflect shifts in global economic power, but these changes tended to lag behind reality, and in any event the institutions themselves were not designed to address many of the challenges that emerged.

One innovation was the G-7, established in the mid-1970s by the United States, West Germany, France, Italy, the United Kingdom, Japan, and Canada. Soon after a representative of the European Community was invited. Two decades later Russia accepted the invitation to join what then became the G-8, which developed into something of an annual opportunity for the leaders of many of the world's wealthiest countries to meet to discuss a broad agenda of issues. Finance ministers of the original G-7 continued to discuss global economic issues in separate meetings, from which Russia was excluded given the nature and relatively small size of its economy.

The G-7 and G-8 mechanisms suffered both from who was still not in the room as well as from the reality that the groups rarely met and had no real staff. The problem of inclusion was mostly resolved in 1999, when the G-20 was established to take on many of the issues that had been in the purview of the G-7 and G-8. China became a member, as did

Mexico, Brazil, and Argentina from Latin America, as well as other countries (many of which are often described as medium powers) such as India, South Korea, Australia, Turkey, and South Africa. The twenty countries represented the lion's share of global population, output, and trade. Like the G-7 and G-8, the G-20 met annually, emphasized an economic agenda, had little in the way of full-time staff, and was a coordinating mechanism rather than a formal institution with clear authority.

The G-20 (which often looked more like a G-25 or G-30 once all the added invitees were counted) could not get around an unavoidable trade-off, namely, that the broader the membership, the more difficult it became to get anything significant accomplished. This was demonstrated repeatedly in such areas as trade and climate, where the requirement for broad and at times near-universal inclusion made it impossible to forge meaningful consensus. One consequence was the explosion of regional and bilateral arrangements in the realm of trade. Another was the emergence of informal groupings of relevant, like-minded governments (often described as coalitions of the willing) to tackle a particular negotiation or problem. Legitimacy and effectiveness often work at cross-purposes.

A consensus as to what constitutes legitimacy is hard to reach for any number of reasons. The most obvious is that different governments see things differently. Specific, short-term national interests almost always take priority over broad and longer-term goals. This can make it difficult if not impossible to convince governments to adopt more ambitious positions on climate change that are in their long-term interest if they fear these will prove costly and slow economic growth in the near and medium terms. Similarly, many governments are wary of anything that conditions sovereignty for fear it will be turned against them if they take actions at home that they see as necessary to maintain internal order but others would see as violations of the rights of their citizens.

There have also been structural changes in the international system. By the late twentieth century, the great powers were not all that great. This was not because of a lack of absolute strength, but rather because their relative positions in many cases were deteriorating as developing countries grew at rates no country with a mature economy could hope to match. China was an obvious exception, a rare example of a developing country and, increasingly, a major power at the same time, something explained in large part by the sheer size of its population.

Closely related to this trend is an associated reality, namely, that the major powers have had to contend with a growing number of state and nonstate entities that could also exert significant power. The word I use to capture this reality of widely distributed power and capacity is "nonpolarity." It is qualitatively and fundamentally different from the nature of the world in the past. The greater distribution of power that characterizes this era makes it more difficult to assemble all the relevant actors in one place and keep such a gathering workable.[1]

It is easy to see how such a world looks nothing like a world dominated by one (unipolar) or two (bipolar) powers. The former is the stuff of empire; it could also be argued that the immediate post–Cold War world had elements of unipolarity given U.S. dominance and an absence of other countries with the means and the desire to oppose it. If such a world did exist after 1989, it was short-lived.[2]

Bipolarity was at the core of the Cold War when the United States and the Soviet Union, along with their respective allies and partners, squared off for four decades. By definition, it waned as Cold War rivalry faded and when the Soviet Union and its external empire both collapsed. What should have disappeared with it is the use of the term "superpower." The term may have captured large elements of the reality that was the Cold War, in that both the United States and the Soviet Union enjoyed considerable sway over their allies and proxies, but it does not correspond to today's world. It is not just that Russia is not the USSR. Today's United States, in part because the discipline brought about by the Cold War is gone, is not as focused or as unified an actor. There is less consensus as to what the United States should do in the world. In addition, alliances are looser and, as is discussed below, power and influence are more distributed than ever before.

Many also make the error of thinking that the subsequent world, the one we live in today, is multipolar. The two are different in important ways. A multipolar world is dominated by several countries. It may seem that we live in one given that the six major powers of this era (the United States, China, Russia, Europe, Japan, and India) account for more than half the world's population, some 70 percent of global economic output, and perhaps 80 percent of global military spending. But this would be a misreading.

First, to describe this world as multipolar ignores the many other centers of meaningful state power. Even a short list would include Brazil, Argentina, Chile, and Venezuela in South America; both Mexico and Canada in North America; Nigeria and South Africa in Africa; Pakistan in South Asia; Australia, Vietnam, and North and South Korea in East Asia and the Pacific; and Saudi Arabia, Iran, Israel, and Egypt in the Middle East. Turkey would also be on this list of countries that qualify as medium powers often figuring prominently in their respective parts of the world.

But meaningful power centers are by no means limited to countries. There are also any number of international organizations with clout: the United Nations and its many offshoots, the International Monetary Fund, the World Bank, and the World Trade Organization all come to mind. There are as

[handwritten margin note: multipolar vs nonpolarity]

well regional bodies (most notably the European Union, but also the African Union, the Organization of American States, and a host of other political and economic organizations with regional membership) and functional bodies, such as the oil cartel OPEC, the International Atomic Energy Agency that monitors NPT-related obligations, and the Shanghai Cooperation Organization, a group of a half dozen countries founded some two decades ago and dominated by China and Russia that promotes common security and economic aims. There are state, provincial, and city governments with a degree of political autonomy and an impact beyond their countries' borders. And then there are corporations, media companies, militias, terrorist organizations, religious institutions and movements, drug cartels, and NGOs of a more benign sort, from the Gates Foundation to Doctors Without Borders, all with an international footprint. Again, this is a world of distributed power, and increasingly power in whatever form is in the hands of entities other than major countries.

But it is not just that the major powers have to share the stage with a large group of other actors. It is also that there is often a large gap between measurable power and relevant power. Major countries have a lot of the former, but they often come up short when it comes to the latter. The reasons can vary—they cannot bring it to bear in distant places for lack of means, their politics will not permit them to commit enough power over a long enough time to deal with specific challenges, or the power that they have can easily be offset by locals who have less power overall but greater capacity at the scene and greater commitment—but the result is often much the same. This is especially the case when it comes to efforts to influence the internal political structures of other societies. Military power can help to create a context, but no occupation or attempt at nation building can transform culture or alter loyalties or entrenched behaviors. Power on paper does not necessarily translate into power in practice.

PART III

8. What Is to Be Done?

The first part of this book traced the evolution of international order from the rise of the modern state system in the mid-seventeenth century to the end of the Cold War. Order, such as it was, revolved around states and above all the major powers of the day. The principal element of the new order was a shared respect for one another's sovereignty, something that reduced the frequency and intensity of meddling in what was understood to be one another's internal affairs and, as a result, the chance of war. Buttressing acceptance of this principle—a common definition of what was legitimate when it came to foreign policy—were a balance of power and a regular diplomatic process that helped manage what could turn out to be challenges to the existing order.

The history of this era, and in particular that of the twentieth century, demonstrated that sustaining order was far easier said than done. The two world wars were evidence that order could all too easily disappear.

The latter half of the twentieth century proved to be more stable, at least in the sense that great-power conflict was avoided. Indeed, the Cold War, for all its risks, failures, and local conflicts, introduced a considerable degree of stability into the world, some of it born of prudence that reflected the understanding that nuclear war would be a catastrophe for all no matter who attacked first, some of it born of creative diplomacy that reduced the chance that lesser differences could set the two powers on an all too easily escalating path of direct confrontation.

Less obvious was a second source of order that evolved in the aftermath of World War II and affected important aspects of global economic, political, and strategic interaction. This second source, involving a degree of international cooperation in certain areas, ended the first part of this book and led off the second. As became all too clear, an era that began brightly and optimistically with the end of the Cold War did not stay that way for long. And today, some twenty-five years later, it would be difficult to argue that the world is orderly or headed in that direction. To the contrary, there are real reasons for concern about the world and its trajectory even though the principal source of disorder over the centuries— major-power conflict—has been absent from the world scene. Instead, the trend toward disorder has been a function of structural changes in the international system—above all, the diffusion of capacity into more hands than ever before— exacerbated at critical times by the action (and inaction) of the United States and other powers. The result is a world not just of more capacity in more hands but also of more decision makers and independent actors. Consequently, a host of global and regional challenges have emerged that are proving to be far more than the major powers can contend with. A short list of these challenges would include the actual and potential spread of nuclear weapons and long-range delivery systems, terrorism, a spike in the number of refugees and displaced persons, a chaotic Middle East, a Europe under siege, a precariously balanced Asia-Pacific, a largely ungoverned cyberspace, an inadequate response to climate change, a growing rejection of free trade and immigration, and the potential for a pandemic that could cost many millions of lives.

challenges we face today.

I appreciate that the thrust of much of this analysis is downbeat, even depressing. I do not mean to be alarmist, but complacency is dangerous. Any comfort derived from viewing things through rose-colored glasses will be short-lived.

I do not want to suggest for a moment, though, that nothing can be done. What is argued in these pages is not fatalism. Little in history is inevitable. To the contrary, what governments and organizations and people do and choose not to do can make a real difference and, over time, make history.

If there is an analogy that comes to mind, it is once again associated with Yom Kippur, the Jewish Day of Atonement. For Jews, the ten holiest days of the year, the Days of Awe,

212 | A WORLD IN DISARRAY

begin with the Jewish New Year (Rosh Hashanah) and end with Yom Kippur. These ten days (which tend to fall in September or October) are a time for intense reflection on the year just past and the year to come. At the end of the ten days, the "Book of Life" for the coming year is sealed. The associated prayer notes that in this book is written, among other things, who shall rest and who shall wander; who shall be tranquil and who shall be harassed; who shall be at ease and who shall be afflicted; who shall be poor and who shall be rich; who shall be brought low and who shall be raised high . . . and, most dramatically, who shall live and who shall die.

This all may seem like fatalism, in that nothing can be done once the Book of Life is sealed as the sun sets on the Day of Atonement, but it is not. Indeed, after noting the range of possible fates, the prayer continues, making clear that the severity of whatever decree is written in the Book of Life can be eased by repentance, prayer, and charity.

The parallels to what is discussed in these pages should be fairly evident. There are fundamental trends afoot that, all things being equal, work against order. But the rationale for statecraft, diplomacy, and foreign policy more broadly is that all things are not equal, that design and execution of policy matter a great deal, and that the nature of international order, the balance between what Hedley Bull termed anarchy and society, can be changed for the better.

This is the assumption of this third, last part of this book, that what is done and how it is done will matter a great deal.

If the previous two parts focused on description and analysis, this part focuses on prescription, on what can and should be done. This section begins with a discussion of major-power relations and how they should be approached. It goes on to make recommendations for what should be done to better meet global and regional challenges. And it ends with what the United States, now and for the foreseeable future the country with the greatest capacity and potential to influence international relations, should do (and avoid doing) both abroad and at home.

9. Thwarting Thucydides

Today's foreign policy must begin with a concerted effort to discourage major-power rivalry, competition, and above all conflict from again becoming the dominant feature of the international system. The reasons are twofold. First, any such deterioration in major-power relations would be extremely costly even if it did not lead to direct conflict and incomparably more costly if it did. Second, adversarial relationships between and among the major powers would prove to be a major distraction that would make it far more difficult for them to work together to deal with the many global and regional challenges that confront them.

Avoiding such an outcome will not be easy; as Thucydides wrote, rivalry between the major power of the day and rising competitors is the natural way of international affairs.[1] Any effort to avoid a significant deterioration in major-power ties must necessarily be conditioned on a degree of reciprocity from other major powers. A desire to avoid confrontation at all costs would lead to a policy of appeasement. Such a posture would only feed the ambitions of the rival power and, in the process, cause other countries either to align with it or to develop additional capacities of their own so that they would be in a better position to look after their own security. The result would be either an order based on unacceptable terms (essentially terms dictated by the most aggressive and strongest among the powers) or mounting disorder.

Here we are mostly talking about U.S. relations with both China and Russia, the only two potential major-power adversaries. (There are other adversaries of import, including North Korea, Iran, and several terrorist groups, but however significant the threat they pose, it is limited in scale or reach. There are as well other major pairings that could go wrong, including Europe and Russia, and China and both Japan and India, which will be discussed in the regional section to follow. These relationships would likely benefit from a course of action similar to what is suggested in this chapter.) The challenge for the United States in shaping relations with both China and Russia is to discourage either from pursuing paths that would result in a new Cold War or worse without bringing about a confrontational relationship that would preclude selective and highly desirable cooperation on global and regional challenges.

Succeeding in such an effort will be no mean feat. It is the diplomatic equivalent of threading a needle. What it requires, on one hand, is effectively shutting down the idea or temptation that coercion or aggression will succeed. Both Russia and China place an emphasis on their respective "near abroads": the European countries to its west in Russia's case, the South and East China seas in China's. Use of force and unilateral actions to alter the territorial status quo need to be resisted and, if deterrence fails, responded to, with the nature of the response depending on local political and military realities. This requires the United States not only to remain strong overall but also to maintain both a local military presence and close ties to neighboring countries.

China and Russia need to know that the United States has both the will and the ability to respond locally to anything they might do. Deterrence is obviously preferable to defense. But deterrence is never far removed from the perception that a government is willing and able to defend its interests. This argues for the stationing of military forces in and around areas that either China or Russia might claim or move against, something that translates into maintaining increased U.S. ground and air forces in Europe and increased air and naval forces in the Asia-Pacific. In the case of Russia, the United States needs to be prepared as well for the sort of "gray area" aggression carried out by irregular forces and armed locals in eastern Ukraine. Such tactics may not trigger NATO's Article 5 common defense clause, but they threaten stability all the same; what is required is training along with arms and intelligence support so that those NATO members near Russia can cope with such challenges should they materialize.[2]

Capabilities can be further enhanced through the regular dispatch of visiting forces and frequent military exercises. Such activity also underscores commitment and concern, thereby reassuring friends and allies and signaling actual or would-be foes. It is important that all this be done locally and with conventional military forces, as the United States never wants to put itself in a position where the only response to a challenge is to escalate, whether by expanding a crisis in terms of geography or in the type of weaponry, or to acquiesce to the results of successful aggression. What the United States is now beginning to do in these regions moves in the direction of what is being advocated here.

It is important to make one additional point. I am not advocating containment, the doctrine that informed U.S. foreign policy during the Cold War and that called for countering any effort by the Soviet Union to expand its influence. I do not assume (as was the case with the USSR) that either China or Russia is motivated, much less consumed, by an ideological or geopolitical imperative to expand in an unlimited manner what they control or influence. Russia's behavior in Ukraine, no matter how regrettable, is not the first phase of a bid for global domination, any more than is China's behavior in the South China Sea. Rather, each has political (nationalist) and security-related concerns that, however large, are not insatiable, and as a result can be influenced and shaped. This reinforces the case for adopting a policy toward them that is best described as "integration." It seeks to in-

help them to also be leaders in the LIEO

volve them in regional and global orders both by giving them a role in defining what constitutes legitimacy and by "hedging," by making clear that they will not benefit from but rather will pay a steep price for pursuing a policy that the United States and its allies view as illegitimate. Another way to say this is that military preparations and signs of strength, while necessary, are not sufficient. The United States does not want to communicate the impression that confrontation and conflict are inevitable. It is thus important to offer and where possible bolster what might be described as diplomatic and economic interdependence.

Diplomatic interdependence is another way of saying that other powers need to be involved in building and operating global and regional orders, that is, in defining what is to be considered legitimate and then ensuring it is carried out in practice. It is a form of geopolitical integration. This is similar to but in fact goes beyond the phrase suggested to China some years back that it become a "responsible stakeholder,"[4] as that notion was viewed by many in China as requiring it to join a U.S.-designed order. The objective being suggested here is for the two governments to work together to come up with rules and arrangements for what would in effect constitute legitimacy for this era. The aims should be realistic and specific.

Doing so will require time-consuming consultations that are more frequent and creative than the increasingly bureaucratic and incremental Strategic and Economic Dialogue launched in 2009 and held annually by senior State Department and Treasury officials with their Chinese counterparts. It will also require a willingness to eschew what was described as "linkage" during the Cold War, namely, a policy approach that consciously tied cooperation in one area (say economic) to the ability to cooperate or at least not compete in another. The thinking behind it was to gain leverage across issues and domains. This was not quite an all-or-nothing approach to relationship management, but it came close. Rather, I am suggesting something fundamentally different: to make the goal of diplomacy to preserve and even expand areas of cooperation amid inevitable areas of disagreement. To be sure, such an approach could become overwhelmed by disagreements that brought the fundamentals of the relationship into question, but the operating principle ought to be to maintain what cooperation there is (along with the potential for more) even when the countries disagree, as they inevitably will from time to time.

The need to avoid linkage has consequences for the use of sanctions as a tool of foreign policy. If sanctions are to be introduced versus Russia or China in response to some action on its part deemed illegitimate, they should be kept as narrow as possible lest the entire relationship suffer and with it the chance for selective cooperation. The good news is that it is increasingly possible to tailor sanctions so that they are smart and focused. It is also important that any sanction be designed so that it can be easily modified or removed if circumstances warrant. I would add here two other points. Sanctions can all too easily become the instrument of choice, a "safe" third way between doing nothing and using military force. History suggests, though, that sanctions alone can rarely accomplish big things. They can also have a range of unintended and undesirable consequences, including hurting civilians and strengthening authoritarian governments. Second, it is equally important that the United States be careful not to turn sanctions into a major source of friction with friends and allies who for one reason or another refuse to sign on to all that Congress or the executive branch desires. Sanctions should be used by the United States when they exact a price from the intended target and do not cause collateral damage to other relationships.[5]

A comprehensive approach to relations with major powers that could become adversaries would require two more things to make that unwanted eventuality less likely. Diplomatic interdependence ought to be buttressed by its economic counterpart. This entails giving China and Russia a stake in maintaining or even expanding bilateral economic ties (trade, investment, technology transfer, and so on) as well as in the regional and global stability that provides a supportive context for their economic growth. The goal is to incentivize them not to do things that would threaten to upset a status quo that serves their overall interest. Ideally, the economic loss that could accrue to them (in particular from sanctions) if they acted badly would deter them.

Second, there also needs to be restraint of a different sort on the American side. The focus of the relationship with both China and Russia would need to be on their external behavior—their foreign policy—rather than on their domestic politics. Focusing on their internal behavior would be unlikely to meaningfully affect it for the better but would almost certainly affect and conceivably poison their view of the United States and the way they see the relationship. The United States can have preferences for how they evolve and criticize them when they violate human rights on any scale, but it has neither the influence with them nor the luxury of placing such concerns at the center of the relationship.

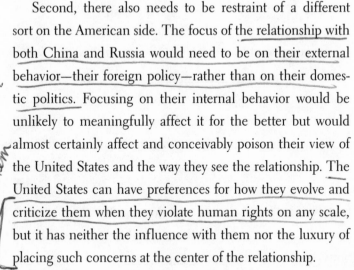

The United States also needs to exercise more traditional foreign policy restraint. NATO membership for either Ukraine or Georgia should be placed on hold. Neither comes close to meeting NATO requirements, and going ahead would not only further alienate or provoke Russia but would also add military commitments that the United States is not in a position to fulfill. Indeed, the United States and NATO would be wise to focus on meeting existing obligations before taking on new ones. The United States should also explore the potential of reviving the arms control dimension of its relationship with Russia. In the case of China, the United States has a self-interest in tempering the behavior of those with competing claims to local islands and seas; they, too, must be pressed not to take unilateral actions that could trigger a crisis.

It must be acknowledged that there is no guarantee any American posture toward China and Russia would have the intended effect. At least as important a factor, one in part or even largely beyond American influence, will be the internal trajectories of both countries and how their leaders choose to deal with their respective challenges. Russia under Vladimir Putin has important decisions to make, above all whether it wants to be a spoiler, one heavily reliant on the use of military force for its external influence, or be part of international society. It also needs to determine whether it wants to remain largely one-dimensional, reliant on oil and gas, or modernize across the board, something that would necessitate less government influence over the domestic economy and increase its integration with the global economy. Recent trends are not encouraging, but there is no reason to give up on Russia given its importance and the possibility of bringing about some change in its behavior.

In the case of China, even a short list of what lies in the inbox of its increasingly centralized leadership includes replacing a heavy reliance on exports with increased domestic demand, reducing overcapacity and speculative bubbles in several economic sectors, reining in corruption, dealing with an aging population, and coping with climate change and environmental degradation. Hovering over everything is the reality that the future will be one of more modest economic growth.[6] China's leaders want the benefits of a modern economy, but they are not willing to create one of the prerequisites, a more open society. A more aggressive foreign policy could create a new source of political legitimacy, but only by placing at risk trade and investment opportunities. How China's leaders will manage this dilemma will be truly consequential for China and the world.

10. World Order 2.0

A big part of how the future unfolds will depend on whether the principal powers of this era can develop a common approach, or at least overlapping approaches, to what constitutes legitimacy. As has been the case previously, legitimacy involves both content and process. The basic approach to legitimacy and, as a result, order ought to begin with the traditional or classic approach to sovereignty but modify it given the challenges and threats of this era. Sovereignty between and among states needs to remain at the center of global order. As the twentieth century showed repeatedly and this century saw in Ukraine, a world in which borders are violated through the use of military force (and, increasingly, through the use of other tools, such as the offensive use of cyber instruments) is a world of increased danger and instability.

But an approach to order premised *only* on respect for the sovereignty of states is not enough. The traditional approach to order, one that speaks only to the rights and prerogatives of states, is increasingly inadequate, even dangerous. A cardinal reality associated with globalization is that little stays local in terms of its consequences. The world is not to be confused with Las Vegas: what happens somewhere rarely remains there. Almost anyone and anything, from tourists, terrorists, and both migrants and refugees to e-mails, weapons, viruses, dollars, and greenhouse gases, can travel on one of the many conveyor belts that are modern globalization and reach any and every corner of the globe. So much of what has historically been viewed as domestic and hence off-limits because it took place within the borders of a sovereign country is now potentially unlimited in its reach and effects. The result is that we no longer have the luxury of viewing all of what goes on in another country as off-limits.

What follows from this argument is a departure not just from traditional thinking but also from the principal existing political and intellectual challenge to a sovereignty-dominated international system. Traditional thinking is that sovereignty is virtually absolute and that it is the prerogative of governments to decide what goes on within their borders. The one prominent (but far from universally embraced) exception to this approach emphasizes the rights of individuals and the possibility that governments that abridge these rights on a large scale run the risk of forfeiting some of the protections sovereignty normally confers on governments and states. This is the essence of the Responsibility to Protect (R2P) doctrine.

I am suggesting something fundamentally different: the

need to develop and gain support for a definition of legitimacy that embraces not just the rights but also the *obligations* of sovereign states vis-à-vis other governments and countries. The world is too small and too connected for borders to provide cover for activities that by definition can affect adversely those who live outside those borders. I call this concept "sovereign obligation."

The notion of sovereign obligation should inform how we think about legitimacy in this era of international relations. Just to be clear, sovereign obligation is fundamentally different from the idea of "sovereignty as responsibility," which involves a government's responsibilities to its own citizens and how it forfeits some of the traditional protections and benefits of sovereignty if it fails to live up to those responsibilities, as in R2P.[1] Not surprisingly, R2P is viewed with unease or outright suspicion by many governments that fear it might be used against them by those with hostile agendas. It can also be cited (as was done by Vladimir Putin in the case of purportedly acting on behalf of ethnic Russians living in Ukraine) as justification for intervening in the domestic affairs of another country.[2] Such an interpretation is reminiscent of pre-Westphalian times. Even R2P's supporters would agree that it constitutes a diminution of sovereignty; the principal difference between backers and critics is their level of comfort with this consequence and more specifically with what conditions would trigger legitimate intervention and what body would have to authorize it.

Again, sovereign obligation is something altogether different. It is about a government's obligations to other governments and through them to the citizens of other countries. The two different notions—sovereignty as responsibility and sovereign obligation—derive from very different and often competing traditions of American foreign policy. The former is an outgrowth of what might be called the idealist or Wilsonian school. Named for Woodrow Wilson, who championed various rights and freedoms around the world in the aftermath of the First World War, it often makes shaping the internal conditions or nature of other societies the principal objective of what this country should do in the world. The purpose can be to promote human rights or democracy or to prevent human suffering. This philosophy is most associated with the presidencies of Jimmy Carter, Ronald Reagan, and George W. Bush. Contemporary adherents of such thinking can be found in both major political parties; indeed, the American foreign policy debate is increasingly waged as much within the Democratic and Republican parties as it is between them.

The other dominant foreign policy tradition tends to fall under the heading of realism. Foreign policy realism (not to be confused with international relations realism, which posits that countries inevitably compete for resources and power at one another's expense) tends to be associated with such presidents as Richard Nixon and George H. W. Bush. Here the

[margin note: focus on foreign policy decisions not domestic decisions]

emphasis is less on what another country is (or does within its borders) as it is on what it chooses to do beyond its borders, that is, in its foreign policy.

There are other foreign policy choices to be made, including the emphasis to be accorded to foreign over domestic policy (this is the classic guns versus butter tension); the matter of how the country should carry out its foreign policy, that is, how much alone (unilaterally) and how much with others (multilaterally); the perennial question about how best to use and blend the various instruments that make up a national security policy; and the issue of how U.S. foreign policy is to be made, which involves more than anything else the balance between the legislative and executive branches of government. But the tension between Wilsonian idealism and realism is in many ways the most intense and enduring foreign policy fault line, because it deals with what the United States is trying to accomplish in the world.

[margin note: The US' place in the world]

Some argue that what is being represented here constitutes a false distinction and that a successful foreign policy must do both: it must try to shape both the internal conditions of other countries and their foreign policies. This is true in principle but less so in practice. Choices must inevitably be made. The administration of George H. W. Bush made such a choice after the Chinese government cracked down on protesters in Tiananmen Square in 1989. It decided that reacting strongly versus China for what it had done would be counterproductive, in part because of everything else on the bilateral agenda. But a different president might have chosen otherwise, with different results.

A more recent example of the inevitable trade-off involved Egypt. The Obama administration was critical of President Sisi of Egypt for various reasons, many tied in one way or another to the government's heavy-handed approach to political opponents associated with the Muslim Brotherhood. At the same time, Egypt's support was seen as critical to regional efforts against terrorism, to stabilize Libya, and to maintain a good relationship with Israel. There was also no certainty that pressing the government would either soften its policies or, if the government were to come to be replaced, lead to something better. The result was a policy that vacillated between support and cooperation on one hand and gestures of criticism (such as withholding certain arms) on the other.

Still others would argue that the choice between realism and Wilsonian idealism is false for a different reason, namely, that democratic countries are more likely to carry out more peaceful foreign policies. For those of this view, the United States should promote democracy and human rights both for "normative" reasons (because Americans believe that political freedom is part of human dignity and hence inherently desirable) and for what are known as "instrumental" reasons— that it will lead others to adopt more moderate and constructive foreign policies.[3]

It is correct that fully democratic countries tend to pursue

more peaceful paths in their relations with others; this judgment is what gives the "democratic peace" advocates their
raison d'être. One problem, though, is that bringing democracy about elsewhere is easier said than done. Not every society is ripe for democracy. Many of the essential prerequisites,
from an educated populace and a sizable middle class to a
developed civil society, a culture of tolerance, and a strong
secular divide, are often missing and not easily created.

the basis for democracy does not exist

Closely related to this argument is that outsiders are
normally limited in what they can do to affect democratic
prospects. While there are successful experiences to point to,
from Germany and Japan in the wake of World War II to
South Korea and Chile more recently, the American efforts
in both Iraq and Afghanistan, where years of occupation were
unable to build political systems approximating functioning
democracies, provide grounds for more than a little caution
and modesty. As we have seen all too often of late in the Middle East, the alternative to a flawed political system can be an
even more flawed political system.

Third, incomplete or what Fareed Zakaria terms "illiberal"
democracies can be dangerous both to those living in the
country and to others.[4] Incomplete democracies such as Russia, Turkey, and Iran have some but in no way all or even
most of the attributes of mature or full democracies. Elections that take place in a context in which opposition figures
are prohibited from standing for office or are denied equal
access to media and resources along with the ability to orga-

nize if they do, or where the process of voting is in one way or another manipulated, can give some countries the appearance of being democratic when in fact they are far from it. Checks and balances on the concentration and exercise of power tend to be inadequate or missing altogether in such countries. As a result, populism and nationalism can all too easily be used to mobilize majority support for domestic intolerance of minorities, foreign adventure, or both.

Fourth, foreign policy (or public policy of any sort, for that matter) involves the need to determine and stick with priorities. To govern is to choose. It is difficult to enlist and sustain the support of a government on some matter of international policy if at the same time it is the target of criticism or sanctions for what it is doing at home. This statement could apply to any number of authoritarian countries in the Middle East as well as to both Russia and China.

To be sure, there is nothing specifically American about any of this, as all governments must decide their foreign policy priorities. What is specifically American, though, is the strength of the Wilsonian tradition, the resulting intensity of the debate through history, and the consequences for the world given the role and influence of the United States.

It is important to underscore that what is being suggested here pertaining to sovereign obligation assumes respect for sovereignty. Sovereignty must remain the bedrock of international order. The pre-Westphalian world was hardly a peaceful one. It is essential to avoid the reemergence of a world of constant interference by one state or entity in the affairs of another. Even more essential is to avoid acts of attempted territorial takeover or conquest. This in turn requires maintaining balances of power at both the global and regional levels. Again, the objective is to maintain or even strengthen what is best about the sovereign order, including broad acceptance of a meaningful zone of autonomy for governments as well as a robust respect for borders and for the principle that they are not to be modified through the use of military force or other forms of coercion. This definition of legitimacy, this approach to international relations, can be summed up as World Order 1.0.

The argument being advanced here is that the requirements for order must be expanded and adapted to the realities of our interconnected world. The goal should be to build consensus around a larger approach to sovereignty, one that includes obligations beyond borders. Call it World Order 2.0.

Sovereign obligation clearly overlaps with realism. But realism, with its emphasis on relations between major powers, is simply too narrow for a world in which global issues, regional states, and all sorts of nonstate actors possess influence. Major-power rivalry is *a* driving force, but, so far at least, not *the* driving force of this century. Another way to think about the concept of sovereign obligation is that it represents realism for a time in which globalization exerts a powerful force on the

A sovereign obligation is foreign policy realism in the globalized context of today

course of history and on the interests of individual countries. Sovereign obligation is realism updated and adapted to meet the exigencies of a global era.

As already suggested, some elements of the traditional order would carry over in a world predicated on the principle of sovereign obligation. The first would be respect for borders and a commitment not to use military force or other coercive means to change them. There is considerable support among the world's governments for this principle, but it is not absolute in practice. When this norm is violated, there will be resistance, be it physical (as was the case when Saddam Hussein invaded Kuwait) or financial (as when Russia annexed Crimea). There will be no way to reach agreement on responses or penalties, but there is a good chance that the principle of nonacquisition of territory by force can be broadly embraced in principle and most if not 100 percent of the time in practice.

A second aspect of the classic or traditional order that needs to be considered is the notion that governments enjoy a relatively free hand to act as they wish within their borders. This concept has been constrained by the Universal Declaration of Human Rights and the Genocide Convention. It has also been conditioned by the promulgation and widespread acceptance of the Responsibility to Protect doctrine. But far from clear is when (and how) such constraints kick in. In particular, what is or should be acceptable for a government to do to maintain domestic order (and the safety of its citizens) and at what point does this cross a line and constitute repression (or worse) that is inconsistent with the obligations of sovereignty? Who decides? What are to be the remedies?

The cold truth is that there will be no way to answer such questions in the abstract. An effort to do so would likely end up not just failing but exposing opposition to the basic concept of R2P. In the aftermath of the Libya intervention, it is doubtful that many countries would support R2P even in principle if it were to come up for a vote. A wiser approach would be to live with R2P as it exists and to meet at the global or regional level when a situation arises that threatens the well-being of a population because of governmental action or inaction. To paraphrase the old saw about a French intellectual being someone who tells you why something cannot work in principle even though it is clearly working in practice, it is sometimes better to attempt to resolve a problem in practice than in principle. All things being equal, regional bodies may be a better bet than global venues to raise such concerns, as local states will have a stake in doing something about a crisis that could lead to massive refugee flows. Regional approaches also tend to reduce the role of great-power politics. This said, and as the Middle East demonstrates, turning to regional approaches to prevent or stop massive civilian suffering and genocide is no panacea when the regional body is hamstrung by disagreement or constrained by a lack of capacity. All of which is to say this issue will have to be approached on a case-by-case basis; nothing can or will be automatic.

Here I would add one additional point. If the United

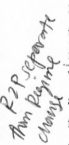

R2P separate from Regime change

States or any other party calls for and carries out an intervention in the name of R2P, it must be limited to a humanitarian intervention. This is also a matter of sovereign obligation. What happened in Libya, where regime change masqueraded as R2P, undermined the very doctrine it sought to fulfill. If for some reason regime change is sought, it ought to be articulated as such and kept apart from R2P even if the motivation is partly or entirely humanitarian.

Reaching consensus on a continuing role for self-determination will not be easy. There is no way to reach agreement around any concrete formula that would determine the stance of the United States or another government toward any and all situations. A good start, though, would be to amend the concept of self-determination away from its inherent unilateralism on the part of the entity seeking a state of its own and to replace it with the notion that statehood is something to be granted as well as asserted. One precedent to fall back on here is the 1978 Camp David Accords between Egypt and Israel, which did not extend the principle of self-determination to the Palestinians but rather supported the notion that "representatives of the Palestinian people should participate in negotiations on the resolution of the Palestinian problem in all its aspects."[5] Support for what has been called self-determination would be less automatic or likely than was the case in the era of decolonization. Existing governments would agree to be open to considering bids for statehood in cases where there is historical justification, a compelling rationale, demonstrated support by the population in question, and viability of the territory, including its potential ability to meet its obligations as a sovereign entity. Also to be considered would be the impact on the viability of the country that would give up a portion of its territory and population. Governments would agree to consult with one another before reaching a decision.

There is likely to be greater international agreement about the unacceptability of terrorism, defined earlier in these pages as the intentional use of armed violence against civilians and noncombatants in pursuit of political objectives. As was noted earlier, the world has moved a considerable ways away from tolerance for terrorists even if their cause was deemed just. There is considerable international condemnation of terrorism on the books as well as authorization for collective action against it. Indeed, there is arguably more consensus on that than on any other threat to order—that states individually or collectively have not just the right but the obligation to act against terrorism as well as against other states that harbor or otherwise support terrorists. It can even be said that governments possess all the legal and political authority they need to strike against terrorists in any mode, be it preventive, preemptive, or reactive, via Article 51 of the UN Charter (which supports the right of self-defense) and numerous resolutions passed over the years by the UN Security Council. What matters is that when governments act under the name of counterterrorism they are striking individuals or groups who are genuinely terrorists and that the attacks are designed in a way that is consistent with legal and ethical standards, including taking steps to protect innocent civilians.

Much more controversial will be bolstering the existing norm against the spread or use of weapons of mass destruction. The importance of doing so should be obvious, as the use of nuclear weapons in particular would have devastating effects. There is as well the danger that materials and weapons could fall into the hands of terrorists, a possibility that increases as more countries gain access to these materials and weapons and as the inventories that they maintain grow in size. The suggestion that proliferation can be assumed to be stabilizing is equal parts fanciful and dangerous.

There is a bias against such "horizontal proliferation," but the essence of the existing international inclination (underscored by the Non-Proliferation Treaty) is to stop it before it happens by limiting the access of countries to the relevant technologies, materials, and weapons. The Iran case suggests that there is considerable support for preventing further proliferation, even if the consensus breaks down when it comes to what precise steps ought to be taken to do so, including the severity of sanctions, interdiction, sabotage, and so on. The problem comes from the demonstrated ability of governments to develop or acquire nuclear weapons if they make it a priority. Israel, India, Pakistan, and North Korea are all proof of this.

There is much less consensus regarding what to do once proliferation has occurred. Here there is no meaningful inter-

except Trump pulled out

[handwritten margin note: regulation of obtaining WMD but none on the proliferation — general consensus - "Don't do it"]

national norm beyond the fact that such possession is inconsistent with the NPT, which may not even pertain if the country in question is a nonsignatory. One option is of course to live with it. This is what happened in the cases of Israel, India, and Pakistan. This approach attempts to discourage or deter actual use and to reduce the likelihood that nuclear weapons will fall into the wrong hands. This can on occasion entail providing certain technologies that increase "command and control" over as well as the operational safety of the weapons and associated delivery systems. Intelligence can also be provided and diplomacy can be activated to help prevent crises from escalating to nuclear use. In the case of obvious foes, deterrence could be activated by ensuring that retaliatory options are in place and by communicating the intent to use them if warranted. Defensive arms (such as antimissile systems) can also be positioned; this was the essence of the July 2016 decision of the United States and South Korea to deploy theater antimissile capabilities to counter the growing North Korean threat.[6] Under this approach, nonproliferation gives way to coping.

The North Korea situation is, however, different. Unlike Israel and India, where there is confidence that nuclear weapons will be managed responsibly, no such condition exists when it comes to North Korea. And unlike Pakistan, there is not the sense that North Korea has passed a point of no return in the size of its arsenal. So there is still the hope in some quarters that North Korea can be persuaded or forced to accept limits on its arsenal of weapons and delivery systems or even agree to give them up altogether. I would describe this approach as one of diplomatic rollback. I would also describe it as wildly optimistic given that North Korea's leaders see their nuclear weapons as the closest thing they have to a guarantee of the regime's survival. They also see nuclear arms as their principal if not only source of leverage, something to be preserved. Indeed, it is revealing that North Korea's leader, Kim Jong-un, speaking in May 2016, described his country's nuclear weapons as a deterrent force.[7]

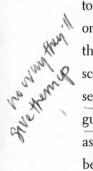

One alternative to the management approach (and a companion or complement to both diplomatic efforts to roll back North Korea's nuclear capability and deployment of antimissile systems) would be to live with proliferation until intelligence suggests that such weapons are about to be used or transferred to a nonstate actor such as a terrorist group. At that point, there is the potential option to undertake a preemptive strike against an imminent threat. What would be required would be receipt of accurate and relatively unambiguous intelligence in a timely manner and the will and the means to act on it.

As was discussed earlier, there is some support in international law for such a posture. It would likely be impossible to gain formal international agreement on the acceptability of such action in advance or in the abstract, but there would likely be considerable understanding as to the legitimacy of acting if it could be demonstrated that the threat was in fact genuine and imminent. Holding such consultations would also be a warning to China that inaction on North Korea could be consequential, possibly leading China to exert more pressure on North Korea to roll back its nuclear program. Advertising the adoption of this policy would also get North Korea's attention and might restrain its behavior even if it never admitted that the policy was having such an effect.

A second alternative for the United States would be to try to gain international support for the legitimacy of preventive action to stop proliferation. As discussed earlier, a preventive (as opposed to preemptive) action is one that targets a gathering rather than an actual, imminent threat. This was the animating idea of the national security strategy published in September 2002 by the administration of George W. Bush. The document made this clear, stating that "in an age where the enemies of civilization openly and actively seek the world's most destructive technologies, the United States cannot remain idle while dangers gather."[8] Prevention in principle provides a means to disrupt a program before it produces nuclear weapons or, even if one or more weapons exist, to prevent the expansion of an arsenal and, more ambitiously, to destroy those weapons that do exist. What was done with malware (allegedly by the United States and Israel) to interfere with the computers central to Iran's enrichment program could likewise qualify as a preventive action. So too would a strike using conventional munitions on suspected nuclear facilities.

Gaining international support or even sympathy for such a stance would almost certainly be impossible, as it would be resisted by those governments that saw it as issuing a license to the United States to attack countries such as North Korea or Iran. It is not certain that it would even be advisable; as noted earlier, a world of frequent preventive attacks would be more violent and dangerous. The United States would not want to hand such a right over to others, and would not want to be denied such an option (as was considered in the case of Iran and might be worthy of consideration again) if it concluded it was the least bad one available.

There are, as it turns out, other problems with a preventive approach that uses military force. First, such an attack would necessarily be based upon incomplete and possibly inaccurate information; the case of Iraqi "WMDs" is a warning here. Second, it is impossible to assume that any preventive attack would in fact accomplish what it set out to do, as the systems are increasingly well hidden and protected. Third, a preventive attack would be an act of war, one likely to trigger some form of retaliatory response. I say "likely" rather than "certain" because Israeli preventive attacks on an Iraqi nuclear facility in 1981 and in 2007 on a Syrian nuclear facility under construction did not lead to retaliation. But a preventive attack on either North Korea or Iran should be undertaken only assuming that it could lead to one or multiple forms of retaliation, although in both cases prospects for retaliation could be influenced if the government in question was warned that any retaliation would open it up to further attack.

What this adds up to is considerable support as a rule for promoting nonproliferation but little for military action to prevent or roll back proliferation once it has occurred. Support for preemptive action in the face of imminent threats would be stronger so long as it could be demonstrated such action was warranted. It could be argued that the NPT, by limiting the right to possess nuclear weapons to five countries (the United States, the United Kingdom, France, Russia, and China) is a statement that other countries have an obligation not to possess nuclear weapons. The five do not have an unlimited right to take action against those beyond the five that have or seek nuclear weapons, but what they do have a right to do, and under what terms, is a necessary question that must be raised. Making this a topic of discussion at bilateral and multilateral meetings makes sense, not so much because it would likely lead to a formal agreement, which it would not, but because it would increase understanding as to what circumstances could or would lead to what one or more governments considered to be legitimate preventive or preemptive action. Knowing this could well influence—that is, increase—what a Russia or a China was prepared to do to make sure an Iran or a North Korea did not reach the point where the United States would contemplate such action; it might also help reduce the scale of any adverse reaction if the

244 | A WORLD IN DISARRAY

United States (the most likely country to undertake a preventive or preemptive attack) were to so act.

Climate change is in many ways the quintessential manifestation of globalization. It reflects the sum total of what is going on; countries are affected unevenly (reflecting everything from changes to their climate to how many people live in areas vulnerable to a rise in water levels) regardless of their contribution to the problem. Borders count for naught. There is broad if not universal agreement that climate change is real, caused in large part by human activity, and that it constitutes a major threat to the future of the planet and its inhabitants. Where consensus breaks down most is when it comes to determining what is to be done and by whom.

In principle, climate change is something that ought to fit well under the rubric of sovereign obligation, as what any country does within its borders in emitting carbon has implications for the whole world. Put differently, climate change is a cumulative consequence of local activity. It is thus fundamentally different from, say, air or water pollution, which is largely a local consequence of local activity.

The problem comes in achieving consensus over what ought to be each country's "share" of combating climate change, either by reducing its own carbon output or helping others reduce theirs, or both. As was discussed previously, attempts to set global ceilings, allocate national shares, or affix a price for carbon have been resisted. The 2015 Paris conference, however, showed some realism and creativity alike by taking a different approach. An overall goal was set for limiting climate change (by setting a goal for the overall rise in the earth's temperature) even though countries were not given their specific share of what needed to be done to meet that goal. It was entirely aspirational rather than mandated. Indeed, what was agreed to was that each country had the obligation to set for itself what it judged to be an ambitious but achievable goal in reducing its carbon output (or reducing the amount of increase in output) and then to do what it could to meet or better that goal. The approach amounts to sovereign best efforts or intent, but it is a step in the direction of sovereign obligation. Incentives (from financial to technology sharing) can and should be provided to help countries reach or better their goals. Greater emphasis will also have to be placed on (and increased resources devoted to) helping countries and societies adapt to those effects of climate change that have already happened or are likely to. This should be a sovereign obligation for wealthier countries that have contributed significantly to climate change over the decades. In extremis, penalties, including sanctions, might need to be threatened or introduced against governments acting irresponsibly.

Cyberspace is in many ways the newest domain of international activity, and as is often the case, what makes it complex is the existence at one and the same time of areas of overlap and cooperation and those of disagreement and potential conflict. Adding to the complexity is that some activity in cyberspace is benign and has little if anything to do with national security, while other activities are intimately connected with foreign policy, intelligence, competitiveness, and more. The goal should be to create international arrangements—a "regime" in the academic jargon—that would encourage certain uses of cyberspace and discourage others. It would become part of a government's obligation to act consistently with this regime and to do all in its power to stop those acting from its territory who do not.

So what would constitute such a regime for cyberspace? It would need to set forth those behaviors permissible in normal times or in specified contexts as well as those to be banned. Ideally, a global arrangement for cyberspace would maintain a single, integrated linked system, limit what governments could do to stop the free flow of information and communication, prohibit commercial espionage and theft of intellectual property, and severely limit what could be done over cyberspace in peacetime to interfere with or disrupt either civilian or military systems that depend on cyberspace, as virtually all systems now do. Presumably espionage trained on governmental activities would be allowed. Exceptions would need to allow for cyberattacks to frustrate both proliferation and terrorism. There could be a cyber annex to the laws of war—that is, what would be considered acceptable wartime uses of cyber and what would not, given their impact on civilians. One could also imagine discussion of if not agreement

all things that may be done before

on responses to cyber behavior at odds with what had been discussed and agreed to.[9]

Governments would have the obligation not just to avoid engaging in prohibited activities but also to do everything in their power to prevent other parties from carrying out those activities from their territory. It would be the cyber equivalent of terrorism: governments would be expected not just to live up to agreed-upon behaviors but also to make sure that no third party carried out prohibited actions from their territory and that any party discovered to be so doing would be stopped and penalized. Achieving even limited consensus on any of these principles would take enormous effort, as would garnering agreement on what, if any, exceptions ought to be allowed and what should be done if and when the principles were violated. These are still relatively early days, however, in figuring out just what ought to be the rules to govern this new set of technologies, and the goal at this point should be to develop and gain adherence to (if not formal acceptance of) a set of behaviors on the part of sovereign governments. Smaller consultations involving critical governments, companies, and NGOs are likely to accomplish more than large formal gatherings of countries at this point.

In the realm of global health, a different set of challenges awaits. There is near-universal recognition that in a global world, an outbreak of infectious disease in one country could very quickly morph into a serious threat to health elsewhere.

This was the experience with SARS and Ebola. Pandemics that could claim millions of lives are anything but science fiction. What needs to be done is to nail down what is expected of governments, that is, to determine just what are the obligations of sovereigns in this realm. Actually, the notion of sovereign obligation is well advanced here and includes the ability to detect infectious disease outbreaks, notify others around the world, and take steps (or ask for assistance) to deal with outbreaks. The challenge is to make sure that governments and the World Health Organization have the capacity to meet it, something that could require technical and financial assistance.[10] But "naming and shaming" (something that would scare off tourism and business and that thus might be viewed as a de facto sanction) will also be required to place pressure on those who refuse to meet their obligations in this area.

Sovereign obligation takes on a different coloring in the economic realm, as the need to maintain a viable currency, ensure that financial institutions keep on hand adequate reserves, enforce honest accounting, push back against corruption, honor contracts, expand trade, and foster an environment that will attract investment provides incentives to governments to act in a responsible manner apart from any sense of obligation to others. Indeed, the obligation, such as it is, is more to a government's own citizens, who require a strong or at least not a weak economy if they are to enjoy a decent standard of living and the prospect of a better future. Expressed differently, there is not so much sovereign obligation to attract investment and keep deficits and debt under control as there is sovereign self-interest.

A few exceptions are worth noting. Trade agreements are by definition pacts of reciprocal sovereign obligation regarding tariff and nontariff barriers and the like. When one party believes that the obligations are not being met, it has recourse; indeed, the principal breakthrough of the World Trade Organization is to provide a standing mechanism for challenges and for settlements. One area of obligation that has not been adequately dealt with is currency manipulation by a government to advantage its exports by lowering their effective price and to disadvantage imports from elsewhere by raising theirs. Another is government subsidy that again can make it possible to make exports more competitive than they would otherwise be. The challenge here will be to devise future trade pacts so that sovereign obligations in these specific areas (as well as in such areas as agriculture and services, which have received scant coverage in many trade pacts, along with labor and environmental practices) are spelled out and to design the accords so that a mechanism exists to hold governments accountable.

Obviously, gaining international consensus for the obligations to be met by governments (and what might be done to see that those obligations are met as well as when they are not) promises to be a diplomatic task that is ambitious and then some. Even more ambitious would be to make such an order operational and bring countries into compliance with their obligations. Beyond persuasion, this could and would require a mix of incentives, assistance, capacity building, sanctions ranging from "naming and shaming" to political and economic penalties, and, on occasion, armed intervention, especially in cases of terrorism and proliferation. Pushing the world in the direction of embracing sovereign obligation as its operating system will take years of consultations and on occasion negotiations, and even then its embrace and impact will be uneven. Still, it is important that the idea gain traction and the conversations begin, as it holds out the best hope for fashioning order for the world in the era of globalization.

It is perhaps obvious but worth saying all the same that sovereign obligation cannot just be something the United States expects of others. It must practice it if it expects to preach it with any effect. To be sure, the United States has a special role and unique obligations in the world, but it must also appreciate that when it appears hypocritical or looks to be guilty of double standards it forfeits influence. Some "opt-outs," such as the U.S. refusal to ratify the Law of the Sea Treaty, should be reconsidered, as the stance is unwarranted on the merits of the issue at the same time it raises questions about U.S. willingness to play by the rules.[11] Other U.S. exceptions, like its refusal to support the International Criminal Court, can be managed through workarounds that allow for tribunals to be created for specific historical events.

Ha!
Not w/
Trump

In some realms, such as climate, U.S. ability to persuade others to act responsibly will reflect in no small part U.S. performance (which happens to be quite good), along with its willingness to make financial and technical resources available to assist others. Much the same holds when it comes to promoting sovereign obligation in the realm of health. In other areas, a willingness to use military force may well be essential if terrorism is to be minimized and proliferation frustrated—although even here a degree of restraint will be required in when and how force is used.

The United States needs to accept special obligations in the economic realm given the role of the dollar as the world's de facto reserve currency. This means taking into account the views of others when deciding on interest rates or asset purchases (quantitative easing). Regular, serious consultations between the Federal Reserve and its central bank counterparts around the world are essential. Trade disputes should be taken to the WTO rather than acted on unilaterally, as well.

Consistent with all this, and to return to a theme that has appeared throughout this book, legitimacy requires a commitment to process as well as policy. A big part of the process of building legitimacy for sovereign obligations will be consultations. In some areas, such as health, the conversation is already far advanced. What mostly remains is building national capacity. In other realms, such as cyber, the world is far from agreement as to what is desirable. In still other areas, such as proliferation, the norms are agreed on, but unresolved is what is permissible or desirable in practice when the norms are ignored.

This all raises another issue, that of authority or approval. In some of these areas, no government will accept that it can act only if it receives "permission" to do so from some international body, such as the United Nations. The General Assembly is the most democratic and representative body, but for these same reasons it is not a viable venue for major powers. "One country, one vote" is the ultimate expression of sovereign equality, but it has nothing to do with strength and the real world. The UN Security Council has greater standing because it is smaller and because it extends a veto to some of the world's major powers, but it suffers both from those countries and relevant nonstate entities that are not represented as well as from the even more basic reality that no major power will submit what it sees as matters central to its national security to the Security Council for decision.

To suggest this should change is a nonstarter. It would be a serious error to think any world body could impose sovereign obligation in any realm on an unwilling power.[12] This is not the intention. A consensus as to what constitutes legitimacy can come about only on a voluntary basis. Governments will have to decide for themselves whether on balance they are better off even if required to forfeit some of their own options or room to maneuver. This is already the case in the trade sphere, and is beginning to materialize with climate and cyber. Prospects are more mixed in the political-military realm.

What could get in the way of building support for making sovereign obligation central to a modern notion of legitimacy? One possible obstacle is that some governments might disagree with a specific objective either as a matter of principle or in certain contexts. A second potential obstacle is that a government might agree in principle but for one reason or another be unable to act. It could lack resources or domestic law or sufficient domestic political support. A third reason would be that it is deemed unacceptable to make the trade-off described in the paragraph just above, namely, that any acceptance of restraint would be unacceptable.

There can be no institutional or procedural solution to these concerns. No adjustment of the UN Security Council would make a difference in providing a mechanism that would bestow authority to act, although a more representative Security Council could facilitate consultations. Absent such reform, consultations are likely to take place in other settings: bilateral and multilateral, informal and formal, general and purpose-specific. Consultations are often overlooked as people focus on negotiations. But many issues are not sufficiently ripe (and may never get there) for negotiations to succeed. Still, consultations can do a lot to generate understanding and tolerance of certain actions, to make clear the limits of what is judged to be reasonable or acceptable and the likely costs and consequences of going beyond those limits, and to reduce the chance of surprise and miscalculation that history so often associates with breakdowns of order.

I will conclude this discussion of process with three thoughts. Multilateralism needs to be rethought and reconfigured if it is to encourage the adoption of sovereign obligation as a central element of what constitutes legitimacy in this era. First, "best practices" multilateralism ought to become the norm for those issues that mostly involve domestic policy but that have global impact. The 2015 Paris climate meeting as well as arrangements in the financial and health realms suggest a way ahead. The goal should be to get governments to commit to adopting certain best practices at home in areas that inevitably affect global efforts to deal with common challenges. Counterterrorism and especially law enforcement is another possible domain. The commitment is not contractual; failure to adopt a certain practice or meet a set goal is not an act of noncompliance (as it would be with a traditional treaty commitment) but rather simply a failure to deliver. The price paid may be to get called out, to be named and shamed, or to receive low ratings and independent assessments. It may discourage investment or tourism. More positively, the approach encourages assistance to help governments that seek to meet their sovereign obligations by what they do at home but for one reason or another cannot.

Second, pragmatism will need to play a large role when it comes to multilateral efforts to deal with collective chal-

[margin note, handwritten: Committing to domestic changes that achieve collective goals.]

lenges. This means bringing together the representatives of those countries (and, as suggested just below, entities other than countries) that are the most relevant and that are both willing and able to address the particular challenge at hand. It matters not whether this is described as "designer multilateralism" or "multilateralism à la carte"; what matters is that the bias favors getting things done with those who matter most rather than favoring inclusion for its own sake. Such coalitions of the willing can become more formal with time, but what matters is that they are forged as needed.

Third, relevant nonstate actors need to be included in whatever process is selected. Multilateralism cannot be a country-only enterprise in a nonpolar era. Obviously, the mix of invitees will vary from issue to issue. But efforts to contend with infectious disease need to give a place at the table to, say, the Gates Foundation, pharmaceutical companies, and NGOs such as Doctors Without Borders alongside health ministers and representatives of the World Health Organization. It would be nonsensical to convene gatherings meant to promulgate rules of the road for cyberspace without the participation of Apple, Microsoft, Google, Facebook, and others. City mayors and governors of states or principalities deserve a seat at many tables. Call it ironic, but room must be found for the meaningful participation of relevant nonsovereign entities in an order predicated on sovereign obligation.

11. Regional Responses

We have already noted the reality that in many ways it makes more sense to speak of world orders than of world order. This is true in the functional domains just discussed, as the degree of consensus in, for example, trade cannot be expected to be mirrored in others such as climate or cyberspace. This same separateness is reflected in the geographic sense as well. There are a number of distinct regions in today's world, including North America, the Asia-Pacific, South Asia, the Middle East, South or Latin America, Africa, and Europe. Indeed, it is another one of those seeming contradictions that at one and the same time the world is experiencing increased globalization and increased regionalization.

The Asia-Pacific is the part of the world that most resembles familiar models. In some ways, it is the inverse of the Middle East. Nation-states are strong, as are national identities. The region has also been quite orderly amid extraordinary economic growth, increased spending on military capabilities, numerous territorial disagreements, and rising nationalism. All of this was hardly automatic. As was discussed previously, it was the result of several factors, including a significant degree of economic interdependence, a decision on the part of many governments to focus the bulk of their attention and resources on their country's economic and political development, and U.S. involvement in the region, which made it unnecessary for several countries to maximize their own military development and made aggressive action by others a high-risk, low-payoff proposition.

The obvious question is whether this can last—or, more usefully, what needs to be done so that it can last. Order has to continue to be rooted in a balance of power and in economic interdependence. As a general proposition, promoting stability in the Asia-Pacific region plays to U.S. strengths. What is called for closely resembles classic statecraft. The challenge is to shape the external behavior of local countries, not to transform them. Realism, not Wilsonian idealism, is the operative framework. The challenges stem from strong states, competing territorial claims, rival nationalisms, historical animosities, and a lack of diplomatic machinery and architecture. If there is a parallel, it is Europe before the outbreak of the First World War. I say this not to be alarmist, but more to warn against complacency and to suggest that stability can likely be maintained if the United States acts with clear purpose.

The Obama administration introduced what I would argue was (and is) a smart idea, namely a rebalancing of U.S. foreign policy toward the Asia-Pacific region. (The original term for what was intended, a "pivot," was unfortunate, as it suggested a sharper turn away from other regions than was a good idea, but the basic concept was correct.) I say it was a smart idea because for too much of the post–Cold War era, U.S. foreign policy has been overly preoccupied with the greater Middle East. This makes little sense, as U.S. interests there, however substantial, are not unlimited. More important, given local realities, there are limits to what the United States can do on behalf of those interests. And there is the obvious additional factor that the United States has vital interests elsewhere, including the Asia-Pacific, where a relatively modest effort can yield significant dividends.

Indeed, it is no exaggeration to say that the trajectory of this part of the world will be central to that of the world writ large. The Asia-Pacific is where several of the major powers of this era are located. It will account for the lion's share of the world's population, wealth, and military might. The ability of countries in or bordering on this part of the world to agree or at least limit their disagreement will go a long way toward determining whether global issues such as climate change and cyberspace can be successfully managed. What happens there will also largely shape the character of relations among the major powers of this era.

One essential ingredient of order will be a regular, visible U.S. presence: diplomatic, economic, and military. Air and naval overflights and patrols that underscore commitments to allies and friends and push back against unilateral claims by China, in particular to territory and air- and sea-space, are one component of what needs doing. The United States maintains formal treaty relationships (alliances) in the area with Japan, South Korea, the Philippines, Thailand, and Australia and New Zealand. The ties to Japan and South Korea are particularly significant, not just in helping to deter aggression against them and helping to keep the peace, but also in reassuring them so that they do not feel they have to take security matters into their own hands. Put differently, a Japan or South Korea that did not feel confident of American will and ability to come to its defense would likely acquire nuclear weapons; the chance that a conflict would happen between Japan and China or between the two Koreas would rise substantially. Those making a narrow calculus of the direct costs of U.S. military presence and commitments in the region (which are relatively modest in normal circumstances and offset in part by allies offering "Host Nation Support") need to take into account the many economic and strategic benefits that accrue to the United States from this being a peaceful and prosperous region.

At the same time, this support for friends and allies cannot be unconditional. They must understand that with U.S. support comes the responsibility on their part not to act recklessly or provocatively. This applies to formal allies as well as to Taiwan. The concept that comes to mind here, one familiar to investors, is "moral hazard." The United States needs to be sufficiently supportive so that other countries will not doubt U.S. commitments and act independently, but not so supportive that other governments will assume that irresponsible behavior will automatically be underwritten by the United States. As should be obvious, getting the balance right between guaranteeing necessary support and not granting license is easier described than implemented.

But as important as military presence and ties are, the U.S. stance in the region cannot be one-dimensional. There need to be regular, high-level consultations, that is, real strategic dialogue. With friends and allies, the subjects can and should range from the contours of a regional security system (more on this just below) and how to approach the threat that is North Korea to coordinating the management of China's rise, fashioning common or at least consistent approaches to global issues, and promoting economic growth.

A regional security system or architecture is long overdue. Such an architecture has existed in Europe for more than four decades. I am referring to the Helsinki Accord, more formally known as the Organization for Security and Cooperation in Europe, or OSCE. This and associated arrangements work to, among other things, discourage the use of military means to change borders and promote measures and arrangements (confidence-building measures, or CBMs) that reduce the chance of accidental military incidents and of escalation if one occurs all the same.

Such a system could and should not simply be overlaid on the Asia-Pacific, which has a very different geography and political composition from Europe's. There is no need, for example, to try to replicate the human rights provisions of the Helsinki arrangements, which would not be acceptable to China and other countries and if pushed on them could make it that much more difficult to put into place arrangements that would reduce the odds of conflict in the region. An Asian architecture would have to be consistent with the U.S. need to meet its alliance commitments, something that was not an obstacle in Europe. As a first step, it would be wiser to emphasize CBMs such as hotlines and the provision of advance notice of exercises rather than constraints on military activities, much less the size of militaries. China should be brought into the conversation once it is clear that the United States and its allies are on the same page. There is also an argument for pushing hard for the establishment of crisis avoidance and management mechanisms between China and Japan as soon as possible rather than waiting for a regional arrangement to be negotiated.

North Korea is a necessary second subject of consultations, again with allies (South Korea and Japan) and with China. The goal should be to pressure North Korea to give up all its nuclear weapons; failing that, there ought to be an understanding as to the conditions under which a preemptive or preventive military attack might be undertaken. Japanese and above all South Korean buy-in would be essential here given that they would bear the brunt of any North Korean retaliation. Other subjects for discussion should be war aims if North Korea does something aggressive, as well as what might be suggested to China so that it would conclude it is better off applying pressure to North Korea now, even if that threatened the regime's stability, than living with a nuclear-armed North Korea and all that could happen as a result.

A common theme here is the need to consult with China and include it in various dialogues. This is in no way meant to be a U.S.-China "G-2" that would seek to run the world (which for many reasons it could not) but rather is part and parcel of a larger policy of trying to integrate China more fully into regional and global arrangements. No regional security system is meaningful without China's participation, as avoiding conflict with the PRC over any number of territorial and sea claims is a priority. The United States will want to urge China not to take unilateral actions or resort to military force; for its part, the United States will need to pledge to work diligently to dissuade its friends and allies from acting unilaterally or provocatively. In many instances, all parties will need to be persuaded of the wisdom of living with rather than resolving differences over competing claims.

When it comes to North Korea, China is critical given

how much of North Korea's economy depends on Chinese subsidy and cooperation. Discussions with the PRC as to the number, kind, and location of any U.S. troops that would be in South Korea after unification of the peninsula could lead China to reconsider its support for North Korea. China also needs to be included in talks about securing North Korean nuclear weapons and materials in the event of the country's collapse. I would also argue for its joining the Trans-Pacific Partnership, a trade pact involving the United States and eleven other countries, if the accord comes into existence and if Beijing can meet the essential standards. In every case, the aim should be to include China in conversations about the region's future and to integrate it into regional arrangements. An Asian-Pacific order that China accepts as legitimate and cannot overturn through force (or, better yet, sees no reason to) is likely to endure even if, as seems certain, many of the competing claims to territory will persist.

South Asia constitutes a very different challenge from East Asia and the Pacific. The region or subregion includes a half dozen states but is dominated by two: India and Pakistan. India is the more important of the two in that it will in a matter of a generation likely overtake China as the world's most populous country. India is also growing at something in the range of 7–8 percent per year, which if sustained could make it one of the world's major economies in two decades. What India does and does not do could also have a major impact on global climate change efforts; with hundreds of millions of Indians lacking regular electricity and hundreds of millions enjoying or closing in on middle-class status, the country's energy choices will have enormous consequences for the world. India's strategic orientation will also matter in that Chinese defense planners will have to take into account their country's contested border with India, along with New Delhi associating itself more with the United States. True strategic consultations at a high level and on a regular basis between U.S. and Indian leaders and officials are a must. One element of these talks should be to urge India to take a more generous approach toward Pakistan, as a favor not to its neighbor but to itself. A more normal relationship between the two dominant countries of South Asia would increase the chances that they will not go to war and free up India to focus on its internal development and its larger role in Asia and the world.

Pakistan, whose close to two hundred million people make it the second most populous country in the Muslim world, unfortunately represents more problem than opportunity. Pakistan maintains what many believe to be the world's fastest-growing nuclear arsenal (now numbering more than one hundred devices) and is home to many of the world's most dangerous terrorist organizations. It has long provided sanctuary to the Taliban, who have used the western part of the country to wage war against the government and people of Afghanistan and those assisting them, including the United States.

What to do about Pakistan has long been a problem for the United States. I recall vividly my first conversation in January 2001 with Colin Powell after he became secretary of state and I took over the State Department Policy Planning Staff. We spent a good hour and a half sitting in his small inner office going around the world, discussing problems and opportunities and what the United States might do about each. Finally, he turned to me and asked, "What worries you most?" I quickly responded, "Pakistan," explaining its toxic mix of nuclear weapons, terrorists, weak civilian authority, and limited governmental capacity, and the intensity of its animosity toward India. Making it all even worse was the frustrating reality that U.S. options for dealing with it were extremely limited.

The sad truth is that I could and would give much the same answer today, although there are arguably several other competing sources of concern in the world. Pakistan represents a difficult foreign policy challenge, namely, what to do about a bad situation that could get worse. Stated differently, as bad as the problems posed by Pakistan might now be, they pale in comparison to a country that loses control over its nuclear weapons or materials, that unleashes terrorist attacks on India that lead to a war between the two countries, or that is taken over by an offshoot of the very same Taliban that

Pakistan has supported for well over a decade in an effort to ensure it has a major say in determining the future of its neighbor Afghanistan. Sanctions and other forms of penalties that weaken the civilian government, as flawed as it is, therefore risk being counterproductive.

What has a better chance of working is a policy that essentially establishes a baseline of support for Pakistan with increased support of one sort or another tied to specific performance. This is the sort of thing recently suggested both in the report of an independent task force sponsored by the Council on Foreign Relations[1] and by some U.S. senators when they agreed to sell Pakistan certain aircraft but linked financing to the level of effort against terrorism. To this approach I would add one element. The United States must retain the willingness and ability to act in and near Pakistan but independent of it. The Obama administration correctly did so when it launched the raid that killed Osama bin Laden. For good reason, Pakistani officials were not given advance notice, as it is nearly certain that one or more would have compromised the mission. Pakistan is not an ally and often not even a partner.

One other country merits mention in this context: Afghanistan. There is little unique about it in the sense that the principal U.S. objective is that the country not again become a base for terrorists who launch attacks against the U.S. homeland or U.S. interests around the world. This same objective applies to literally dozens of countries. This argues against an ambitious U.S. effort to remake Afghanistan, but it also argues against leaving it to its own devices. Instead, what makes sense is a long-term, open-ended effort to bolster the government with economic and military help. A military presence (along the lines of what was announced by the United States in July 2016) is also called for to reassure, to train, and to advise. Peace talks can be pursued, but expectations should be held firmly in check. Afghanistan is more akin to a situation to be managed than a problem to be resolved.

The Middle East constitutes the greatest challenge to policymakers of any region in the world. It is the region experiencing the greatest level of violence. The previous section (Part II) explained both where it is and how it got there. To argue for an ambitious set of objectives amid such circumstances, though, is to embrace fantasy over reality. There are times in statecraft when to set modest goals is to squander opportunity; this is not one of those times. To the contrary, even the most modest goals promise to be ambitious.

Another way to think of the situation in the contemporary Middle East is that there are situations in which it is right and appropriate to think about what might be created. There is a case for going on the diplomatic offensive. Again, this is not one of them. One parallel that comes to mind is financial markets, in that there are moments when investors would be advised to invest because there are sound reasons to believe there is money to be made—and there are moments when for whatever reason or reasons markets should be avoided and cash held in reserve.

Today's Middle East most resembles the latter. The Middle East now and for the foreseeable future is a region to be thought of less in terms of what might be accomplished than what might be avoided. As was just said about Afghanistan, it is more a condition to be managed than a problem to be solved.

To argue for an approach steeped in modesty is not to suggest that the region should be avoided or ignored. It cannot be. First, the United States and other outsiders continue to have critical interests in the region. Second, U.S. interests elsewhere will be affected by what happens in the Middle East. A case in point is the refugee crisis that has significantly added to Europe's burdens. Another example is terrorism carried out in the United States or elsewhere by people who have left the region or been inspired by people and events there.

The most obvious local interest is oil. The Middle East is home to more than half the world's proven oil reserves and is responsible for more than a third of world oil production. This is unlikely to change appreciably for decades to come. Indeed, the only factor that could dramatically affect the region's energy importance would be technological breakthroughs that made oil far less central to the world's economy.

The importance of the region's oil still very much affects

the United States. Much has been said and written about the changed American energy picture, and much of it is wrong, in the sense that the revolutions in technology and practices that have led to stunning increases in oil and natural gas output have not ushered in an era of American energy independence. The United States may not need Middle East oil for itself, but it does need to import some four million barrels a day, as there is a mismatch between domestically produced oil and domestic refineries. The price of this oil is heavily affected by developments in the Middle East. More important, even if what might be described as net or overall U.S. energy sufficiency exists, the United States is not economically an autarky, and if the rest of the world suffers because of inadequate energy supplies, high prices, or both, the United States will suffer as well given its reliance on the rest of the world to buy American exports, invest in the United States, and help fund its debt.

Energy, though, is by no means the only continuing interest of the United States in the Middle East. Another is the well-being of Israel. There has long been a debate as to whether this is rooted in history or morality or strategy, and the only honest answer is all of the above. A third set of interests is the well-being and orientation of countries long friendly to the United States, whether for reasons of regional stability, counterterrorism, nonproliferation, energy security, a willingness to live in peace with Israel, humanitarian considerations, or some combination thereof. This may mean on occasion countering what Iran or Russia does, but such a calculation should be made on a situation-by-situation basis, as the possibility of selective cooperation with either should not be ruled out.

So what to do? There can be no single or overriding approach to the Middle East, as there is no common threat to order. One approach to be dismissed out of hand is to walk away from the region in the belief that it doesn't matter or that it can find an acceptable measure of order on its own. This is a dangerous pipe dream, one sometimes put forward by critics of past interventions.[2] What they miss is that bad situations can and in this case certainly would get worse.

Two figures in children's literature, not normally associated with strategy, come to mind. The first is Humpty Dumpty. If all the king's horses and men could not put Humpty together again, then all this country's soldiers and all its dollars cannot make the Middle East whole. The Middle East that has existed since the aftermath of World War I, one devised by Messrs. Sykes and Picot (representing Great Britain and France respectively) in 1916 and captured in countless maps and globes by those who followed Messrs. Rand and McNally, is likely gone. The lines drawn reflected more the preferences of outsiders than the realities of those living there. More than anything else, the Sykes-Picot Middle East created a number of countries with heterogeneous societies, often with little national tradition, history, identity, or practice of tolerance.

That Middle East is, as suggested above, largely of the

past. Identities now are at one and the same time sub- and transnational; they are based more on religion, tribe, ethnicity, and ideology. Reversing this trend would require a mixture of brute force and the ability to effect a change in political culture. It would require today's illiberalism to be replaced by liberalism, today's intolerance by tolerance, and today's spirit of revenge by forgiveness.

All of which brings us to the second figure from the world of children's books: Goldilocks. Goldilocks was the ultimate centrist, avoiding the extremes of porridge that were either too hot or cold, chairs too big or small, and beds too hard or soft. That said, Goldilocks had it relatively easy (at least until the three bears showed up) in that the middle choice was both presented to her and happened to be "just right."

The United States faces a similar task in the Middle East—to avoid doing too much or too little. Doing too much would mean trying to bring back a region of defined and viable countries; it would also mean trying to transform these same countries into something approximating functioning democracies. Doing too little would essentially mean leaving the region to its own devices.

When it comes to the Middle East, though, there is no obvious "just right" option. The task of foreign policy is to discern what is both desirable and feasible at a cost that is acceptable. Such a policy begins with counterterrorism, as terrorists can harm U.S. interests in the region, they can

ME Foreign Policy   ④ military force
① counterterrorism
② denuclearization (Iran)   REGIONAL RESPONSES | 273
③ support for Israel

travel beyond the region, and they can inspire over the Internet. An effective policy would entail putting terrorists on the defensive by attacking them directly (from the air and with special forces) and by strengthening select local actors (be they governments, tribes, or ethnic groups) so that they can either take the fighting to the terrorists, be less vulnerable to them, or both. What is said in schools, in mosques, and over the Internet can affect whether young men and women make the decision to become terrorists or stick to their career choice once they have made it; this will likely require a degree of government intervention. The counterterrorism effort can and should involve a range of tools, including the provision of arms, intelligence, and training; economic aid; and the deft use of social media and more traditional forms of public diplomacy. Coordinated efforts are required to slow the flow of funds and recruits and to track suspected groups and individuals. Support would also be provided to governments so they could better withstand the pressure being brought to bear by Iran and proxy forces backed by Iran. Again, this support should involve a variety of foreign policy tools. It may not be realistic to eradicate terrorism, as desirable as this would be, if only because terrorism is part of the new normal, a result of social, religious, and political factors that have gained considerable traction. But what is realistic is to reduce terrorism to a level that limits what it can achieve and how often it succeeds so that it does not affect the basics of our way of life. This will require a sustained, comprehensive approach that blends elements of prevention, protection, and resilience.

A second aim of any Middle East policy should include a major effort to discourage the further nuclearization of the region, a possibility in the wake of the Iran nuclear agreement that reduced but did not eliminate Iran's nuclear capabilities and then only for a limited time. It is possible and arguably probable that several of Iran's neighbors will hedge against the possibility that Iran might either cheat or simply wait until the limits on centrifuges and enriched uranium expire (in 2025 and 2030 respectively) and start developing nuclear options for themselves. Such doubts reflect a sober assessment of Iran but also a diminution of confidence in the value of U.S. assurances and in U.S. trustworthiness in the wake of both the Syrian red line debacle and the Iran nuclear pact. Stopping regional proliferation from happening will at a minimum require providing defense against Iranian missiles and aircraft. It could also require providing defense guarantees, including that Iran would face the threat of U.S. military action (potentially including nuclear forces) if it were to threaten or use nuclear-armed systems against its neighbors. The policy would also include a diplomatic dimension, that is, using diplomacy and the threat of new sanctions to extend the limits in the 2015 joint agreement that are otherwise mostly set to expire in 2025 or 2030. Consultations with regional states as well as with Russia, China, and Europe on all facets of Iran's nuclear policy (including, of course, its compliance with the current agreement) need to be a high priority.

Policy toward Iran cannot be one-dimensional, however, as important as the nuclear dimension might be. Indeed, the nuclear agreement failed to address most aspects of the challenge posed by Iran, and arguably even exacerbated them by making available resources that had previously been denied. Iran may not be a major global power, but it is by any standard a major regional one. Only Israel and to a lesser extent Saudi Arabia and Turkey can compete with it in the Middle East. It is also a highly complex and problematic actor, with a divided government (making it particularly hard to negotiate with), a strong ideology, multiple proxy forces, a capable military, and ties to Shia populations in the region.

There is as well the reality that the Islamic Republic, approaching four decades in age, is secure. A policy that would seek to transform it is unrealistic; the emergence with time of a more moderate Iran is possible but cannot be counted on. The most sensible policy might be a variant of what has been suggested here for dealing with China and Russia: a mixture of selective cooperation (say in Afghanistan, where cooperation has proved possible in the past) and diplomacy (such as in the nuclear realm) with hedging and, where required, containment using sanctions, extending assistance to Iran's neighbors, or military action when Iranian actions threaten core U.S. interests in the region.

A third dimension of the policy would be support for

Israel. This goes beyond maintaining or selectively increasing military, economic, and intelligence support. It also involves reestablishing and maintaining a close consultative relationship on questions ranging from Iran and averting the region's nuclearization to what might be done in response to a crisis of stability in, say, Jordan or Saudi Arabia. The United States already maintains a strategic dialogue with Israel, but like almost all such dialogues, it has become captured by the respective bureaucracies. I noted earlier that any country that contains "democratic" in its name rarely is; much the same holds for dialogues that call themselves strategic. To the contrary, real strategic cooperation normally takes place outside of formal dialogues. In January 1991, for example, President George H. W. Bush persuaded Israeli prime minister Yitzhak Shamir not to retaliate against Iraq even after Iraqi missiles hit Tel Aviv. At the core of the argument was that Israel should trust the United States to do the right thing, which included acting to protect Israel's interests along with its own. It was an extraordinary ask; no less extraordinary was Israel's willingness to stand down.[3] The two countries should aim to get back to such a place of trust, given the range of difficult contingencies, from Iran's nuclear program to a collapse of authority in Jordan or Saudi Arabia, that they may well have to contend with.

A fourth dimension of policy involves the use of military force. My recommendation is not to rule out military intervention per se. Interventions of one sort or another can make sense for a range of purposes, including to defend a friendly country against external aggression, to attack terrorists, to prevent proliferation or preempt the launch of (or loss of control over) weapons of mass destruction, to avoid or ease a humanitarian nightmare, to maintain the free movement of shipping and oil tanker traffic, or to protect oil-producing areas. What matters, though, are two things if any discretionary use of military force (what I have termed "wars of choice") is to be warranted: first, the likely benefits of acting militarily must outweigh the likely human, economic, diplomatic, and military costs; and second, this balance between projected benefits and costs must be better than what could be expected to result from other policies over a reasonable time frame. Such calculations would have argued against undertaking the 2003 Iraq War and the Libya intervention but in favor of the Gulf War and for carrying out a set of punitive strikes in the wake of the Syrian government's use of chemical weapons.

But just as important is what any policy toward the Middle East would not include. It would not place a large emphasis on reforming local societies anytime soon, as desirable as this might be in principle. Desirability is never enough as a determinant of foreign policy; there is a sharp distinction between what is desirable and what is essential. In addition, a proposed action, be it military or otherwise, must pass the test outlined above, namely, the likely results and benefits need to outweigh the likely costs and compare favorably to what could be reasonably expected from other policies. Transforming Middle Eastern societies meets none of these criteria.[4]

Again, this is not to say the United States should ignore what is going on inside Middle Eastern societies. There may be situations where some form of humanitarian intervention is warranted. Countries such as Jordan and Lebanon deserve help to meet the burden of refugees and the threat from terrorists. In lesser situations, there may be a case for a degree of diplomatic intervention, public or private, to urge one set of behaviors and discourage another. This is the case today with Egypt, less for humanitarian reasons and more for the goal of promoting social and political stability. In many countries, the agenda the United States should promote should be less one of "democracy" (much less elections, which in the absence of checks and balances and strong constitutions can have antidemocratic outcomes) than one of reforms that reduce corruption, increase opportunity for girls and women and the space for civil society, increase the rule of law, introduce educational reform away from rote learning and toward critical thinking, and promote economic reform that reduces the role of government and the energy sector. Such change will reduce the gap between governments and their citizens and make these countries less vulnerable to the appeals of radicals. Over time such reforms could set the stage for a gradual transition to a more open society and a political system with some or even many of the trappings of democracy.

It also does not make sense for the United States to consider it a matter of vital interest to preserve the current national borders of the region. To the contrary, it is more reasonable to accept the high likelihood that the near-term Middle East will likely be made up of as many autonomous areas within countries as countries themselves. This is certainly true for Syria, Iraq, and Libya, where national governments may be national in name but are unlikely to be so in terms of area under their control. Cantons more than countries may well be the norm.

It would make no sense, though, to try to get this emerging reality reflected in any formal arrangement. There is no need for a reprise of the Paris Peace Conference, which followed the First World War and the dissolution of the Ottoman Empire. Such an effort would surely fail, as few if any governments would want to set such a precedent, and even if they were so willing, there is little or no chance that there would be agreement on where to draw borders. For the foreseeable future, the reality of the Middle East will be far more de facto than de jure.

Two stateless groups merit separate treatment. The first is the Kurds. They lost out at the Paris Peace Conference; when the music stopped, they were left without the sovereign equivalent of a chair. Today, a century later, there are some twenty-five to thirty-five million Kurds, mostly living in Turkey, Iran, Iraq, and Syria. The United States has historically held off supporting Kurdish statehood out of concern that it could destabilize the region and alienate Turkey, a NATO ally. But today the region is already destabilized, the Kurds in Syria and Iraq have proven to be the best local fighters against ISIS, and Turkey under its current leadership is an ally more in name than in reality. Also, U.S. support for a Kurdish state could be limited to Iraq and Syria. In Turkey the U.S. position should be limited to supporting peaceful dialogue between the government and Kurds along with a healthy degree of autonomy for the Kurds if they pursue their aims peacefully.

The Palestinians are of course the second stateless people. I would not place a great emphasis on bringing about a comprehensive peace between Israel and the Palestinians. No one should misinterpret this statement. Such a formal peace would be highly desirable for Israelis and Palestinians alike. There is a strong case to be made that both peoples would be well served by an agreement that created a Palestinian state prepared to live in peace alongside Israel. Palestinians would at long last have a state to call their own. Such an agreement would also provide the best guarantee that Israel will endure as a secure, Jewish, prosperous, and democratic country.

But as is often the case, what is missing is not ideas for a conceivable agreement. To the contrary, the outlines of such an accord are painfully familiar: they include a Palestinian state on land equal in amount to that gained in 1967 by Israel but adjusted to take into account the large settlement blocs that would remain part of Israel; some sharing of an undivided Jerusalem; special arrangements, including limits on

Palestinian arms and possibly allowances for an Israeli military presence on Palestinian territory, for Israeli security; and only a limited number of Palestinians who would be able to "return" to Israel, but compensation provided to the many who could not. There would of course be many difficult matters to resolve, but the bigger question is whether there would be leadership on all sides of the table both willing and able to make the necessary compromises. I define this mix of capacity and willingness as the principal factors determining "ripeness," that is, whether a dispute is poised to be resolved. When such factors are present, it makes sense for those with a stake in the outcome to devote time and effort to bringing about an accord; when such prerequisites are absent, it is futile to proceed as if it were otherwise. Instead, time is better spent developing the prerequisites, aiming for more modest progress, or working on other issues. As Edgar notes in Shakespeare's *King Lear*, "Ripeness is all."[5]

For now and for the foreseeable future, such prerequisites are likely to be missing from the Israeli-Palestinian equation. Israel's coalition government is not prepared to make significant compromises; only a different coalition could do so, and this would happen only if the prime minister or some other political figure was able and prepared to build such a coalition. If he was, then Israel could presumably be a full partner in any negotiation. As of now, this is not in the cards.

The Palestinian side is also a question, if for different reasons. Making the situation particularly difficult is the divided nature of the Palestinian polity, split as it is between the Palestinians residing in the West Bank and those in Gaza. The problem is less geographic than political, as the Palestinians in control of the West Bank lack political strength, while Hamas, the radical organization that rules Gaza, has shown no interest in accepting Israel or negotiating with it.

The price of a lack of progress mostly affects the parties themselves. For decades it was held as a matter of conviction by many that if the Israel-Palestinian conflict could be resolved it would lead to a broader Middle East peace. This may or may not have been true, but now it is nearly irrelevant, as the many sources of instability and conflict in the Middle East, including the events in Syria, Iraq, Yemen, and Libya as well as between Arabs and Persians and between ISIS and others, would not be meaningfully affected even if there were a Palestinian state living in peace alongside Israel. Indeed, such an agreement would be attacked by the radical groups who are laying siege to much of the region on the grounds that it embraced compromise with Israel.

Again, this is not meant as an argument for leaving the situation alone or allowing matters to drift. Neither the Middle East nor what prospects there are for peace will benefit from neglect or from a diplomatic vacuum that leads the Palestinian side to turn to the United Nations as a substitute venue, something that would only further alienate Israel. In the case of Israel and the Palestinians, there is an argument for diplomatic efforts that would aim to keep the situation from deteriorating and to keep alive diplomatic prospects for a more propitious moment or, better yet, to bring such a moment closer. A minimal approach would bring together Saudi Arabia, Jordan, West Bank Palestinian leaders, and Israel to focus on rules of the road to minimize the chance of there being an explosive incident involving Jerusalem's holy places. A somewhat more ambitious approach would emphasize such things as the economic development of the West Bank and forging a pact with Israel to limit settlement development to those already developed blocs or areas, thereby making a peace agreement involving territorial exchanges more feasible when the political context changed. There remains a strong argument for building up the capacity of the Palestinian Authority, both so it could withstand a challenge from Hamas and so that it would have the ability to meet its sovereign obligations were the Palestinians to gain statehood. Only under such circumstances could Israel be expected to go along.

Latin America and Africa could not be more different from the other three regions just discussed. Geopolitics do not figure prominently in either. Most policy should be focused on encouraging domestic policies known to foster good governance and economic growth. In some countries, though, the additional challenge will be to help build state capacity so authorities can better contend with terrorists, drug cartels, and criminal organizations. What would also help is the fostering of regionalism in two senses: economically, through trade pacts, and in the security sphere, to help weak or failed states cope with humanitarian and security challenges. This latter aim could best be advanced by strengthening the capacities of regional and subregional organizations (through the provision of relevant arms, training, and intelligence) that do not require unanimity to act.

Europe, as noted earlier, has in a short span of time gone from being the most predictable and stable region to something dramatically different. That said, the ability of the United States to influence Europe's trajectory is relatively limited. Much of what needs doing in Europe can be done only by Europeans. They should spend more on defense, but even more important is that they coordinate their spending so the result is additive rather than duplicative. This will require far more specialization. There is also a pressing need to bolster the capacity of those NATO members bordering Russia. And as already mentioned, NATO enlargement ought to be put on hold until the alliance is in a position to fulfill its current obligations and prospective members can meet theirs. This reality also argues for NATO focusing on "in area" challenges rather than those "out of area" for the foreseeable future.

Europe must also change how it goes about tackling terrorism. Part of what is needed is greater integration and cooperation between governments in the realms of law enforcement and intelligence sharing. The same need for greater coordination also applies to many countries when it comes to their internal counterterrorism and law enforcement agencies. In addition, Europe has not as a rule done as well as the United States in integrating immigrant populations into its social mainstream. Initiatives that among other things build ties with community and religious leaders, add to what is taught in schools, and promote employment among young men need to be a higher priority, as even a small number of alienated individuals can cause disproportionate disruption and damage.

As for the EU, there is an obvious need for reform. Possibilities include imposing some constraints on the free movement of people to and within Europe, instituting some version of collective deposit insurance conditioned on countries and banks accepting specific reforms and controls, and instituting real discipline over fiscal policies if countries are to join or remain in the Eurozone. Politics and above all the ideology favoring greater integration have been allowed to triumph over economic realities, but as recurring fiscal crises in several countries of southern Europe show, this stance has hurt the EU politically as well as economically. Dealing with this gap between political and economic realities may require a future EU that offers several levels of membership, possibly a version of what already exists in terms of an inner core of countries participating in the Eurozone. Such flexibility could prove essential if the EU is to remain intact.

There is a limit to what the EU can do if it is forced to operate in a context of low economic growth. Reforms that promote growth, including increased flexibility for employers when it comes to hiring and firing workers, targeted tax and entitlement reductions, and increased infrastructure spending, are worth exploring and arguably adopting. Politics permitting, one initiative the United States could advance that would help Europe and bolster U.S.-European ties is a transatlantic trade pact.

More broadly, there is a compelling case for close U.S.-European consultation and coordination on the full agenda of global and regional issues as well as relations with China and Russia. Consultations and collaboration can take place in NATO, in Brussels, or in capitals, with the emphasis determined by what venue is likely to yield the best results. History shows that the United States benefits from a close partnership with Europe; the real question is whether European governments will have the capacity and the focus to be meaningful partners.

12. A Country in Disarray

A large portion of the burden of creating and maintaining order at the regional or global level will fall on the United States. This is inevitable for several reasons, only one of which is that the United States is and will likely remain the most powerful country in the world for decades to come. The corollary to this point is that no other country or group of countries has either the capacity or the mind-set to build a global order. Nor can order ever be expected to emerge automatically; there is no invisible hand in the geopolitical marketplace. Again, a large part of the burden (or, more positively, opportunity) falls on the principal power of the day. There is more than a little self-interest at stake. The United States cannot remain aloof, much less unaffected by a world in disarray. Globalization is more reality than choice. At the regional level, the United States actually faces the opposite problem, namely, that certain actors do have the mind-set and means to shape an order. The problem is that their views of order are in part or in whole incompatible with U.S. interests. Examples would include Iran and ISIS in the Middle East, China in Asia, and Russia in Europe.

It will not be an easy time for the United States. The sheer number and range of challenges is daunting. There are a large number of actors and forces to contend with. Alliances, normally created in opposition to some country or countries, may not be as useful a vehicle in a world in which not all foes are always foes and not all friends are always friendly. Diplomacy will count for a great deal; there will be a premium on dexterity. Consultations that aim to affect the actions of other governments and their leaders are likely to matter more than negotiations that aim to solve problems.

Another reality is that the United States for all its power cannot impose order. Partially this reflects what might be called structural realities, namely, that no country can contend with global challenges on its own given the very nature of these challenges. The United States could reduce its carbon footprint dramatically, but the effect on global climate would be modest if India and China failed to follow suit. Similarly, on its own the United States cannot maintain a world trading system or successfully combat terrorism or disease. Adding to these realities are resource limits. The United States cannot provide all the troops or dollars to maintain order in the Middle East and Europe and Asia and South Asia. There is simply too much capability in too many hands. Unilateralism is rarely a serious foreign policy option. Part-

[handwritten margin note: because by nature they are created globally]

[handwritten note at bottom: doesn't work, US can't do it alone]

ners are essential. That is one of the reasons why sovereign obligation is a desirable compass for U.S. foreign policy. Earlier I made the case that it represents realism for an era of globalization. It also is a natural successor to containment, the doctrine that guided the United States for the four decades of the Cold War. There are basic differences, however. Containment was about holding back more than bringing in and was designed for an era when rivals were almost always adversaries and in which the challenges were mostly related to classical geopolitical competition.[1] Sovereign obligation, by contrast, is designed for a world in which sometime rivals are sometime partners and in which collective efforts are required to meet common challenges.

Up to this point, we have focused on what the United States needs to do in the world to promote order. That is what one would expect from a book about international relations and American foreign policy. But a focus on foreign policy is not enough. National security is a coin with two sides, and what the United States does at home, what is normally thought of as belonging to the domestic realm, is every bit as much a part of national security as foreign policy. It is best to understand the issue as guns *and* butter rather than guns *versus* butter.

When it comes to the domestic side, the argument is straightforward. In order to lead and compete and act effectively in the world, the United States needs to put its house in order. I have written on what this entails in a book titled

Foreign Policy Begins at Home.[2] This was sometimes interpreted as suggesting a turn away from foreign policy. It was nothing of the sort. Foreign policy begins at home, but it ends there only at the country's peril.[3]

Earlier I mentioned that the United States has few unilateral options, that there are few if any things it can do better alone than with others. The counterpart to this claim is that the world cannot come up with the elements of a working order absent the United States. The United States is not sufficient, but it is necessary. It is also true that the United States cannot lead or act effectively in the world if it does not have a strong domestic foundation. National security inevitably requires significant amounts of human, physical, and financial resources to draw on. The better the United States is doing economically, the more it will have available in the way of resources to devote to what it wants and needs to do abroad without igniting a divisive and distracting domestic debate as to priorities. An additional benefit is that respect for the United States and for the American political, social, and economic model (along with a desire to emulate it) will increase only if it is seen as successful.

The most basic test of the success of the model will be economic growth. U.S. growth levels may appear all right when compared with what a good many other countries are experiencing, but they are below what is needed and fall short of what is possible. There is no reason why the United States is not growing in the range of 3 percent or even higher other than what it is doing and, more important, not doing.[4]

Such optimism is well founded. The United States has any number of innate strengths and advantages, including a balanced demography that avoids the youth and age bulges that hold back so many societies; the best universities in the world; effective capital and stock markets; a legal system that encourages and protects invention and allows for orderly bankruptcy; a rich endowment in energy and minerals; climate and land that allow for ample food production; political stability; and excellent relations with its neighbors to the north and south.

What would it take to increase current U.S. rates of growth? There is no universally accepted answer to this question, but my list would include better education at every level from preschool through K-12 through all forms of postsecondary education and on to lifelong learning. To this I would add a robust infrastructure program, something that would provide jobs, increase U.S. competitiveness, and make the society more resilient in the face of natural disasters or terrorism. Immigration reform that created greater opportunity for those with advanced degrees and needed skills to come and stay would help; also helpful would be immigration reform that included a conditional path to legal status or citizenship for many of the twelve million or so people living in the country now without the necessary documentation. Tax reform that lowers corporate rates (among the world's highest) is desirable, as are other reforms that would lower individual rates, as well as reduce so-called tax expenditures, such as being able to deduct what is spent on mortgage interest and charitable donations or not being taxed on employer health care contributions.

All of which brings me to the debt problem. What makes this issue particularly difficult is that it is part of a class of what I would describe as slow-motion crises. Climate change is another. Slow-motion crises are just that: phenomena or processes that are under way and have potentially substantial or even devastating consequences that will kick in gradually or, even if suddenly at some point, only after the passage of considerable time. They are thus unlike an infectious disease outbreak or a financial collapse.[5]

There is both good and bad news in this. The good news is that to a large degree we know where things are heading. We also have time to do something about it. We can see the iceberg in our path, and there is ample time to turn the ship around. The bad news is that slow-motion crises generate little or no sense of priority but rather tend to promote complacency. The temptation is to put them aside, to focus on today's crisis, and to allow the urgent to take precedence over the important. The problem with this is that not only will we forfeit the opportunity to prevent a crisis from materializing, but we will also deny ourselves those remedies that are not severe. The medical equivalent would be to ignore the symptoms in a patient when the sickness was relatively easy to treat and to do something only when it became life-threatening.

The problem is fairly straightforward. According to *The 2016 Long-Term Budget Outlook* of the Congressional Budget Office and the CBO's January 2016 ten-year *Budget and Economic Outlook: 2016 to 2026*, the public debt of the United States is fast approaching $14 trillion.[6] It now is equal to roughly 75 percent of GDP and in a decade will rise to between 80 and 90 percent of GDP. Depending upon spending and revenue assumptions, it is a question of when and not if the amount of debt comes to exceed or far exceed GDP. This could well happen by 2030. The cost of servicing the debt will begin to rise rapidly, consuming an ever-larger percentage of GDP and federal spending.

Some contend that this analysis of U.S. debt is too negative.[7] They tend to predict higher revenues, continued low interest rates, and larger than expected cost savings in the medical domain. Such a future is of course possible, but so too is a worse than expected future based on slower growth, higher rates, higher than expected medical costs owing to a larger aging population, and much higher than imagined costs associated with adapting to the many effects of climate change.

The causes of the debt problem are somewhat more controversial but still fairly straightforward. Although the federal deficit is considerably lower than it was five years ago, it is once again increasing, due to greatly increased spending (in particular on entitlements) and low rates of economic growth. Some would say that taxes, or rather the lack of them, are to blame as well, but U.S. corporate rates are high by global standards and individual rates are not conspicuously low.

All things being equal, the problem will not only not fix itself but will grow worse. There are two reasons. First, the principal driver of spending increases, spending on entitlements such as Medicare, Medicaid, and Social Security, will likely become more and not less of a factor as Americans retire in large numbers and live longer lives. Second, interest rates are near historic lows and are far more likely to rise than fall over future decades. Specific projections as to the size of the debt and what it will cost to finance necessarily vary depending on assumptions regarding economic growth, spending, taxation, inflation, and interest rates, but the trend is clear, and the trend is not our friend. Nor is time.

The strategic consequences of growing indebtedness are many and worrisome. The need to finance the debt will absorb an ever-increasing number of dollars and an ever-increasing share of the U.S. budget. This will mean that proportionately fewer resources will be available for national security, including defense, intelligence, homeland security, and foreign assistance. There will as well be fewer dollars available for discretionary domestic programs ranging from education and infrastructure modernization to scientific research and law enforcement. What this portends is an in-creasingly sharp and destructive debate over guns versus butter while the two fastest-growing parts of the budget, debt service and entitlements, remain largely off-limits.

Mounting debt will raise questions around the world about the United States. U.S. inability to deal with its debt challenge will detract from the appeal of the American po-litical and economic model. It will make others less likely to want to emulate the United States and more wary of depend-ing on it as it will raise questions about this country's ability to come together and take difficult decisions. The result will be a world less democratic and increasingly less deferential to U.S. concerns in matters of security. To some extent this is already happening; U.S. failure to deal with its debt promises to accelerate a worrisome evolution.

Mounting debt will leave the United States more vulner-able than it should be to the whims of markets and the mach-inations of governments. Already nearly half of U.S. public debt is held by foreigners, with China one of the two largest lenders. It is of course possible that China will be constrained by its stake in not seeing its own huge pool of dollars lose its value and by its need for the United States to continue to buy its exports. The result, according to this line of thinking, is the financial equivalent of nuclear deterrence. This may be true, but I for one am not sanguine that China would not decide to slow or stop accumulating U.S. debt as a signal of displeasure or even to sell debt amid, say, a crisis over Taiwan or one involving its claims in the South or East China seas. In such circumstances, Chinese leaders might well judge it to be worth paying a financial price to protect what they viewed as their vital national interests. Interestingly, it was American threats aimed at the pound sterling that more than anything else persuaded a British government that was fearful of the need to devalue its currency to back off its ill-fated venture to regain control of the Suez Canal in 1956.

Mounting debt could absorb funds that could otherwise be usefully invested at home or abroad. This will in turn depress already modest levels of economic growth. Making matters worse is that high levels of debt and debt financing will increase concerns about the government's willingness to maintain the dollar's value or, worse yet, meet its obligations. This will cause foreigners in particular to demand high returns on their loans, something that will increase the cost of debt financing and further crowd out other spending and depress growth. This is a vicious, not a virtuous, cycle.

Mounting debt limits American flexibility and resilience. There is no way of stating in the abstract what constitutes the right level of debt for the country or knowing with precision what level is sustainable. But the United States does not want to make high levels of debt the new normal, if only because it removes flexibility if, for example, there were to be another financial crisis that required large-scale fiscal stimulus or a major national security challenge that demanded a costly response. Keeping debt levels low enough to allow for a surge without triggering a debt crisis seems to be a prudent hedge and, as is the case with preventive medicine or insurance, worth paying a reasonable premium for.

Let me just add one more prediction. Mounting debt will hasten the demise of the dollar as the world's reserve currency. This will happen due to loss of confidence in U.S. financial management and the related concern that what the United States will need to do to finance its debt will be at odds with what it should be doing to manage the domestic and, indirectly, world economy. It is possible that such a move away from the dollar would have happened were it not for the EU's problems and China not being prepared to free up the yuan. Granted, there is no alternative to the dollar on the immediate horizon, but the United States cannot depend forever on the weaknesses and errors of others, and a postdollar world will be both more costly (as it will require the United States to move in and out of other currencies) and one of less leverage when it comes to imposing dollar-related sanctions.[8]

What needs doing? Given that a big driver of the debt will be the cost of entitlements, it makes a lot of sense to raise the current and projected retirement age so that Social Security better reflects economic and demographic realities. It would also make sense to subject Social Security to a means test and reduce payments to the relatively wealthy for whom by definition such payments are not essential, to make moderate cost-of-living adjustments, and to reform the fast-growing disability program.

Medicare and Medicaid are even more responsible for the entitlement burden. Some changes that could help here include accelerating the move away from a system based on fee for service and toward one that reflects quality of outcomes, increasing copayments, limiting malpractice torts, and introducing some means testing of benefits.

Congress should avoid false "solutions." The sequester is one of them. It ignores entitlements and favors spending over investment and the present over the future. It should be jettisoned once and for all. The same holds for threats not to raise the debt ceiling. As every member of Congress knows or should know, failure to raise the debt ceiling does nothing to limit debt already incurred but does raise major doubts in markets and around the world as to whether the United States is reliable and serious. Ironically, failure to raise the debt ceiling would trigger reactions that would lead to an increase in rates, something that in turn would slow growth and exacerbate the debt burden.

Congress needs to be similarly careful about defense spending. Current and projected defense spending is around 3 percent of GDP, far below historic averages for the past seventy years. What is more, it is an increasingly dangerous and precarious world, and if the world becomes messier, there is no way the United States will be able to wall itself off from consequences partly brought about by its doing less. Isolationism will once again prove to be folly. There is no other country willing and able to make a sizable contribution to order, and the world cannot order itself. Only the United States can play this role. This will require a military that possesses a range of capabilities, considerable flexibility, and an ability to surge. It must be able to handle contingencies and conflicts of different type, scale, and duration in different places (possibly simultaneously) and against foes ranging from dangerous terrorist organizations to powerful nation-states. More, not less, defense spending is required, especially if Congress continues to insist on keeping select bases and assembly lines open for reasons that have more to do with politics than national security. The good news is that the country can do more in the defense realm and tackle the debt challenge at one and the same time if it is willing to make some choices and spend its resources wisely. The argument that what the country is doing abroad explains the slow growth at home is simply untrue.

Several pages back I noted what I thought could be done to raise rates of economic growth. I purposefully left one item off that list that I want to raise here. It is free trade. Trade pacts do many positive things, including create relatively high-paying export-oriented jobs, increase consumer choice, lower inflation, promote economic development around the world, bolster friends and allies, and create ties of interdependence that can constrain would-be foes. And, as noted, trade pacts contribute (however modestly) to economic growth; the consensus seems to be that once it went into effect, the Trans-Pacific Partnership would add up to half a percent a year to U.S. growth.[9]

Trade pacts and trade more generally can also cause specific jobs to disappear. The smart response is not to deny Americans the strategic and economic benefits of trade but to help those whose jobs have disappeared. Several things can and should be done, including adopting a more aggressive posture in the WTO toward foreign governments that unfairly subsidize industries or "dump" products abroad, increasing the availability of wage insurance, making sure that critical benefits are more portable and extended for longer periods, and increasing opportunities and financial support for education and retraining.

Technological innovation is an even bigger culprit when it comes to job disappearance.[10] The future promises more of the same, as such innovations as artificial intelligence, robotics, and 3-D printing add to productivity but eliminate some existing jobs, even if they also create new ones. Again, it will be essential to help citizens deal with the inevitable turbulence through various forms of assistance and a mix of education and retraining.[11]

Education is a recurring theme when it comes to what the United States must focus on to put its domestic house in order. It is critical for economic growth, for assisting those workers hurt by trade and technological changes, and for attacking inequality. Much is being said and written about the danger of inequality. Yes, inequality is growing, but the real problem is not that a few are extraordinarily wealthy, but that many are poor and not seeing their living standards or prospects improve. The policy prescription is not to try to reduce inequality per se through massive subsidies and new taxes intended to redistribute wealth. This will surely fail, and any transfer of wealth will not increase the capacity of recipients to be productive but will decrease the productivity of those who are. Rather, the aim must be to make upward mobility a reality. This will come about only if there is more access to quality education, not just for young people but for all citizens as they go through their lives. The alternative, a country increasingly defined by class, would lead to lower economic growth and higher social friction, in turn producing more populism in American politics and less support for the sort of foreign policy that is required if this era is to be one of more stability than not.

Education also merits mention in another sense. This book has argued that the world matters to Americans and the United States, and that what the United States chooses to do (and not to do) in the world matters in return. Understanding these realities and judging the policies being put forward requires a citizenry that is globally literate and that appreciates the potential benefits of global involvement and the potential risks that come from globalization as well as from either too much or too little involvement in the world—or, more accurately, from too much of the wrong kind of involvement and too little of the right kind. Including global civics as a matter of course in high school and college, offerings that made clear why the world matters and the choices that face the United States, would be a good investment in the country's future.

I want to make one last point in this context. What becomes all too apparent is that prospects for doing most of what needs doing at home in the economic and other spheres is determined not so much by economics as by politics. And the result of developments in recent decades has been to make politics more difficult. The extremes are gaining at the expense of the center. Compromise has become something of a dirty word in many quarters.

What explains this shift? The weakening of political parties is one explanation, as politicians can appeal directly to the most motivated and often most ideological sources of support. Increasingly, individual politicians are becoming what amounts to their own political parties, with direct access to voters, money, and media. Coalitions are fleeting; as one astute political observer wrote, "Washington doesn't have a crisis of leadership; it has a crisis of followership."[12] Primaries whose outcome similarly depends on a narrow base of party members are another factor. The proliferation of cable and satellite channels, radio stations, and Internet sites has brought about an era of narrowcasting that has largely superseded broadcasting that by definition needed to appeal to a wider audience. Organized special interests that act with great intensity on behalf of a narrow cause can bring great pressure to bear on candidates or incumbents who fail to toe a line that rejects any real compromise.[13]

Any number of procedural reforms could improve things, including taking the drawing of congressional districts out of the hands of state legislatures, opening up primaries to all voters and not just party members, and moving away from winner-take-all outcomes both in primaries and in the selection of delegates that each state sends to the electoral college. Constraints on political spending could have a positive effect but are highly unlikely to come about in the current political and legal environment.[14]

Procedural reforms that affect governing are also called for. In the Senate, the goal should be to make it harder for senators to place holds and carry out filibusters, and to reduce the need for supermajorities. As for the House of Representatives, it would help to jettison the so-called Hastert Rule, which requires that a majority of the majority party favor a bill before it can be brought up for a vote. Getting such a majority can be difficult given that both political parties are getting more, not less, partisan and ideological; in addition, this requirement stands in the way of passing legislation that could muster a coalition constituting an overall majority of members of the House even if the bill could not attract a majority within either party. Almost by definition, compromise legislation would fall in this category.

The consequences are worrisome, as continued or even worse political dysfunction is the most likely result. We have seen all too many examples of just this in recent years: difficult but important issues not tackled, a reduction in legislative output, threats to close down government and default on debt, personnel actions delayed, international agreements left unapproved. The result is a United States that is less able to act in its own self-interest and less certain to act consistently at home or abroad.

Not all reforms are desirable. Here the British decision to decide a profoundly important policy, namely, the country's relationship with Europe, by a popular referendum is instructive. It is for good reason that the founders of the American political system created a representative government and made it difficult to amend the Constitution. Direct democracy can all too easily be dominated by the passions of the moment and false representations without regard to enduring interests and relevant facts. And if for some reason referenda cannot be avoided, they should be advisory, require a supermajority, or both.

Bringing about real reform would require a sustained demonstration of leadership, beginning with the president. It would require both an inside game, in which the president would work closely with politicians from both parties in both the Senate and the House, and an outside game, in which the president would meet with representatives of various constituencies and interest groups. Also required would be for the occupant of the Oval Office to speak frequently and honestly to the American people, to level with them about the realities of living in a global world and what can and must be done to make Americans competitive and secure. If there is a model that comes to mind here, it is FDR's "fireside chats" of the late 1930s and early 1940s, which were designed to explain the deteriorating international situation, ready the American people for joining the Second World War on the side of the Western democracies, and then help them endure the war and prepare for its aftermath.

Absent such a sustained effort, and possibly even with one, the sort of political dysfunction that has characterized so much of American politics of late is likely to continue or grow worse. This would come at a considerable price. The United States has to be wary of sudden or sharp departures in what it does in the world. Consistency and reliability are essential attributes for a great power. Friends and allies who depend on the United States for their security need to know that this dependence is well placed. If America comes to be doubted, it will inevitably give rise to a very different and much less orderly world. One would see two reactions: either a world of increased "self-help," in which countries take matters into their own hands in ways that could work against U.S. objectives, or a world in which countries fall under the sway of more powerful local states, in the process undermining the balance of power. This is a prescription for greater instability at the regional level, less concerted action at the global level, and heightened chance for great-power competition.

"Stare decisis" is a legal concept in which judges and courts emphasize precedent and allow existing decisions to stand unless there is strong reason to overturn them. Such a bias is meant to discourage individual courts from "doing their own thing," which could create a dysfunctional patchwork quilt of rulings. More generally, the notion reflects an understanding that the integrity, reputation, and legitimacy of the legal system would suffer were the law to shift with any frequency.

There is much to be said for a foreign policy equivalent of stare decisis. To say so is not to argue against all change, as all policies should be reviewed regularly and revised if there is reason to do so, as much of this book has argued. But wholesale, frequent reversals run the risk of unnerving friends and emboldening adversaries. Disarray at home is thus inextricably linked to disarray in the world. The two together are nothing short of toxic.

There is a school of thought that argues that crisis is the necessary midwife of reform. This school holds that absent crisis, decision makers will be unwilling or unable to do things differently. The problem with such thinking is that history suggests that crises do not automatically generate the impetus for necessary change on the scale that is required.

There is as well the problem that crisis by definition can be extremely costly. Conflict between two or more powers, a nuclear event brought about by a state or terrorists, significant climate change, a global pandemic, the collapse of the world trade system—it would be hard to exaggerate the costs if any of these were to happen.

Surely a better way would be to start moving toward an international order without waiting for a crisis. The case and the potential for doing so could hardly be more compelling.

Acknowledgments

Every book is to one degree or another a collaborative effort, and *A World in Disarray* is no exception. There are many people I want and need to thank for what they did to help bring it about.

As noted in the introduction, the book had its origins in a phone call from Richard Dearlove (then the master of Pembroke College) and in the lectures I subsequently gave at Cambridge University in the spring of 2015. Not only did I enjoy the beauty of Cambridge at that time of year and relish the chance to attend evensong at various colleges, but preparing the lectures and learning from the feedback set me on a path that ultimately led to this book. It is not easy for an Oxford man to go on the record praising Cambridge, but I want to do just that.

I want to give a special shout-out to my editor, Scott Moyers, of Penguin Press. This is the first time Scott and I have worked together, and the good news, for me at least, is that it will not be the last. He was a real partner, be it in e-mails, in conversation, and in comments about drafts. He was supportive and smart every step of the way.

Others at Penguin Press also helped a great deal. I especially want to acknowledge associate editor Christopher Richards, production editor Bruce Giffords, copy editor Roland Ottewell, indexer Do Mi Stauber, Oliver Munday for the cover design, and Gretchen Achilles for the interior design.

Also deserving of thanks is my agent, Andrew Wylie. He believed in me and this project from the outset.

Big thanks go as well to Polly Colgan, my hardworking and talented research associate here at the Council on Foreign Relations. Polly found much of the background material, prepared the endnotes, and read and reread the manuscript, offering suggestions along with checking facts and quotes.

I benefited tremendously from the reactions and suggestions of friends good enough to take the time to read an early draft. "Friend" is the operative word, because only a true friend would be prepared to devote the time and effort to reading a manuscript and commenting on it. Roger Altman, Roger Hertog, Zach Karabell, and Richard Plepler did just that, and I am in their debt.

Several of my colleagues—Jim Lindsay, Meghan O'Sullivan, and Gideon Rose—also were good enough to give me detailed and what turned out to be extremely useful feedback. The final product is considerably better (not to be confused with good) for all their reactions and suggestions.

And last but hardly least, I want to thank my wife, Susan Mercandetti, an experienced and hugely talented book editor, for giving me her take on the manuscript. I have been known to point out that husbands incline toward the position that there can be such a thing as too much constructive criticism, but here it was welcome and invaluable.

Several people labored hard to increase the odds that the book would get some notice. At CFR I want to single out Irina Faskianos, Melissa Guinan, Samantha Tartas, and Iva Zoric. At Penguin

Press, Sarah Hutson and Brooke Parsons took the lead on publicity, while Matt Boyd, Grace Fisher, and Caitlin O'Shaughnessy shepherded marketing. It is no fun to produce the proverbial tree that falls without notice, and the efforts of one and all are appreciated.

I want to say something about the five men to whom this book is dedicated. Two were professors of mine at Oberlin College. Robert Tufts provided my first classroom experience with foreign policy, and Tom Frank, my introduction to religion in the academic sense, which then took me to Israel and started a lifelong interest in the Middle East. The other three individuals were all tutors of mine at Oxford University. Albert Hourani deepened my interest in (and extended my knowledge of) Middle Eastern history, while both Alastair Buchan and Michael Howard introduced me to and then helped guide me through the arcane world of strategic studies, adding rigor to my thinking and some style to my prose along the way. Anyone who knew one of these men, much less all five, will immediately grasp just how fortunate I was.

I wrote much of this book at my desk—I should say my standing desk, a first for me—in my office at the Council on Foreign Relations, where I am in my fourteenth year as president. CFR is dedicated to being a resource for its members, government officials, business executives, journalists, educators and students, civic and religious leaders, and other citizens to help them better understand the world and the foreign policy choices facing the United States and other countries. I never anticipated being here this long, and it has been one of the great experiences of my life.

I did the bulk of the writing early in the morning and on weekends. My immediate staff—Kathleen McNally, Jeff Reinke, Natasha Gabby, as well as Polly Colgan and Melissa Guinan—did all they could to protect these hours and to make sure I made the most of the remaining ones. I want to underscore, though, that the result is entirely mine, in particular when it comes to the book's flaws and shortcomings. I also want to make clear that I do not speak for CFR, an extraordinary institution that takes no positions on matters of policy and that remains independent and nonpartisan to its core.

Notes

INTRODUCTION

1. Richard N. Haass, *War of Necessity, War of Choice: A Memoir of Two Iraq Wars* (New York: Simon & Schuster, 2009).
2. George H. W. Bush, "Address Before a Joint Session of Congress on the Persian Gulf Crisis and the Federal Budget Deficit," Washington, DC, September 11, 1990, George Bush Presidential Library and Museum, https://bush41library.tamu.edu/archives/public-papers/2217.
3. See, for example, Steven Pinker, *The Better Angels of Our Nature: Why Violence Has Declined* (New York: Penguin, 2011); G. John Ikenberry, "The Myth of Post–Cold War Chaos," *Foreign Affairs* 75, no. 3 (May/June 1996), www.foreignaffairs.com/articles/1996-05-01/myth-post-cold-war-chaos; James Dobbins, "Reports of Global Disorder Have Been Greatly Exaggerated," *Foreign Policy*, July 22, 2015, http://foreignpolicy.com/2015/07/22/reports-of-our-global-disorder-have-been-greatly-exaggerated-russia-china-us-leadership/; Michael A. Cohen, "Despite Bloody 2015, the World Really Is Safer Than Ever," *World Politics Review*, December 23, 2015, www.worldpoliticsreview.com/articles/17537/despite-bloody-2015-the-world-really-is-safer-than-ever; and Christopher A. Preble and John Mueller, eds., *A Dangerous World? Threat Perception and U.S. National Security* (Washington, DC: Cato Institute, 2014).
4. Chairman of the Joint Chiefs of Staff, *The National Military Strategy of the United States 2015*, June 2015, i, www.jcs.mil/Portals/36/Documents/Publications/2015_National_Military_Strategy.pdf.
5. *Worldwide Threat Assessment of the US Intelligence Community: Hearing Before the Senate Armed Services Committee*, statement of James R. Clapper, Director of National Intelligence, 114th Congress, February 9, 2016, www.armed-services.senate.gov/imo/media/doc/Clapper_02-09-16.pdf.

6. Henry A. Kissinger, "Kissinger's Vision for U.S.-Russia Relations," *National Interest,* February 4, 2016, http://nationalinterest.org/feature /kissingers-vision-us-russia-relations-15111.
7. Tony Barber, "This Verdict Is a Grievous Blow to the World Order," *Financial Times,* June 25–26, 2016.

1. FROM WAR THROUGH WORLD WAR

1. Henry A. Kissinger, *World Order* (New York: Penguin, 2014).
2. Hedley Bull, *The Anarchical Society: A Study of Order in World Politics* (New York: Columbia University Press, 1977).
3. Henry A. Kissinger, *A World Restored: Metternich, Castlereagh and the Problems of Peace, 1812–1822* (London: Weidenfeld & Nicholson, 1957; New York: Universal Library, 1964). Citations refer to the Universal Library edition.
4. Ibid., 1.
5. Ibid., 318.
6. Peter Wilson, *The Thirty Years War: Europe's Tragedy* (Cambridge, MA: Harvard University Press, 2011), 753–54.
7. For background, see Kissinger, *A World Restored,* as well as Harold Nicolson, *The Congress of Vienna: A Study in Allied Unity: 1812–1822* (New York: Harcourt Brace Jovanovich, 1946).
8. For background, see René Albrecht-Carrié, ed., *The Concert of Europe, 1815–1914* (New York: HarperCollins, 1968); and A. J. P. Taylor, *The Struggle for the Mastery of Europe, 1848–1918* (New York: Oxford University Press, 1971).
9. Mark Mazower, *Governing the World: The History of an Idea, 1815 to the Present* (New York: Penguin, 2013), 5.
10. On Bismarck, see Jonathan Steinberg, *Bismarck: A Life* (New York: Oxford University Press, 2011). Also see Henry A. Kissinger, "The White Revolutionary: Reflections on Bismarck," *Daedalus* 97, no. 3 (Summer 1968): 888–924, www.jstor.org/stable/20023844.
11. For a sampling of the enormous literature on the origins of World War I, see Christopher Clark, *The Sleepwalkers: How Europe Went to War in 1914* (New York: HarperCollins, 2012); Margaret MacMillan, *The War That Ended Peace: The Road to 1914* (New York: Random House, 2013); and Barbara Tuchman, *The Guns of August* (New York: Random House, 1962).
12. For the conceptual background, see Robert O. Keohane and Joseph S. Nye, *Power and Interdependence,* 2nd ed. (Glenview, IL: Scott, Foresman, 1989). As for the argument made in the late nineteenth century that commerce would help prevent war, see Richard Cobden, *The Political Writings of Richard Cobden,* vol. 1 (New York: Cambridge University Press, 2011).
13. See Michael Walzer, *Just and Unjust Wars: A Moral Argument with Historical Illustrations,* 3rd ed. (New York: Basic Books, 2000).

14. John Maynard Keynes, *The Economic Consequences of the Peace* (New York: Harcourt, Brace & Howe, 1920).

15. "Treaty Between the United States and Other Powers Providing for the Renunciation of War as an Instrument of National Policy," August 27, 1928, Avalon Project, Yale University, http://avalon.law.yale.edu /20th_century/kbpact.asp.

2. COLD WAR

1. Three books I would suggest are John Lewis Gaddis, *The United States and the Origins of the Cold War, 1941–1947* (New York: Columbia University Press, 1972); Daniel Yergin, *Shattered Peace: The Origins of the Cold War*, rev. ed. (New York: Penguin, 1990); and Martin McCauley, *Origins of the Cold War, 1941–1949*, rev. 3rd ed. (New York: Routledge, 2013).

2. There are fewer books on the Korean War than are warranted; not for nothing is it often referred to as "the forgotten war." One history I would suggest is David Halberstam, *The Coldest Winter: America and the Korean War* (New York: Hyperion, 2007). Also worth reading on the impact of the Korean War on the subsequent conduct of the Cold War is John Lewis Gaddis, "Was the Truman Doctrine a Real Turning Point?," *Foreign Affairs* 52, no. 1 (January 1974), www.foreignaffairs.com/articles/russian -federation/1974-01-01/reconsiderations-cold-war-was-truman-doctrine -real-turning.

3. Albert Carnesale and Richard N. Haass, eds., *Superpower Arms Control: Setting the Record Straight* (Cambridge, MA: Ballinger, 1987).

4. "Treaty Between the United States of America and the Union of Soviet Socialist Republics on the Limitation of Anti–Ballistic Missile Systems," May 26, 1972, U.S. Department of State, www.state.gov/www/global/arms /treaties/abm/abm2.html.

5. X [George F. Kennan], "The Sources of Soviet Conduct," *Foreign Affairs* 25, no. 4 (July 1947), www.foreignaffairs.com/articles/russian -federation/1947-07-01/sources-soviet-conduct.

6. "Text of the 'Basic Principles of Relations Between the United States of America and the Union of Soviet Socialist Republics,'" May 29, 1972, American Presidency Project, www.presidency.ucsb.edu/ws/?pid=3438. Also see Henry A. Kissinger, *White House Years* (Boston: Little, Brown, 1979).

7. "Conference on Security and Co-operation in Europe Final Act," August 1, 1975, OSCE, www.osce.org/mc/39501?download=true.

8. Paul Kennedy, *The Rise and Fall of the Great Powers* (New York: Random House, 1987).

9. X [Kennan], "The Sources of Soviet Conduct."

10. See Jon Meacham, *Destiny and Power: The American Odyssey of George Herbert Walker Bush* (New York: Random House, 2015); George H. W.

Bush and Brent Scowcroft, *A World Transformed* (New York: Knopf, 1998); and James A. Baker III with Thomas M. DeFrank, *The Politics of Diplomacy: Revolution, War and Peace, 1989–1992* (New York: Putnam, 1995).

3. THE OTHER ORDER

1. G. John Ikenberry, *Liberal Leviathan: The Origins, Crisis, and Transformation of the American World Order* (Princeton, NJ: Princeton University Press, 2011).
2. See Benn Steil, *The Battle of Bretton Woods: John Maynard Keynes, Harry Dexter White, and the Making of a New World Order* (Princeton, NJ: Princeton University Press, 2013); Harold James, *International Monetary Cooperation Since Bretton Woods* (New York: Oxford University Press, 1996); and Barry Eichengreen, *Globalizing Capital: A History of the International Monetary System*, 2nd ed. (Princeton, NJ: Princeton University Press, 2008).
3. "Charter of the United Nations," June 26, 1945, Chapter VI, Article 33, and Chapter VII, Article 42, www.un.org/en/charter-united-nations /index.html.
4. "Treaty on the Non-Proliferation of Nuclear Weapons," July 1, 1968, U.S. Department of State, www.state.gov/www/global/arms/treaties /npt1.html#2.
5. "Convention on the Prohibition of the Development, Production and Stockpiling of Bacteriological (Biological) and Toxin Weapons and on Their Destruction (BWC)," April 10, 1972, U.S. Department of State, www.state.gov/t/isn/4718.htm#treaty.
6. "Convention on the Prohibition of the Development, Production, Stockpiling and Use of Chemical Weapons and on Their Destruction (CWC)," January 13, 1993, U.S. Department of State, www.state.gov/t/avc /trty/127917.htm.
7. Albert Hourani, "A Moment of Change: The Crisis of 1956," in *A Vision of History: Near Eastern and Other Essays* (Beirut: Khayats, 1961).
8. "Universal Declaration of Human Rights," UN General Assembly, Resolution 217A(III), December 10, 1948, www.un-documents.net /a3r217a.htm.
9. Convention on the Prevention and Punishment of the Crime of Genocide, December 9, 1948, United Nations, https://treaties.un.org/doc /Publication/UNTS/Volume%2078/volume-78-I-1021-English.pdf; Rome Statute of the International Criminal Court, July 17, 1998, International Criminal Court, www.icc-cpi.int/nr/rdonlyres/ea9aeff7-5752-4f84-be94 -0a655eb30e16/0/rome_statute_english.pdf.
10. For data on the world economy, see Angus Maddison's "Historical Statistics of the World Economy: 1–2008 AD," www.ggdc.net/maddison /Historical_Statistics/horizontal-file_02-2010.xls. For data on world trade

volume, see UN Conference on Trade and Development STAT (UNCTADSTAT), http://unctadstat.unctad.org/wds/ReportFolders /reportFolders.aspx. Extreme poverty is calculated as those living on less than $1.25/day. For data on poverty levels, see François Bourguignon and Christian Morrisson, "Inequality Among World Citizens: 1820–1992," *American Economic Review* 92, no. 4. (2002): 732, www.jstor.org /stable/3083279.

11. See John F. Kennedy, "Commencement Address at American University," Washington, DC, June 10, 1963, John F. Kennedy Presidential Library and Museum, www.jfklibrary.org/Asset-Viewer /BWC7I4C9QUmLG9J6I8oy8w.aspx; and John F. Kennedy, "Address to the Nation on the Nuclear Test Ban Treaty," Washington, DC, July 26, 1963, John F. Kennedy Presidential Library and Museum, www.jfklibrary.org/Asset-Viewer/ZNOo49DpRUa-kMetjWmSyg.aspx.

4. THE POST–COLD WAR WORLD

1. See Graham Allison, "The Thucydides Trap: Are America and China Headed for War?," *Atlantic*, September 24, 2015, www.theatlantic.com /international/archive/2015/09/united-states-china-war-thucydides -trap/406756/; and Richard N. Rosecrance and Steven E. Miller, eds., *The Next Great War?: The Roots of World War I and the Risk of U.S.-China Conflict* (Cambridge, MA: MIT Press, 2014). For a relatively sanguine perspective, see Stephen G. Brooks and William C. Wohlforth, "The Rise and Fall of the Great Powers in the Twenty-first Century: China's Rise and the Fate of America's Global Position," *International Security* 40, no. 3 (Winter 2015/16): 7–53. More pessimistic are John J. Mearsheimer, *The Tragedy of Great Power Politics* (New York: Norton, 2001); and especially Michael Pillsbury, *The Hundred-Year Marathon: China's Secret Strategy to Replace America as the Global Superpower* (New York: Henry Holt, 2015).

2. Wayne M. Morrison, *China-U.S. Trade Issues*, Congressional Research Service Report No. RL33536 (Washington, DC: Congressional Research Service, 2015), 3, www.fas.org/sgp/crs/row/RL33536.pdf.

3. See Bush and Scowcroft, *A World Transformed*, chapter 4, and Baker, *The Politics of Diplomacy*, chapter 7.

4. "Joint Statement Following Discussions with Leaders of the People's Republic of China," February 27, 1972, U.S. Department of State, Office of the Historian, https://history.state.gov/historicaldocuments/frus1969 -76v17/d203.

5. "Joint Communiqué on the Establishment of Diplomatic Relations Between the People's Republic of China and the United States of America," December 16, 1978, Embassy of the People's Republic of China in the U.S., www.china-embassy.org/eng/zmgx/doc/ctc/t36256.htm; "Joint Communiqué of the People's Republic of China and the United States of

America," August 17, 1982, Embassy of the People's Republic of China in the U.S., www.china-embassy.org/eng/zmgx/doc/ctc/t946664.htm.

6.   Taiwan Relations Act, Public Law 96-8, April 10, 1979, www.gpo.gov /fdsys/pkg/STATUTE-93/pdf/STATUTE-93-Pg14.pdf.

7.   See, for example, Robert D. Blackwill and Kurt M. Campbell, *Xi Jinping on the Global Stage: Chinese Foreign Policy Under a Powerful but Exposed Leader*, Council on Foreign Relations Special Report No. 74 (New York: Council on Foreign Relations Press, 2016).

8.   Fu Ying and Wu Shicun, "South China Sea: How We Got to This Stage," *National Interest*, May 9, 2016, http://nationalinterest.org/feature/south -china-sea-how-we-got-stage-16118.

9.   Basic information about the Asian Infrastructure Investment Bank can be found at its Web site, www.aiib.org.

10. See Xi Jinping, *The Governance of China* (Beijing: Foreign Languages Press, 2014), 306–8; and Fu Ying, "The US World Order Is a Suit That No Longer Fits," *Financial Times*, January 6, 2016, www.ft.com/intl /cms/s/0/c09cbcb6-b3cb-11e5-b147-e5e5bba42e51.html.

11. One advocate for generous U.S. support for Russia at this time was former president Richard Nixon. See Richard Nixon, "Yeltsin Needs Us. We Need Yeltsin," *New York Times*, June 12, 1992, www.nytimes .com/1992/06/12/opinion/yeltsin-needs-us-we-need-yeltsin.html.

12. See Josef Joffe, "Is There Life After Victory? What NATO Can and Cannot Do," *National Interest*, Fall 1995, http://nationalinterest.org /article/is-there-life-after-victory-what-nato-can-and-cannot-do-827.

13. Mary Elise Sarotte, *1989: The Struggle to Create Post–Cold War Europe* (Princeton, NJ: Princeton University Press, 2009); Mary Elise Sarotte, "A Broken Promise?: What the West Really Told Moscow About NATO Expansion," *Foreign Affairs* 93, no. 5 (September/October 2014), www.foreignaffairs.com/articles/russia-fsu/2014-08-11/broken-promise; and Joshua R. Itzkowitz Shifrinson, "Deal or No Deal?: The End of the Cold War and the U.S. Offer to Limit NATO Expansion," *International Security* 40, no. 4 (Spring 2016): 7–44. For an official account, see Baker, *The Politics of Diplomacy*, especially chapter 14.

14. NATO enlargement triggered an intense, sustained debate in the foreign policy community. For background to the decision and the debate, see James Goldgeier, *Not Whether but When: The U.S. Decision to Enlarge NATO* (Washington, DC: Brookings Institution Press, 1999). Also see G. John Ikenberry, *After Victory: Institutions, Strategic Restraint, and the Rebuilding of Order After Major Wars* (Princeton, NJ: Princeton University Press, 2001), especially 235–39; Ronald D. Asmus, *Opening NATO's Door: How the Alliance Remade Itself for a New Era* (New York: Columbia University Press, 2002); and Eugene Rumer, "NATO Expansion: Strategic Genius or Historic Mistake?," *National Interest*, August 21, 2014, http://nationalinterest.org/feature/nato-expansion-strategic-genius-or -historic-mistake-11114.

15. See Charles King, "The Five-Day War: Managing Moscow After the Georgia Crisis," *Foreign Affairs* 87, no. 6 (November/December 2008), www.foreignaffairs.com/articles/russia-fsu/2008-11-01/five-day-war.

16. "Vladimir Putin Submitted Appeal to the Federation Council," March 1, 2014, President of Russia, http://en.kremlin.ru/events/president /news/20353; "Telephone Conversation with U.S. President Barack Obama," March 2, 2014, President of Russia, http://en.kremlin.ru/events /president/news/20355.

17. "Package of Measures for the Implementation of the Minsk Agreements," February 12, 2015, United Nations, http://peacemaker.un.org/sites /peacemaker.un.org/files/UA_150212_MinskAgreement_en.pdf.

18. For a good overview of Russian foreign policy and the deterioration in U.S.-Russian relations, see Jeffrey Mankoff, *Russian Foreign Policy: The Return of Great Power Politics*, 2nd ed. (Lanham, MD: Rowman & Littlefield, 2012). For a minority view that places the onus for deterioration on the United States, see Stephen F. Cohen, *Failed Crusade: America and the Tragedy of Post-Communist Russia* (New York: Norton, 2000).

19. Dmitry Medvedev, "Dmitry Medvedev's Speech at the Panel Discussion," Munich Security Conference, February 13, 2016, Russian Government, http://government.ru/en/news/21784/.

5. A GLOBAL GAP

1. For all of the UN Security Council resolutions dealing with the Gulf War, beginning with Resolution 660, see www.un.org/Docs/scres/1990/scres90 .htm and www.un.org/Docs/scres/1991/scres91.htm.

2. See Laura Silber and Allan Little, *Yugoslavia: Death of a Nation* (New York: Penguin, 1997); Tim Judah, *Kosovo: War of Revenge* (New Haven, CT: Yale University Press, 2002); Ivo H. Daalder and Michael O'Hanlon, *Winning Ugly: NATO's War to Save Kosovo* (Washington, DC: Brookings Institution Press, 2000); and Richard Holbrooke, *To End a War* (New York: Modern Library, 1998).

3. Michael Mandelbaum, "Foreign Policy as Social Work," *Foreign Affairs* 75, no. 1 (January/February 1996), www.foreignaffairs.com/articles /haiti/1996-01-01/foreign-policy-social-work.

4. Haass, *War of Necessity, War of Choice*, 134–44.

5. Richard N. Haass, *Intervention: The Use of American Military Force in the Post–Cold War World*, rev. ed. (Washington, DC: Brookings Institution Press, 1999): 47–48, 120–21.

6. See Samantha Power, *A Problem from Hell: America and the Age of Genocide* (New York: Basic Books, 2002); Roméo Dallaire, *Shake Hands with the Devil: The Failure of Humanity in Rwanda* (Boston: Da Capo, 2004); and Philip Gourevitch, *We Wish to Inform You That Tomorrow We Will Be Killed with Our Families: Stories from Rwanda* (New York: Farrar, Straus & Giroux, 1998).

7. For the text establishing the Responsibility to Protect, see "2005 World Summit Outcome," Resolution 60/1, paragraph 138–40, October 24, 2005, UN General Assembly, http://undocs.org/A/RES/60/1. For background, see Gene M. Lyons and Michael Mastanduno, eds., *Beyond Westphalia?: State Sovereignty and International Intervention* (Baltimore: Johns Hopkins University Press, 1995).

8. Haass, *War of Necessity, War of Choice*; for President Bush's account of what led up to his decision, see George W. Bush, *Decision Points* (New York: Crown, 2010), especially chapter 8.

9. *The National Security Strategy of the United States of America*, September 2002, White House, www.state.gov/documents/organization/63562.pdf.

10. Walzer, *Just and Unjust Wars*, 74–85.

11. For background, see Avner Cohen, *Israel and the Bomb* (New York: Columbia University Press, 1998).

12. For background, see George Perkovich, *India's Nuclear Bomb: The Impact on Global Proliferation* (Berkeley: University of California Press, 1999); Ashley J. Tellis, *India's Emerging Nuclear Posture: Between Recessed Deterrent and Ready Arsenal* (Santa Monica, CA: Rand Corporation, 2001); and Jasjit Singh, ed., *Nuclear India* (New Delhi: Knowledge World, 1998).

13. "Report by the Director General on the Implementation of the Resolution Adopted by the Board on 25 February 1993 (GOV/2636) and of the Agreement Between the Agency and the Democratic People's Republic of Korea for the Application of Safeguards in Connection with the Treaty on the Non-Proliferation of Nuclear Weapons (INFCIRC/403)," April 1, 1993, International Atomic Energy Agency Board of Governors, www.securitycouncilreport.org/atf/cf/%7B65BFCF9B-6D27-4E9C-8CD3-CF6E4FF96FF9%7D/Disarm%20GOV2645.pdf.

14. Arnold Kanter and Brent Scowcroft, "Korea: Time for Action," *Washington Post*, June 15, 1994, www.washingtonpost.com/archive/opinions/1994/06/15/korea-time-for-action/73e7cb5b-73e9-4503-916f-9b601b67087d/; Richard N. Haass, "Keep the Heat on North Korea," *New York Times*, June 17, 1994.

15. "Agreed Framework of 21 October 1994 Between the United States of America and the Democratic People's Republic of Korea," November 2, 1994, International Atomic Energy Agency, www.iaea.org/sites/default/files/publications/documents/infcircs/1994/infcirc457.pdf.

16. Dennis Ross, "Nothing in the Middle East Happens by Accident—Except When It Does," Washington Institute, December 7, 2015, www.washingtoninstitute.org/policy-analysis/view/nothing-in-the-middle-east-happens-by-accident-except-when-it-does.

17. "Joint Comprehensive Plan of Action," July 14, 2015, U.S. Department of State, www.state.gov/documents/organization/245317.pdf.

18. "Adoption of the Paris Agreement," December 12, 2015, UN Framework Convention on Climate Change, https://unfccc.int/resource/docs/2015/cop21/eng/l09.pdf.

19. See Adam Segal, *The Hacked World Order: How Nations Fight, Trade, Maneuver, and Manipulate in the Digital Age* (New York: PublicAffairs, 2016).

20. "Safe Harbor Privacy Principles," July 21, 2000, Council of Europe, www.coe.int/t/dghl/standardsetting/dataprotection/National%20laws/USA_SAFE%20HARBOR%20PRIVACY%20PRINCIPLES.pdf.

21. *International Strategy for Cyberspace: Prosperity, Security, and Openness in a Networked World*, May 2011, 8, White House, www.whitehouse.gov/sites/default/files/rss_viewer/international_strategy_for_cyberspace.pdf.

22. "Fact Sheet: President Xi Jinping's State Visit to the United States," September 25, 2015, White House, www.whitehouse.gov/the-press-office/2015/09/25/fact-sheet-president-xi-jinpings-state-visit-united-states.

23. "EU-U.S. Privacy Shield Principles," February 23, 2016, U.S. Department of Commerce, www.commerce.gov/sites/commerce.gov/files/media/files/2016/eu_us_privacy_shield_full_text.pdf.pdf.

24. *International Health Regulations (2005)*, 2nd ed., June 15, 2007, World Health Organization, http://apps.who.int/iris/bitstream/10665/43883/1/9789241580410_eng.pdf.

25. "Nations Commit to Accelerating Progress Against Infectious Disease Threats," February 14, 2014, U.S. Department of Health and Human Services, www.hhs.gov/about/news/2014/02/13/nations-commit-to-accelerating-progress-against-infectious-disease-threats.html.

26. "Agreement Establishing the World Trade Organization," April 15, 1994, World Trade Organization, www.wto.org/english/docs_e/legal_e/04-wto.pdf.

27. For data see World Trade Organization Statistical Program (Time Series data) for total world merchandise trade, http://stat.wto.org/StatisticalProgram/WSDBStatProgramHome.aspx?Language=E.

28. "Financial Stability Board Charter," September 25, 2015, Financial Stability Board, www.fsb.org/wp-content/uploads/r_090925d.pdf?page_moved=1.

29. Two books give the world's governments relatively high marks for their performance in this area. See Daniel W. Drezner, *The System Worked: How the World Stopped Another Great Depression* (Oxford: Oxford University Press, 2014); and Padma Desai, *From Financial Crisis to Global Recovery* (New York: Columbia University Press, 2011).

6. REGIONAL REALITIES

1. See, for example, Ron Suskind, *The One Percent Doctrine: Deep Inside America's Pursuit of Its Enemies Since 9/11* (New York: Simon & Schuster, 2006).

2. Scott Anderson, "Fractured Lands: How the Arab World Came Apart," *New York Times Magazine*, August 14, 2016, http://nyti.ms/2bkjcnv.

3. Mahmoud Abdel-Fadil et al., *Arab Human Development Report 2009:*

Challenges to Human Security in the Arab Countries (New York: United Nations Publications, 2009), www.arab-hdr.org/publications/other/ahdr /ahdr2009e.pdf.

4. "Statement of President Barack Obama on Egypt," February 10, 2011, White House, www.whitehouse.gov/the-press-office/2011/02/10/statement -president-barack-obama-egypt.

5. Resolution 1973, March 17, 2011, UN Security Council, www.undocs.org /S/RES/1973(2011).

6. The phrase "leading from behind" was first articulated by an unnamed Obama administration official in Ryan Lizza, "The Consequentialist: How the Arab Spring Remade Obama's Foreign Policy," *New Yorker*, May 2, 2011, www.newyorker.com/magazine/2011/05/02/the-consequentialist.

7. See Alan J. Kuperman, "Obama's Libya Debacle: How a Well-Meaning Intervention Ended in Failure," *Foreign Affairs* 94, no. 2 (March/April 2015), www.foreignaffairs.com/articles/libya/obamas-libya-debacle. For an account of decision making, see Jo Becker and Scott Shane, "Hillary Clinton, 'Smart Power' and a Dictator's Fall," *New York Times*, February 27, 2016, www.nytimes.com/2016/02/28/us/politics/hillary -clinton-libya.html.

8. Jeffrey Goldberg, "The Obama Doctrine," *Atlantic*, April 2016, www .theatlantic.com/magazine/archive/2016/04/the-obama-doctrine/471525/.

9. "Statement by President Obama on Syria," August 18, 2011, from Macon Phillips, "President Obama: 'The Future of Syria Must Be Determined by Its People, but President Bashar al-Assad Is Standing in Their Way,'" White House blog, August 18, 2011, www.whitehouse.gov/blog/2011/08/18 /president-obama-future-syria-must-be-determined-its-people-president -bashar-al-assad.

10. Barack Obama, "Remarks by the President to the White House Press Corps," Washington, DC, August 20, 2012, White House, www .whitehouse.gov/the-press-office/2012/08/20/remarks-president-white -house-press-corps.

11. Barack Obama, "Statement by the President on Syria," Washington, DC, August 31, 2013, White House, www.whitehouse.gov/the-press -office/2013/08/31/statement-president-syria.

12. "Framework for Elimination of Syrian Chemical Weapons," September 14, 2013, U.S. Department of State, www.state.gov/r/pa/prs /ps/2013/09/214247.htm.

13. Goldberg, "The Obama Doctrine."

14. John F. Kennedy, speech, Americans for Democratic Action Convention, Washington, DC, May 12, 1961, quoted in "Times Call for Liberal Action, Says Kennedy," *Lodi (CA) News-Sentinel*, May 13, 1961, https://news.google.com/newspapers?id=QOgzAAAAIBAJ&sjid= g4HAAAAIBAJ&dq=americans+for+democratic+action&pg= 7056,2944411&hl=en.

15. Vladimir Putin, "70th Session of the UN General Assembly," speech,

New York, September 28, 2015, President of Russia, http://en.kremlin.ru
/events/president/news/50385.

16. See Richard N. Haass, *The Reluctant Sheriff: The United States After the
Cold War* (New York: Council on Foreign Relations Press, 1998). Barack
Obama clearly belongs to the category of presidents who favored
retrenchment over the expansion of U.S. power. See Steven Sestanovich,
Maximalist: America in the World from Truman to Obama (New York:
Knopf, 2014), especially chapter 12.

17. Resolution 2254, December 18, 2015, UN Security Council, www.undocs
.org/S/RES/2254(2015).

18. "Joint Statement of the United States and the Russian Federation, as
Co-chairs of the ISSG, on Cessation of Hostilities in Syria," February 22,
2016, U.S. Department of State, www.state.gov/r/pa/prs/ps/2016/02/253115
.htm.

19. Adel Al-Jubeir, interview by Christiane Amanpour, *Amanpour*, CNN,
February 19, 2016, http://transcripts.cnn.com/TRANSCRIPTS/1602/19
/ampr.01.html.

20. James A. Baker III et al., *The Iraq Study Group Report* (December 6,
2006), http://bakerinstitute.org/media/files/Research/88085bb4
/iraqstudygroup_findings.pdf.

21. See George W. Bush, "President's Address to the Nation," Washington,
DC, January 10, 2007, George W. Bush White House, https://
georgewbush-whitehouse.archives.gov/news/releases/2007/01/20070110-7
.html; and "Fact Sheet: The New Way Forward in Iraq," January 10, 2007,
George W. Bush White House, https://georgewbush-whitehouse.archives
.gov/news/releases/2007/01/20070110-3.html. See also Bush, *Decision
Points*, chapter 12.

22. "Agreement Between the United States of America and the Republic of
Iraq on the Withdrawal of United States Forces from Iraq and the
Organization of Their Activities During Their Temporary Presence in
Iraq," December 14, 2008, U.S. Department of State, www.state.gov
/documents/organization/122074.pdf.

23. Barack Obama, "Remarks of President Barack Obama—Responsibly
Ending the War in Iraq," Camp Lejeune, Jacksonville, NC, February 27,
2009, White House, www.whitehouse.gov/the-press-office/remarks
-president-barack-obama-ndash-responsibly-ending-war-iraq.

24. Emma Sky, *The Unraveling: High Hopes and Missed Opportunities in Iraq*
(New York: PublicAffairs, 2015).

25. There is no end to the literature that examines foreign policy decision
making. Some of the best books include Richard Neustadt and Ernest
May, *Thinking in Time: The Uses of History for Decision-Makers*
(New York: Free Press, 1986); Graham Allison and Philip Zelikow,
Essence of Decision: Explaining the Cuban Missile Crisis (Boston: Addison
Wesley, 1999); Morton H. Halperin and Priscilla A. Clapp with Arnold
Kanter, *Bureaucratic Politics and Foreign Policy*, 2nd ed. (Washington,

DC: Brookings Institution Press, 2006); and Gordon Goldstein, *Lessons in Disaster: McGeorge Bundy and the Path to War in Vietnam* (New York: Times Books, 2008). On the role and functioning of the National Security Council under different presidents, see Ivo H. Daalder and I. M. Destler, *In the Shadow of the Oval Office: Profiles of the National Security Advisors and the Presidents They Served—from JFK to George W. Bush* (New York: Simon & Schuster, 2009). For insider accounts of the dynamics of the George H. W. Bush administration, see the memoirs of Bush and Scowcroft, *A World Transformed*; Baker, *The Politics of Diplomacy*; and Haass, *War of Necessity, War of Choice*. For the Clinton administration, see Madeleine Albright, *Madame Secretary* (New York: Miramax, 2003); and Bob Woodward, *The Agenda: Inside the Clinton White House* (New York: Simon & Schuster, 1994). For the George W. Bush administration, see Bush, *Decision Points*; Condoleezza Rice, *No Higher Honor: A Memoir of My Years in Washington* (New York: Random House, 2011); and Robert M. Gates, *Duty: Memoirs of a Secretary at War* (New York: Knopf, 2014). For the Obama administration, see Gates, *Duty*; Hillary Rodham Clinton, *Hard Choices* (New York: Simon & Schuster, 2014); Leon Panetta, *Worthy Fights: A Memoir of Leadership in War and Peace* (New York: Penguin, 2014); Vali Nasr, *The Dispensable Nation: American Foreign Policy in Retreat* (New York: Doubleday, 2013); and David Samuels, "The Aspiring Novelist Who Became Obama's Foreign-Policy Guru," *New York Times Magazine*, May 5, 2016, www.nytimes.com/2016/05/08/magazine/the-aspiring-novelist-who-became-obamas-foreign-policy-guru.html.

26. Hillary Clinton, "America's Pacific Century," *Foreign Policy*, October 11, 2011, www.foreignpolicy.com/articles/2011/10/11/americas_pacific_century; Tom Donilon, "America Is Back in the Pacific and Will Uphold the Rules," *Financial Times*, November 27, 2011, www.ft.com/cms/s/0/4f3febac-1761-11e1-b00e-00144feabdc0.html#axzz1lvbgzfyEc; Barack Obama, "Remarks by President Obama to the Australian Parliament," Canberra, Australia, November 17, 2011, White House, www.whitehouse.gov/the-press-office/2011/11/17/remarks-president-obama-australian-parliament.

27. "TPP Full Text," Office of the U.S. Trade Representative, https://ustr.gov/trade-agreements/free-trade-agreements/trans-pacific-partnership/tpp-full-text.

28. See Zheng Bijian, *China's Peaceful Rise: Speeches of Zheng Bijian, 1997–2005* (Washington, DC: Brookings Institution Press, 2005). Also see Thomas J. Christensen, *The China Challenge: Shaping the Choices of a Rising Power* (New York: Norton, 2015).

29. Sheila Smith, *Intimate Rivals: Japanese Domestic Politics and a Rising China* (New York: Columbia University Press, 2015).

30. Richard Katz, "Mutual Assured Production: Why Trade Will Limit Conflict Between China and Japan," *Foreign Affairs* 92, no. 4 (July/August

2013), www.foreignaffairs.com/articles/china/2013-06-11/mutual-assured
-production.

31. United States and India Nuclear Cooperation, Public Law 109-401,
December 18, 2006, www.congress.gov/109/plaws/publ401
/PLAW-109publ401.pdf.

32. See Daniel S. Markey, *No Exit from Pakistan: America's Tortured
Relationship with Islamabad* (New York: Cambridge University Press,
2013).

33. Haass, *War of Necessity, War of Choice*, 194–200. Also see Ahmed Rashid,
*Descent into Chaos: The United States and the Failure of Nation Building
in Pakistan, Afghanistan, and Central Asia* (New York: Viking, 2008).

34. Barack Obama, "Remarks by the President in Address to the Nation on
the Way Forward in Afghanistan and Pakistan," Washington, DC,
December 1, 2009, White House, www.whitehouse.gov/the-press-office
/remarks-president-address-nation-way-forward-afghanistan-and-pakistan.

35. Barack Obama, "Statement by the President on Afghanistan,"
Washington, DC, October 15, 2015, White House, www.whitehouse.gov
/the-press-office/2015/10/15/statement-president-afghanistan; Barack
Obama, "Statement by the President on Afghanistan," Washington, DC,
July 6, 2016, White House, www.whitehouse.gov/the-press
-office/2016/07/06/statement-president-afghanistan.

36. "Treaty on European Union," February 7, 1992, European Union,
http://europa.eu/eu-law/decision-making/treaties/pdf/treaty_on_european
_union/treaty_on_european_union_en.pdf.

37. "Treaty of Lisbon," December 13, 2007, European Union, eur-lex.europa
.eu/legal-content/EN/TXT/PDF/?uri=CELEX:11992M/TXT&from=EN.

38. "Treaty for the Prohibition of Nuclear Weapons in Latin America and
the Caribbean," February 14, 1967, UN Office of Disarmament Affairs,
http://disarmament.un.org/treaties/t/tlatelolco/text.

39. Elizabeth C. Economy and Michael Levi, *By All Means Necessary: How
China's Resource Quest Is Changing the World* (New York: Oxford
University Press, 2014).

7. PIECES OF PROCESS

1. There is a large body of work on the contours and characteristics of the
post–Cold War world. See, among others, Richard N. Haass, "The Age of
Nonpolarity: What Will Follow U.S. Dominance," *Foreign Affairs* 87,
no. 3 (May/June 2008), www.foreignaffairs.com/articles/united
-states/2008-05-03/age-nonpolarity; "Prospectives," in *Strategic Survey
2007*, International Institution for Strategic Studies (New York: Routledge,
2007); "The New Game," *Economist*, October 17, 2015, www.economist
.com/news/leaders/21674699-american-dominance-being-challenged-new
-game; Fareed Zakaria, *The Post-American World* (New York: Norton,
2008); Charles A. Kupchan, *The End of the American Era: U.S. Foreign*

Policy and the Geopolitics of the Twenty-first Century (New York: Alfred A. Knopf, 2002); Joshua Cooper Ramo, *The Age of the Unthinkable: Why the New World Disorder Constantly Surprises Us and What We Can Do About It* (New York: Little, Brown, 2009); Moisés Naím, *The End of Power: From Boardrooms to Battlefields and Churches to States, Why Being in Charge Isn't What It Used to Be* (New York: Basic Books, 2013); Charles A. Kupchan, *No One's World: The West, the Rising Rest, and the Coming Global Turn* (New York: Oxford University Press, 2012); and Ian Bremmer, *Every Nation for Itself: Winners and Losers in a G-Zero World* (New York: Portfolio/Penguin, 2012).

2. Charles Krauthammer, "The Unipolar Moment," *Foreign Affairs* 70, no. 1 (1990), www.foreignaffairs.com/articles/1991-02-01/unipolar-moment.

9. THWARTING THUCYDIDES

1. Thucydides, *The History of the Peloponnesian War*, translated by Richard Crawley, MIT Classics, http://classics.mit.edu/Thucydides/pelopwar.html.
2. A step in this direction was the announcement in July 2016 of the decision to send an additional thousand U.S. troops to Poland. See Barack Obama and Andrzej Duda, "Remarks by President Obama and President Duda of Poland After Bilateral Meeting," Warsaw, July 8, 2016, White House, www.whitehouse.gov/the-press-office/2016/07/08/remarks-president -obama-and-president-duda-poland-after-bilateral.
3. For a discussion of "integration," see Richard N. Haass, *The Opportunity: America's Moment to Alter History's Course* (New York: PublicAffairs, 2005), 24.
4. Robert B. Zoellick, "Whither China: From Membership to Responsibility?," speech, New York, September 21, 2005, U.S. Department of State Archive, http://2001-2009.state.gov/s/d/former/zoellick/rem/53682.htm.
5. See Jacob Lew, "Remarks of Secretary Lew on the Evolution of Sanctions and Lessons for the Future at the Carnegie Endowment for International Peace," Washington, DC, March 30, 2015, U.S. Department of the Treasury, www.treasury.gov/press-center/press-releases/Pages/jl0398.aspx; Gary Clyde Hufbauer et al., *Economic Sanctions Reconsidered*, 3rd ed. (Washington, DC: Peterson Institute for International Economics, 2007); and Meghan O'Sullivan, *Shrewd Sanctions: Statecraft and State Sponsors of Terrorism* (Washington, DC: Brookings Institution Press, 2003).
6. See David Shambaugh, *China's Future* (Cambridge: Polity Press, 2016).

10. WORLD ORDER 2.0

1. Francis M. Deng et al., *Sovereignty as Responsibility: Conflict Management in Africa* (Washington, DC: Brookings Institution Press, 2006).
2. Vladimir Putin, "Address by President of the Russian Federation,"

Moscow, March 18, 2014, President of Russia, http://en.kremlin.ru/events
/president/news/20603.

3. See Michael E. Brown, Sean M. Lynn-Jones, and Steven E. Miller, eds.,
Debating the Democratic Peace (Cambridge, MA: MIT Press, 1996);
Natan Sharansky with Ron Dermer, *The Case for Democracy: The Power
of Freedom to Overcome Tyranny and Terror* (New York: PublicAffairs,
2004); and Elliott Abrams et al., "U.S. Must Put Democracy at the Center
of Its Foreign Policy," *Foreign Policy*, March 16, 2016, http://foreignpolicy
.com/2016/03/16/the-u-s-must-put-democracy-at-the-center-of-its-foreign
-policy/.

4. Fareed Zakaria, *The Future of Freedom: Illiberal Democracy at Home and
Abroad* (New York: Norton, 2003).

5. "The Camp David Accords: The Framework for Peace in the Middle
East," September 17, 1978, U.S. Department of State Archive,
http://2001-2009.state.gov/p/nea/rls/22578.htm.

6. "Republic of Korea and the United States Make Alliance Decision to
Deploy THAAD to Korea," July 7, 2016, U.S. Department of Defense,
www.defense.gov/News/News-Releases/News-Release-View/Article/831178
/republic-of-korea-and-the-united-states-make-alliance-decision-to-deploy
-thaad.

7. For the transcript of Kim Jong-un's statement, see "Kim Jong Un Calls for
Global Independence," Pyongyang, May 7, 2015, National Committee on
North Korea, www.ncnk.org/resources/news-items/kim-jong-uns-speeches
-and-public-statements-1/KJU_Speeches_7th_Congress.pdf. Also see
Choe Sang-Hun, "North Korea Claims Its Nuclear Arsenal Is Just a
'Deterrent,'" *New York Times*, May 7, 2016, www.nytimes.com/2016/05/08
/world/asia/north-korea-claims-its-nuclear-arsenal-is-just-a-deterrent.html;
and Mitchel B. Wallerstein, "The Price of Inattention: A Survivable North
Korean Nuclear Threat?," *Washington Quarterly* 38, no. 3 (Fall 2015),
21–35, http://dx.doi.org/10.1080/0163660X.2015.1099023.

8. *The National Security Strategy of the United States of America*,
September 2002.

9. Some of this is covered in the *Report of the Group of Governmental
Experts on Developments in the Field of Information and
Telecommunications in the Context of International Security*, prepared for
the UN General Assembly, July 22, 2015, www.undocs.org/A/70/174.

10. Suerie Moon et al., "Will Ebola Change the Game?: Ten Essential
Reforms Before the Next Pandemic. The Report of the Harvard-LSHTM
Independent Panel on the Global Response to Ebola," *Lancet* 386,
no. 10009 (November 22, 2015), http://dx.doi.org/10.1016/S0140
-6736(15)00946-0.

11. "United Nations Convention on the Law of the Sea," December 10, 1982,
United Nations, www.un.org/depts/los/convention_agreements/texts
/unclos/unclos_e.pdf. The United States signed but never ratified the Law
of the Sea Treaty, which established rules for territorial seas, navigational

rights, economic zones, and resource exploitation. U.S. strategic interests would be well served by ratification and full participation in arrangements relating to the treaty, but the Senate has refused to do so, alleging (unconvincingly) that the treaty would infringe U.S. sovereignty. See Stewart M. Patrick, "Everyone Agrees: Ratify the Law of the Sea," *The Internationalist* (blog), CFR.org, June 8, 2012, http://blogs.cfr.org /patrick/2012/06/08/everyone-agrees-ratify-the-law-of-the-sea/; and Thomas Wright, "Outlaw of the Sea: The Senate Republicans' UNCLOS Blunder," ForeignAffairs.com, August 7, 2012, www.foreignaffairs.com /articles/oceans/2012-08-07/outlaw-sea.

12. It is for this reason that China's rejection of the ruling administered by the Permanent Court of Arbitration on the South China Sea in July 2016 was to be expected. See "Press Release: The South China Sea Arbitration," The Hague, July 12, 2016, Permanent Court of Arbitration, https://assets.documentcloud.org/documents/2990864/Press-Release-on -South-China-Sea-Decision.pdf; and "Full Text of Statement of China's Foreign Ministry on Award of South China Sea Arbitration Initiated by Philippines," *Xinhua*, July 12, 2016, http://news.xinhuanet.com /english/2016-07/12/c_135507744.htm.

11. REGIONAL RESPONSES

1. Alyssa Ayers et al., *Working with a Rising India: A Joint Venture for the New Century*, Council on Foreign Relations Independent Task Force Report No. 73 (New York: Council on Foreign Relations Press, 2015).
2. Jeffrey D. Sachs, "A New Century for the Middle East," *Project Syndicate*, December 19, 2015, www.project-syndicate.org/commentary/middle -east-sustaining-development-by-jeffrey-d-sachs-2015-12.
3. See Haass, *War of Necessity, War of Choice*, 117–20, for a detailed account of what took place between the United States and Israel in 1991.
4. For a similar conclusion, see Michael Mandelbaum, *Mission Failure: America and the World in the Post–Cold War Era* (New York: Oxford University Press, 2016).
5. William Shakespeare, *King Lear*, act 5, scene 2. For a discussion of "ripeness," see Richard N. Haass, *Conflicts Unending: The United States and Regional Disputes* (New Haven, CT: Yale University Press, 1990).

12. A COUNTRY IN DISARRAY

1. X [Kennan], "The Sources of Soviet Conduct."
2. Richard N. Haass, *Foreign Policy Begins at Home: The Case for Putting America's House in Order* (New York: Basic Books, 2013).
3. It is for this reason that a poll conducted by Pew Research in spring 2016 is troubling. A majority of Americans were wary of global involvement, preferring that the United States let others deal with their own problems

as best they could. A plurality of Americans thought this country was doing too much to solve the world's problems. See "Public Uncertain, Divided over America's Place in the World," May 5, 2016, Pew Research Center, www.people-press.org/files/2016/05/05-05-2016-Foreign-policy -APW-release.pdf.

4. There is a robust debate taking place about why the United States is growing as slowly as it is—if in fact it is growing as slowly as official statistics suggest. See N. Gregory Mankiw, "One Economic Sickness, Five Diagnoses," *New York Times*, June 17, 2016, www.nytimes.com/2016/06/19 /upshot/one-economic-sickness-five-diagnoses.html.

5. Much of this treatment of the debt issue is drawn from the testimony I delivered before the Senate Committee on Foreign Relations on April 6, 2016. See *The Strategic Implications of the U.S. Debt: Hearing Before the Senate Committee on Foreign Relations*, statement of Richard Haass, President, Council on Foreign Relations, 114th Congress, April 6, 2016, www.foreign.senate.gov/imo/media/doc/040616_Haass_Testimony.pdf.

6. Ed Harris et al., *The 2016 Long-Term Budget Outlook*, July 2016, Congressional Budget Office, www.cloo.gov/publication/51580; *The Budget and Economic Outlook: 2016 to 2026*, January 2016, Congressional Budget Office, www.cbo.gov/sites/default/files/114th-congress-2015-2016 /reports/51129-2016Outlook_OneCol-2.pdf.

7. See *The Strategic Implications of the U.S. Debt: Hearing Before the Senate Committee on Foreign Relations*, statement of Neera Tanden, President, Center for American Progress, 114th Congress, April 6, 2016, www.foreign.senate.gov/imo/media/doc/040616_Tanden_Testimony%20 REVISED2.pdf.

8. For a thoughtful book on the dollar's past, current, and future role, see Barry Eichengreen, *Exorbitant Privilege: The Rise and Fall of the Dollar and the Future of the International Monetary System* (Oxford: Oxford University Press, 2011).

9. For varying analyses, see both Jose Signoret et al., *Trans-Pacific Partnership Agreement: Likely Impact on the U.S. Economy and on Specific Industry Sectors*, May 2016, United States International Trade Commission, www.usitc.gov/publications/332/pub4607.pdf; and Peter A. Petri and Michael G. Plummer, *The Economic Effects of the Trans-Pacific Partnership: New Estimates*, Peterson Institute of International Economics Working Paper Series, January 2016, https://piie.com/system/files /documents/wp16-2_0.pdf.

10. See Robert Z. Lawrence and Lawrence Edwards, "Shattering the Myths About U.S. Trade Policy," *Harvard Business Review*, March 2012, www.hks.harvard.edu/fs/rlawrence/ShatteringMyths.pdf; Robert Z. Lawrence and Lawrence Edwards, "US Employment Deindustrialization: Insights from History and the International Experience," Peterson Institute for International Economics, October 2013, https://plie.com/sites/default /files/publications/pb/pb13-17.pdf; and Gregg Easterbrook, "When Did

Optimism Become Uncool?," *New York Times*, May 12, 2016, www
.nytimes.com/2016/05/15/opinion/sunday/when-did-optimism-become
-uncool.html.

11. See Aaron Smith, Janna Anderson, and Lee Rainie, "AI, Robotics, and the Future of Jobs," Pew Research Center, August 6, 2014, www.pewinternet .org/files/2014/08/Future-of-AI-Robotics-and-Jobs.pdf; Tom Standage, "The Return of the Machinery Question," Special Report: Artificial Intelligence, *Economist*, June 25, 2016, www.economist.com/news/special -report/21700761-after-many-false-starts-artificial-intelligence-has-taken -will-it-cause-mass; and Michael Chui, James Manyika, and Mehdi Miremadi, "Where Machines Could Replace Humans—and Where They Can't (Yet)," *McKinsey Quarterly*, July 2016, www.mckinsey.com /business-functions/business-technology/our-insights/where-machines -could-replace-humans-and-where-they-cant-yet.

12. Jonathan Rauch, "How American Politics Went Insane," *Atlantic*, July /August 2016, www.theatlantic.com/magazine/archive/2016/07 /how-american-politics-went-insane/485570/.

13. The classic treatment of this phenomenon is Mancur Olson, *The Rise and Decline of Nations: Economic Growth, Stagflation, and Social Rigidities* (New Haven, CT: Yale University Press, 1982).

14. See, for example, Ryan Lizza, "The Center Is Dead in American Politics," *New Yorker*, October 21, 2015, www.newyorker.com/news/news-desk /the-center-is-dead-in-american-politics; and Jane Mansbridge, "Three Reasons Polarization Is Here to Stay," *Washington Post*, March 11, 2016, www.washingtonpost.com/news/in-theory/wp/2016/03/11/three-reasons -political-polarization-is-here-to-stay/.

Index

and NATO enlargement, 93–96
post–Cold War, 92–93
and Syrian crisis, 99–100, 166,
169, 171
Ukraine crisis, 97–99, 136, 149,
162, 191, 196, 227
Rwanda crisis, 113–15, 116–17

Safe Harbor agreement, 142–43
SALT (Strategic Arms Limitations
Talks), 43
sanctions, 3, 83, 98, 100, 104, 110,
126, 129–30, 220–21
Saudi Arabia, 3, 159, 160, 167, 169,
172–73
Schengen area, 189
Schuman, Robert, 61
Scowcroft, Brent, 4–5, 127
self-determination, 62, 71, 107–8, 110,
236–37
September 11, 2001, terrorist
attacks, 119, 120–21, 122,
123, 153
Serbian crisis. See Yugoslav transition
el-Sisi, Abdel Fattah, 158, 159, 230
Snowden, Edward, 143
Somalia, 112–13
South Asia, 70, 183–88, 264–68
and decolonization, 62
nuclear capabilities in, 125–26,
128–30, 183, 184, 185
South China Sea, 9, 89, 90, 181,
182, 328n12
South Korea, 263
sovereign obligation, 226–55, 289
sovereignty, 19–20, 149, 232–33
and Cold War, 45–46, 51

and European integration, 189
and legitimacy, 201
post–World War II, 56, 58–59,
67, 72
and Responsibility to Protect,
115–16, 162, 226
and self-determination, 108
and United Nations, 58–59
and Westphalian order, 23–24
Soviet Union, 52–53, 58, 70–71, 92,
105–6, 121, 129
See also Cold War
spheres of influence, 47–48
START (Strategic Arms Reduction
Treaty), 43
states. See sovereignty
Strategic and Economic Dialogue,
219–20
Suez Crisis (1956), 63
Syrian crisis, 9, 117–19, 163–72
chemical weapons use in, 69, 137,
164–67
Russian role in, 99–100, 166,
169, 171

Taiwan, 58, 84–87, 90
Taliban. See Afghanistan
terrorism, 10, 237–38, 269, 272–74,
284–85
and civil conflict, 119–22
September 11, 2001, attacks, 119,
120–21, 122, 123, 153
and South Asia, 184, 185, 265–66
and Syrian crisis, 118
and weapons of mass
destruction, 130
See also ISIS/ISIL